CANADIAN SOCIAL ORGANIZATION

CANADIAN SOCIAL ORGANIZATION

Gordon F. N. Fearn

Holt, Rinehart and Winston of Canada, Limited
Toronto   Montreal

Care has been taken to trace ownership of copyright material contained in this text. The publishers will gladly receive information that will enable them to rectify any reference or credit in subsequent editions.

HN
103.5
F28
1973   23,230

Printed in Canada
1 2 3 4 5   77 76 75 74 73

To my parents

Acknowledgements

Many persons have guided me in the task of sorting what I know from what I do not know. Many have helped in the related task of sorting what I know and what I do not know from the content of what has been committed to paper during the preparation of this book.

I owe an intellectual debt to many persons who have directly or indirectly contributed to the outline and content of the book. This debt is acknowledged throughout by citation and reference.

I owe many debts to friends and associates across Canada. To trace the "ownership" of ideas is perilous fishing in a sea which is saturated with so many books and journals, so many discussions with students and so many contacts with others. I am most aware of the more direct contacts, especially with students and colleagues at The University of Alberta, but also with those who have been members of university classes which I have taught in rural Alberta and the Northwest Territories. These students are remembered for the many discussions which have helped to temper my academic enthusiasm, not to mention my urban bias.

Citation and reference alone fail to cover many who have shaped my excitement for this project. I especially wish to name Art Davis, Peggy Garritty, Dhara Gill, George and Geneva Kupfer, Gordon Hirabayashi, Gurbachan Paul and Tony Simmons. The encouragement of David Godden, John Holt, Noble Irvine and Carole Ross of Holt, Rinehart and Winston has been much appreciated. My son is still too young to realize that the typewriter which he pounds at will can, by others, be stroked with purpose. I owe him much, too, although that particular debt has less to do with this book and more to do with the proper role of fatherhood. His mother, Lorraine, is more than a person to be acknowledged, for she is the reason behind the effort.

Gordon F. N. Fearn

Edmonton, Alberta
January 29, 1973

Preface

Society and Sociology

University departments of sociology seem to offer many more courses about sociology than they do about society. This is perhaps a reflection of the widespread academic tendency to reify the subject material, or to regard academic models as real phenomena. If we depend upon course titles, for example, introductory courses tend to introduce sociology, not society. While sociology distinguishes itself as the study of society, there is a noteworthy difference between the two pursuits. The difference is confused by statements which relate the development of sociology to the development of society. For example, "the rapid emergence of sociology in Canada might be a reflection of the rapid emergence of Canada as an industrial-urban social system" (Rossides, 1968, p. 47).

Sociology seeks to develop analytical models of society which are valid reflections of that society, but models none the less. Models in sociology are always abstractions. Sociology is like any other academic discipline in that it tries to develop models of society in order to increase man's understanding of the dynamic system which is the social world. Sociology develops models in large part because society *per se* is beyond comprehension. Science tries to build comprehensible models of the things it studies because those things, in their raw form, are beyond reach. The crucial issue for science is thus the issue of validity: how isomorphic is the model with the reality, or how closely does the model resemble the reality?

The labels "Canadian society" or "Canadian social organization" suggest we are in trouble from the start, for we are pushed into making a series of direct observations and analyses concerning society, using the tools of sociology to filter our perceptions and thoughts. Such a direct and immediate approach is a little terrifying, because it necessarily tests the adequacy of sociology's base of knowledge. We should not be surprised when we find that sociology has an incomplete knowledge base, and that other disciplines are just as relevant when we go about the business of studying society.

Sociology and the other social sciences take on a different tone when we emphasize the difference between sociology and society. As individuals, living in community and society, we feel we are all experts when it comes to observing social reality. Lay people must often be excused when they express opinions on their various interpretations of society, although it is somewhat more difficult to excuse them when they extend the commentary to other societies, especially those with dramatically different cultures. But at home *everybody* knows *something* concerning such things as the composition of the population, the distribution of ethnic groups, problems of expanding cities, poverty and other inequalities, regional differences, and social services such as health care and pension benefits. We *all* have social prejudices which we unobtrusively construe as social data. In brief, we quite naturally seem to employ a kind of naive sociology when we observe and analyse the society in which we live. This is hard to overcome. It is also dangerous, for it makes us less responsive to seeing the value in developing models which can provide a more systematic and less prejudiced analysis of society. Sociology will be justified in part when it provides such a systematic and objective perspective.

Concerning This Book

This volume has been prepared with two broad goals in mind: to provide an under-graduate-level text which enables the student to expand acquaintance with the contributions of those who have analysed aspects of Canadian society; and to organize and present material in such a way that the critical skills of students are furthered. These skills include an objective awareness of social structures and social processes which operate in society, and a subjective awareness of the need and consequences of individual involvement in those structures and processes.

The book is subdivided into four parts. Part I contains two short chapters on social analysis; the first of these deals generally with the nature and problems of analysis, while the second chapter reviews selected interpretations of Canadian society.

Part II contains material on social origins, social institutions and social actors. Its three chapters can be read as a unit; they are designed to flow from the general to the specific.

Part III is concerned with social dynamics at various levels of analysis. The first of its three chapters deals with social actors in charge (or in relative charge, or seemingly in charge) of their social destinies. The other two chapters in this part discuss the nature and consequences of social participation in large and impersonal aggregates.

Part IV contains questions and challenges regarding social studies on the practical or applied level. There are provocations concerning social and personal values, their relations to the social future, and the need to learn to view the obvious things around us in terms of the hints they provide concerning society and its operation.

A number of biases are made obvious throughout the volume, but one which is not as obvious must be noted. This is an overriding interest in Canadian subjects, not so much because to be Canadian in content is to be pure in these days of material and cultural nationalism, but because to be Canadian is to be *interesting*. Although a young nation, Canada boasts a heritage which is so complicated as to make it challenging; indeed, there are those who look upon Canada as a workshop for the resolution of those twentieth-century problems which are faced by many nations.

To come to see Canadian society as interesting is partly to come to know facts and interpretations about it. This book seeks at every turn to present facts and interpretations which may then lead to further inquiry. If a few eyes are opened, or if some are opened wider, then much has been accomplished.

Reference

Rossides, Daniel W., SOCIETY AS A FUNCTIONAL PROCESS: AN INTRODUCTION TO SOCIOLOGY, Toronto: McGraw-Hill Company of Canada Limited, 1968.

TABLE OF CONTENTS

Chapter 8   Social Macrodynamics II   152

Part IV   Social Action

Chapter 9   Social Consciousness and Responsibility   181

Chapter 10   Postscript   204

Index   207

Part I
Social Analysis

Chapter 1

Social Analysis

Societies are not easy things to understand. They are complex and ever changing, their scope extending far beyond the comprehension of single individuals. But nevertheless individuals are frequently called upon to be social analysts. Because these individuals are uniquely located in their societies, the possibility of bias lurks about as an occupational hazard, always present and always making analysis susceptible to error.

The general purpose of this chapter is to discuss the most common biases in social analysis. There is a discussion of the problem that what we say is very much determined by our definitions of terms. And further, that what we say and the definitions we adopt are both very much determined by the prior assumptions we make. The biases in social analysis will be discussed following a brief introduction to the nature of theoretical thought.

Social Reality and Sociological Concepts

Philosophers of science have repeatedly demonstrated that more than one theoretical construction can always be placed upon a given collection of data. History of science indicates that, particularly in the early developmental stages of a new paradigm, it is not even very difficult to invent such alternatives. But that invention of alternatives is just what scientists seldom undertake except during the pre-paradigm stage of their science's development and at very special occasions during its subsequent evolution. So long as the tools a paradigm supplies continue to prove capable of solving the problems it defines, science moves fastest and penetrates most deeply through confident employment of those tools. The reason is clear. As in manufacture so in science — retooling is an extravagance to be reserved for the occasion that demands it. The significance of crises is the indication they provide that an occasion for retooling has arrived (Kuhn, 1962, p. 76).

As students we often feel that theoretical thought is mysterious and elusive, to be avoided at all costs. Such an attitude should be overcome since theoretical thought is essential for the comprehension of anything. We are always theorizing about one thing or another. Our goal should be to cultivate an enthusiastic attitude for theory, for it is our ally in the study of Canadian society.

To think theoretically is to simplify the complex nature of social reality. The argument goes something as follows. We cannot possibly understand all the intricacies of a modern society. We cannot possibly comprehend all the relations between people in a society, how relations change with passing time, and how relations historically give rise to organizations such as businesses and hospitals, and to institutions such as religion and education. We typically respond to complex things by employing abbreviations. They are a form of shorthand, which are meant to be symbolic of the more complex reality. Theoretical abbreviations are called concepts.

A concept is a "word or set of words that expresses a general idea concerning the nature of something or the relations between things, often providing a category for the classification of phenomena. Concepts provide a means of ordering the vast diversity of empirical phenomena, are essential in the process of generalizing, and form the basis of language. However, concepts are not inherent in nature itself, waiting to be discovered, as it were. Concepts, including scientific concepts, are mental constructs reflecting a certain point of view and focusing upon certain aspects of phenomena while ignoring others. Therefore, the concepts a person uses have an important effect upon his perceptions of reality" (Theodorson and Theodorson, 1969, p.68).

4

Take the example of an aircraft which skids off a runway during a thunder storm. There are many concepts which might help to understand this event. The layman might suggest that the runway surface was slippery. A concept has been invoked to explain why the plane skidded off the runway. The physical scientist might agree with the layman in principle while suggesting a different concept, friction. The scientist argues that the wet runway created a condition of insufficient friction between the runway and the aircraft's wheels. While both concepts help to make sense of the event, these concepts are not necessarily suggestive of the actual cause of the mishap. There may have been poor visibility or the aircraft may have landed at too excessive a speed.

Concepts, then, are not necessarily explanations of some event. They are simply ways of ordering complex events and observations into some comprehensible form. While concepts may simplify, reality may elude us completely without them. We should continually show caution when using concepts; they may impose a false order on reality, or we may be tempted to assume that our concepts are perfect representations of reality. These and other problems are frequent subjects for debate in the philosophy of science.

Cohn (1967) discussed the relationship between concepts and reality (see pp. 12-15). His presentation can be divided into the following four points. First, theoretical concepts rarely, if ever, represent the constantly changing nature of reality. As a consequence, concepts tend to be more arbitrary and less dynamic than the reality they represent, but this is not to deny that concepts may closely approximate some aspects of reality.

The second point is that a concept of reality is not reality. To have a concept of reality is to know a shorthand for one possible characterization of reality. We should guard against committing the fallacy of reification, that is, to avoid assuming that a concept of reality exists as a phenomenon independent of the reality it is supposed to represent.

Next, science is, or ought to be, forever engaged in resolving contradictions between its concepts and reality. The contradictions develop because reality changes, or because a concept of reality was not a good one in the first place. To resolve the contradictions frequently means to revise or even to replace concepts.

Finally, conceptualizations are all the more complex because they are made by the human species. If we accept that the human person is an active rather than a passive possessor of information, and if we further accept that individuals are limited in their understandings by the concepts which they know, then we see that people contribute to the changing nature of reality while at the same time trying to conceptualize it. Perhaps it is not unfair to say that we are bound to get caught up in the confusion which we in part create.

Sociologists have not been unaware of these issues and problems. Berger and Luckmann (1967) began an important book on sociological theory by contending that "reality is socially constructed" and that reality is a "quality appertaining to phenomena that we recognize as having a being independent of our own volition (we cannot 'wish them away')" (p. 1). By implication, there is no fixed concept of reality; both concept and reality vary across individuals and social relations. Through learning, some aspect of reality may become a subjective part of an individual, and several individuals may share a consensus on some aspect of reality, but reality is still beyond the individual.

Any discussion of concepts and reality is philosophical and complex. When sociologists develop concepts to help specify one or more aspects of reality, they must do so by first demonstrating that their concepts are valid tools for analysing social reality. No matter how careful they are, there are always assumptions which must be made. To cope with reality we must make assumptions concerning its nature; we must also make assumptions concerning our imperfect ability to study it.

The need to make assumptions arises for many reasons. People assume things about reality because they sense that it affects their routine activities in important ways. People make assumptions because they possess imperfect knowledge of reality. We assume things because we cannot possibly perceive all the stimuli which exist in reality and which impinge in some manner upon our lives and activities. That we make assumptions about the social world undoubtedly helps to rationalize something that is characterized by considerable differentiation and heterogeneity. So often it is economical to pass over the many contradictions which exist in reality. Our assumptions, in brief, help to find or to falsely infer some order in chaos. By making assumptions we steer a course around obstacles and sometimes forge new pathways.

Consider an example. A man may wish to purchase some green fabric. He visits a dimly lighted store only to find that the lighting distorts the fabric colours. The customer may be willing to buy under such conditions because he is willing to assume that the store's dim lighting has some predictable effect upon the colour which is perceived. On the basis of such an assumption, consistent with past experience, he comes to realize that fabric which in fact is green appears blue or gray or some other shade. Making the assumption permits action because it permits the individual to make the following type of rationalization. "I assume that this piece of fabric is the color I wish, and that my assumption would be verified if I could see the fabric under normal lighting conditions."

A second example concerns the complexity of making inferences concerning the personality of a stranger. When we first meet another person we experience certain impressions, for example, "Susan seems to be a sincere, warm person." It is likely that the personality of this individual is not homogeneously characterized by sincerity and warmth. Nevertheless, we may make such an assumption. It is economical to do so because it gives us some real impression while allowing us to bypass the many complexities and variations which characterize the person in fact. "One of the most fundamental biases in person perception is that other individuals tend to be seen as constant, unchanging entities. Although in reality, an individual is never exactly the same person at any two moments in time, and in some instances is markedly different, he is usually seen as an enduring entity. He is the same person this week as he was last week; he is the same person even when behaving very differently in different situations. This is obviously an economy; it eliminates the necessity for perceiving behaviors of the other which deviate from his assumed character." (Secord and Backman, 1964, p. 84).

It should be obvious that the assumptions we frequently make about reality are just as frequently not well-founded in the facts. Just to keep moving ahead we assume things and thereby we sometimes falsify. And perhaps most of the time we are not consciously aware of what we are doing.

Dilemmas in Social Theory

> In all modes of thought, efforts to simplify and systematize make it impossible to include the diversity that is characteristic of real life situations. Consequently, if the demands of logical consistency block our insight into reality, we should be ready to sacrifice the logic (Drews and Lipson, 1971, p. 28).

Ideally, social theory is constituted by "systematically organized, lawlike propositions about society that can be supported by evidence" (Zetterberg, 1965, p. 22). Social theory often takes the form of explicit propositions which depend in part upon stated assumptions. At the heart of any proposition and thus basic to any theory are the concepts which represent one or more aspects of perceived reality. Thus we may have a proposition such as "the alienation of young people increases as the perceived credibility of political leaders decreases." The concepts of alienation and credibility are thus related in what could be a hypothetical or verified proposition.

In practice, social theory rarely takes the form of verified, systematically organized, lawlike propositions about society. The situation is further complicated by a number of dilemmas which confront the analyst, several of which are discussed briefly in this section.

There is, in the first instance, the agonizing dilemma of determining validity. As long as we agree that concepts are but partial representations of selected aspects of reality, there must remain with us the nagging possibility that concepts are imperfect representations. To put this dilemma in the form of a question: to what degree can we generalize that the operations in our concepts are representative of the operations in reality? The dilemma of determining validity is always with us, in science and in life.

Secondly, if we approach situations without preconceived theoretical ideas, we sometimes see things more as they, in fact, are. It is impossible to de-theorize ourselves completely; it is impossible to look at things without preconceptions. But it is possible to look without having first articulated an explicit theory concerning the thing to be examined.

An illustration of this is a book in the area of psychiatric sociology (Strauss, Schatzman, Bucher, Ehrlich and Sabshin, 1964). A reviewer of this volume made the following observations. "The authors clearly began their study by imposing on themselves a degree of conceptual open-mindedness which is rare in sociological research. They carefully avoided the temptation of evaluating the psychiatric setting by standards derived from psychiatry itself or of drawing a convenient set of hypotheses from among the various studies of formal organization, and, therefore, they avoided the error, so common in projects of this sort, of mistaking the structure of their argument for the structure of the institution they were exploring" (Erikson, 1966, p. 226).

On the other hand, because of conceptual open-mindedness, the authors "had no settled base line from which to mount their expedition into the hospital world." (p. 226). They did not articulate a theory before beginning their study. This is not to say they did not have a theory, but simply that they did not articulate a theory in a formal sense. In short, there is probably some scholarly merit in having systematic rather than implicit or unknown preconceptions. To state theoretical preconceptions clearly can help us to see things above and beyond our personal preconceptions and ideological biases.

The second dilemma thus lies in the value of articulating theoretical preconceptions versus the value of being able to take a fresh view of the subject matter. In practice, it is common and perhaps even wise to mix a little of both. In such a way, systematic thought protects us from our personal biases, while our own initiative to observe and analyse maintains our inventiveness.

The discussion thus far has revolved around topics in the philosophy of science. The final dilemma is of a different nature. It is largely the issue of differing ideological orientations in social theory. There are, in brief, different theories of social reality, and the differences between them emphasize the different ideological ways of looking at social reality. Some people look at the social world and see in it an overriding order and structure. Other people look and see such things as conflict and change. The dilemma is created when we endeavour to remember that social reality is characterized by order and conflict, structure and change.

One scholar argued that there are three fundamental forms of social thought; no more, no less. "A social philosopher can either maintain that a social system is a unity rather than a multiplicity, that it is one rather than many; or he can take the view that it is a multiplicity rather than a unity, that it is many rather than one; or, finally, he can try to develop a definition of social life which does justice, both to the real integration of the social order and to the real independence of the individuals comprised by it. In other words, to use a well-known cliché, he can either see the wood rather than the trees; or he can see the trees rather than the wood; or he can endeavour to remember that the wood is made up of trees and that the trees between them make up a wood" (Stark, 1962, p. 1).

While each of the three positions outlined in the statement above is viable in its own right, Stark argued that the third possibility is the superior one, that is, a definition of social life which is both holistic and atomistic. At the same time, the most appropriate position is often a function of the task to be completed. For example, if we wish to study the topic of social control, it might be wise to begin our study in a holistic fashion by examining such things as the federal system of criminal law and legal procedure. On the other hand, if we wish to study whether or not a school system is achieving its goal of educating young people, it might be best to begin in an atomistic fashion by examining the levels of motivation and achievement of individual students and teachers. Even then, some might wish to examine the school system as a system in society and history.

The third position might be most defensible if our purpose is to appraise, for example, the operation of some formal organization. We can look holistically at the formal structure of the organization as seen, for instance, in organizational charts.

And we can look atomistically at the various parts of the organization and ask, among other things, whether the arrangements that ought to exist because of the formal structure do, in fact, exist in the more informal structure.

The third position, frequently called interactionism, does not imply theoretical synthesis or integration. This position, which itself is a bias, simply emphasizes the obvious, that it is usually possible to think about things in at least two distinct ways. One of these ways is to study aspects of the discrete parts which compose some whole. If, for example, the whole in question is a forest or a group, we can study the discrete trees which compose the forest or the discrete individuals who compose the group. The other way is to study the whole of things together. We would concentrate not upon trees or individuals, but upon those broader aspects which exist only when trees grow together or individuals meet together, that is, the forest or the group. These two positions are respectively termed nominalism and realism.

Homans (1964) suggested "it must be that the general explanatory principles even of sociology are not sociological . . . but psychological, propositions about the behavior of men, not about the behavior of societies" (p. 815). Homans is being nominalistic in his conviction. Durkheim, on the other hand, symbolizes realism. He argued that social facts are a "category of facts with very distinctive characteristics: it consists of ways of acting, thinking, and feeling, external to the individual, and endowed with a power of coercion, by reason of which they control him. These ways of thinking could not be confused with biological phenomena, since they consist of representations and of actions; nor with psychological phenomena, which exist only in the individual consciousness and through it. They constitute, thus, a new variety of phenomena; and it is to them exclusively that the term 'social' ought to be applied" (1964, p. 3; first published 1895). Interactionism is represented as follows. "Rather than settling the issue as to whether the individual or the group is the ultimate unit in terms of which social life must be analyzed, the main stream of sociological and social-psychological thought has forgotten this issue and proceeded to analyze social phenomena as complexes of the meaningfully oriented actions of persons reciprocally related to one another" (Wirth, quoted by Warriner, 1956, pp. 549-550).

Two qualifications should be noted concerning this discussion. The first is that people are likely predisposed in a psychological way toward either a nominalist or a realist position. It is characteristic of people that, when they look out at the trees in the forest, they will see either some trees or the forest. That which they see becomes foreground; the remainder remains background. The fact that people exhibit such perceptual biases is reason for the theorist to remember the separate virtues of nominalism and realism.

The second qualification is an academic one in that it is possible and sometimes helpful to conceive of the individual realistically. In other words, the person can be viewed as a whole which is constituted by discrete parts. This argument can be extended into such fields as biology and anthropology. Our discussion focused only upon the sociological level of analysis.

In conclusion, consider once again the significance of Stark's words. The student of society should "try to develop a definition of social life which does justice, both to the real integration of the social order and to the real independence of the individuals comprised by it."

Types of Social Analysis

> Perhaps we were afraid that, if we studied the commonplace, we should lay ourselves open to the familiar charge that a sociologist is a man who discovers at infinite pains what everybody knows. . . . We should have had enough self-confidence and enough sense to forget such fears. . . . Far from discovering facts that are too familiar, we have not discovered facts that are familiar enough (Homans, 1950, p. 5).

Olsen (1968) suggested that four questions typify the main types of social analysis. Referring to a social phenomenon such as an organization or even a society, we may ask: what is it like (a question concerning *structure*), how does it occur (a question concerning *process*), what caused it (which obviously questions *causation*), and what are its social consequences (a question concerning *function*)?

As the most widespread body of assumptions and definitions in contemporary social science, functional analysis is perhaps the most difficult to fully understand. The word "function" refers broadly to the contribution made by parts to the maintenance of the whole. With intellectual roots in biology, functional analysis has been widely adopted as a method of investigation in both cultural anthropology and sociology. Functional analysis forces an examination of the functional needs of a society — if such is our object of study — so that, among other things, the analyst can decipher the social and cultural mechanisms which are operating to satisfy (or not to satisfy) the functional needs, themselves determined by the goals or objectives of the society. Timasheff (1967) provided an appraisal of functional analysis, especially in terms of the theme, to be expanded in Chapter 3, that the social development of any society (or other grouping) is the story of a selective process (see pp. 222-223).

The four types of social analysis — structural, process, causal and functional — frequently overlap in one or another combination according to the design of specific analysts. Structural analysis, for example, is frequently combined with functional analysis. Structural-functional analysis approaches the structure of some social phenomenon mainly in terms of the antecedent conditions which gave rise to it; changes in structure are viewed in terms of adjustments to ongoing social activities which may or may not increase the chances for the structure's survival.

With the frequent exception of causal analysis, all the types of analysis are biased in favour of description. Causal analysis usually requires methodological and statistical sophistication; thus it is often biased in favour of empiricism.

Given the complex nature of social reality and the varying qualities of the men and women who live within it, we might sensibly expect that social analysis is further complicated by variations in emphasis. Such is indeed the case. The dominating perspective of functionalism comes to us in both a conservative and radical formulation. Both are concerned with structure and function, but there the similarity ends. Lenski (1966) summarized the conservative and radical variations (see pp. 22-23).

Conservatives are "distrustful of man's basic nature and have emphasized the need for restraining social institutions." Conservatives view society as a "social system with various needs of its own which must be met if the needs and desires of its constituent members are to be met." Conservatives argue that "inequality arises as a necessary consequence of consensus (i.e., because of values which are shared widely throughout society, even by the less privileged elements) and/or innate differences among men" and that "coercion plays only a minor role" in the development and perpetuation of inequality. Conservatives minimize the degree to which inequalities generate conflicts. Conservatives argue that rights and privileges are acquired through such means as hard work and the delegation of authority. Conservatives view the state and law as "organs of the total society, acting basically to promote the common good." Finally, "conservatives have tended to regard the concept of class as essentially a heuristic device calling attention to aggregations of people with certain common characteristics."

Radicals are distrustful of social institutions. They have taken an "optimistic view of man's nature." Radicals view society "more as the setting within which various struggles take place; it is significant chiefly because its peculiar properties affect the outcome of the struggles." Radicals argue that coercion is the "chief factor undergirding and maintaining private property, slavery, and other institutions which give rise to unequal rights and privileges." Radicals place great emphasis on the degree to which inequalities generate conflicts. Radicals also emphasize the roles played by "force, fraud, and inheritance" in the acquisition of rights and privileges. Radicals view the state and law as "instruments of oppression employed by the ruling classes for their own benefit." Finally, radicals have been "much more inclined to view classes as social groups with distinctive interests which inevitably bring them into conflict with other groups with opposed interests."

In his presidential address on the subject of functionalism, delivered to the American Sociological Association, Davis (1959) argued that "functionalism is *not* a special method within sociology or social anthropology," and that functionalism is "synonymous with sociological analysis" (p. 757). Basing his argument around a number of issues which are beyond the scope of the present discussion, Davis concluded that functional analysis is what sociological analysis is all about, and that functionalism addresses itself to central questions of sociological concern: how does social order develop, and how is social order changed or maintained in the face of various pressures for its disruption?

Rossides (1968), in one of the first textbooks on Canadian society, seemed to agree with Davis. Rossides assumed that "functionalism is not a special perspective or school in sociology but that it is synonomous with science itself" (p.x.). At the same time, Rossides argued that "it is no longer scientifically strategic to think of Canada as a congeries of ethnic-religious groups or of provinces or regions, or to think of it as a set of issues focussed around rural vs. urban or federal vs. provincial differences" (p.xi). The first of these statements is accepted here. The second statement cannot be accepted, for it eliminates any consideration of basic dialectical elements in Canadian society. If we eliminate consideration of these elements from the start, our analysis would be falsified because the effect would be to prejudge the validity of the conservative perspective. The importance of recent events in Canadian society would also be neglected. The second statement is reminiscent of the following commentary which appeared in TIME in 1967. "In the early 1960's French separatism, including cells of bearded conspiratorial terrorists, was a major threat to Canada's very fabric as a nation. There was serious worry that Canada might disintegrate. The most striking fact about the present Canadian scene is that this threat has for all practical purposes disappeared" (May 5, 1967). Much has happened since the centennial year of 1967. Perhaps we simply are much more aware of those things which reflect differences in our society. It must be argued, however, that the various things which reflect differences — regional and provincial disparities, ownership of the means of production, minority-group identifications, multilingualism and so on — tell the analyst a great deal if he wishes to fully understand the dynamics which underlie the structure of Canadian society. There is, in brief, a certain viability in both the conservative and radical formulations of functionalism.

In summary, then, it has been noted that sociological analysis for the most part is biased in favour of description. The task of description frequently assumes a dynamic aspect. Functional analysis, for instance, demands that the investigator examine the consequences of various social activities and other factors, in terms of their contribution to the maintenance of social structure. It is to be expected that some happenings increase the survival chances of the structure (they are functional), while other happenings decrease the survival chances (they are dysfunctional).

It is assumed that functional analysis is sociological analysis, and that functionalism comes in both a conservative and radical formulation. Both formulations are essential. It is true, for example, that social inequalities are inevitable in society if the various tasks of that society are to be accomplished (the conservative formulation). It is also true that social inequalities generate conflicts in society, and that conflicts can have a major impact upon the course of events in that society (the radical formulation). We have been through the argument already, but consider it once again in different words. Recall that Durkheim was a social realist; he viewed social facts as having independent effects upon individuals. Weber's approach, on the other hand, has been called voluntaristic. Berger (1963) argued that "Durkheim stresses the externality, objectivity, 'thing'-like character of social reality. . . . Against this, Weber always emphasizes the subjective meanings, intentions and interpretations brought into any social situation by the actors participating in it. Weber, of course, also points out that what eventually happens in society may be very different from what these actors meant or intended. But he asserts that this entire subjective dimension must be taken into consideration for an adequate sociological understanding (*Verstehen* is the technical term used to denote the latter . . .). That is, sociological understanding involves the interpretation of meanings present in society" (pp. 125-126).

Berger continued his argument with an important comment. "The Durkheimian and Weberian ways of looking at society are not logically contradictory. They are only antithetical since they focus on different aspects of social reality. It is quite correct to say that society is objective fact, coercing and even creating us.

12

But it is also correct to say that our own meaningful acts help to support the edifice of society and may on occasion help to change it. Indeed, the two statements contain between them the paradox of social existence: That society defines us, but is in turn defined by us. . . . In other words, it is not only ourselves but society that exists by virtue of definition" (pp. 128-129).

References

Berger, Peter L., INVITATION TO SOCIOLOGY: A HUMANISTIC PERSPECTIVE, Garden City, N.Y.: Anchor Books, 1963.

Berger, Peter L. and Thomas Luckmann, THE SOCIAL CONSTRUCTION OF REALITY: A TREATISE IN THE SOCIOLOGY OF KNOWLEDGE, Garden City, N.Y.: Anchor Books, 1967.

Cohn, Georg, EXISTENTIALISM AND LEGAL SCIENCE, Dobbs Ferry, N.Y.: Oceana Publications, 1967.

Davis, Kingsley, "The Myth of Functional Analysis as a Special Method in Sociology and Anthropology, "AMERICAN SOCIOLOGICAL REVIEW, 24 (December, 1959) 757-772.

Drews, Elizabeth Monroe and Leslie Lipson, VALUES AND HUMANITY, New York: St. Martin's Press, 1971.

Durkheim, Emile, THE RULES OF SOCIOLOGICAL METHOD, New York: The Free Press of Glencoe, 1964.

Erikson, Kai T., Review of PSYCHIATRIC IDEOLOGIES AND INSTITUTIONS, AMERICAN JOURNAL OF SOCIOLOGY, 72 (September, 1966) 225-226.

Homans, George C., THE HUMAN GROUP, New York: Harcourt, Brace & World, Inc., 1950.

Homans, George C., "Bringing Men Back In," AMERICAN SOCIOLOGICAL REVIEW, 29 (December, 1964) 809-818.

Kuhn, Thomas S., THE STRUCTURE OF SCIENTIFIC REVOLUTIONS, Chicago: Phoenix Books, 1962.

Lenski, Gerhard E., POWER AND PRIVILEGE: A THEORY OF SOCIAL STRATIFICATION, New York: McGraw-Hill Book Company, 1966.

Olsen, Marvin E., THE PROCESS OF SOCIAL ORGANIZATION, New York: Holt, Rinehart and Winston, Inc., 1968.

Rossides, Daniel W., SOCIETY AS A FUNCTIONAL PROCESS: AN INTRODUCTION TO SOCIOLOGY, Toronto: McGraw-Hill Company of Canada Limited, 1968.

Secord, Paul F. and Carl W. Backman, SOCIAL PSYCHOLOGY, New York: McGraw-Hill Book Company, 1964.

Stark, Werner, THE FUNDAMENTAL FORMS OF SOCIAL THOUGHT, London: Routledge & Kegan Paul, 1962.

Strauss, Anselm, Leonard Schatzman, Rue Bucher, Danuta Ehrlich and Melvin Sabshin, PSYCHIATRIC IDEOLOGIES AND INSTITUTIONS, New York: The Free Press of Glencoe, 1964.

Theodorson, George A. and Achilles G. Theodorson, A MODERN DICTIONARY OF SOCIOLOGY, New York: Thomas Y. Crowell Company, 1969.

Timasheff, Nicholas S., SOCIOLOGICAL THEORY: ITS NATURE AND GROWTH, New York: Random House, 1967.

Warriner, Charles K., "Groups Are Real: A Reaffirmation," AMERICAN SOCIOLOGICAL REVIEW, 21 (October, 1956) 549-554.
Zetterberg, Hans L., ON THEORY AND VERIFICATION IN SOCIOLOGY, Totowa, N.J.: The Bedminster Press, 1965.

For Further Reading

Boulding, Kenneth E., A PRIMER ON SOCIAL DYNAMICS: HISTORY AS DIALECTICS AND DEVELOPMENT, New York: The Free Press, 1970.
Cuzzort, R. P., HUMANITY AND MODERN SOCIOLOGICAL THOUGHT, New York: Holt, Rinehart and Winston, Inc., 1969.
McGee, Reece, POINTS OF DEPARTURE: BASIC CONCEPTS IN SOCIOLOGY, Hinsdale, Ill.: The Dryden Press Inc., 1972.
Mills, C. Wright, THE SOCIOLOGICAL IMAGINATION, New York: Oxford University Press, 1959.

Chapter 2

Sociological Interpretations of Canadian Society

Three fundamental interpretations of society were established in Chapter 1. The language of the chapter suggested conservative functionalism, radical functionalism, and a third interpretation which attempts, not to reconcile the conservative and radical interpretations, but to remember that there are theoretical approaches which are sensitive to the tone of both conservative and radical interpretations. Granted, sociological interpretations of this last type are rare, perhaps because it is extremely difficult for analysts to remember and to apply theoretical approaches which do not fit the shape of their biases.

The general purpose of the present chapter is to briefly illustrate these three interpretations of Canadian society by selecting and outlining examples from the sociological literature. The fit between theory and example is far from perfect, as will be seen; yet the illustrations are sufficiently to the point that they manage to communicate the tone of the various approaches. Material to be introduced in later chapters will also be seen to relate to one or another of the three sociological interpretations.

Conservative and Radical Functionalism

> In order for us to understand anything, we have to fail to perceive a
> great deal that is there. Knowledge is always purchased at the expense
> of what might have been seen and learned and was not (Oppenheimer,
> quoted by Inkeles, 1964, p. 45).

The conservative variation of functionalism tends to emphasize the systematic
nature of social reality. Various aspects of social reality are viewed in terms of how
adequately they contribute to the ongoing systemic structure. The conservative
variation tends to assume that one of the driving forces behind systems of social
action is survival. The group or society can be committed to tangible goals such as,
for a society, the achievement of a certain minimum per capita income; but survival
itself looms large as a social goal, perhaps to such a degree that functions which
enhance the chances for survival take precedence over other functions.

Vallee and Whyte (1968) published a wide-ranging review of the functional
bases of Canadian society. They began their paper by specifying the structural
nature of the advanced industrial society. It is a familiar story, having to do with
the application of steadily expanding technology to serve the social goals of production and growth, and the consequent effects for the social organization of society.
There are numerous consequences of continued technological and economic
growth, some having to do with the organization and preparedness of the labor
force, others having to do with the increasing difficulty of a society to review and
redirect its social activity in terms of new priorities. "For the industrialization
process to become self-sustaining, there must evolve an institutional framework and
value system which are responsive to the impulses and opportunities for subsequent
economic and social development. The features embodied in such an institutional
and cultural framework are, in turn, preconditions for post-industrial development"
(p. 834).

Vallee and Whyte then proceeded to analyse Canadian society in terms of
specific criteria which represent the industrial or even postindustrial stage of social
development. The tone of their discussion is reflected in their statements about
each of these criteria. Start with population. "Numerous studies show the rapid rate
of urbanization; the flow of population towards regions of economic opportunity,
both within Canada and to the United States; the decline of the labour force in
agriculture and other primary industries and its swelling in managerial, professional,
and clerical services. Regional variations reveal the uneven distribution of opportunities within the country. . . . The evidence from economic and demographic
studies is that Canada is an advanced industrial society with certain peculiarities [a
high birth rate, for example, when compared with other countries in an advanced

stage of industrialization] that can be explained by her geographical and historical circumstances" (p. 835).

With respect to values, Canadians exhibit a conservative syndrome made up of a "tendency to be guided by tradition; to accept the decision-making functions of *élites*, many of whom virtually or actually inherit their positions; to put a strong emphasis on the maintenance of order and predictability. Such values are regarded by many sociologists as incongruent with the requirements of an advanced industrial or a post-industrial society" (p. 836). There are signs of change, however, suggesting that Canada is slowly adjusting to the demands of an advanced industrial society. The province of Quebec, for example, is making significant advances in the area of provincial culture, especially in the field of education. "Evidence from public opinion polls reveals that an increasing proportion of Canadians believe that the influence of religion on Canadian life is decreasing. It is noteworthy that the most marked changes during the last decade have occurred in Quebec, the Atlantic Provinces, and the rural areas, those parts of the society which have most recently experienced the impact of industrialization" (p. 839). Finally, signs of change are reflected in such debates as the new flag and constitutional change, both national issues during the 1960's. Changes of symbolism suggest a "gradual working out of new and distinctive symbolic forms to replace the traditional ones" (p. 840).

When we turn to the technological and economic spheres of Canadian society, we again detect evidence of a basically conservative value syndrome gradually changing in the direction of adaptation to an advanced industrial society, at the same time influencing the rate of advance in these spheres. . . . Sociologists who have compared Canadian patterns with those said to characterize the Americans argue that the sorting out of people in Canada proceeds in terms of ascriptive criteria much more than it does in the United States. For instance, in Canada gender is a clearer indicator of where men or women will be located in the labour force than it is in American society (p. 840). Among others, Porter has demonstrated the persistence of an ascriptive stress in several spheres of activity. For example, on the basis of studies of occupational distribution by ethnic origin, he has argued that the cultural pluralism ideal [in Canada], in contrast to the so-called melting pot ideal [in the United States], results in unequal placement of ethnic groups. In Canada, according to him, there has developed 'a reciprocal relationship between ethnicity and social class. A given ethnic group appropriates particular roles and designates other ethnic groups for the less preferred ones' (p. 841).

Another feature of societies beyond the earliest stages of industrialization is the growth in number and influence of a vaguely defined middle class. This is concomitant with the reduction of the need for masses of unskilled and semi-skilled labour and the expansion of wealth. . . . Using the conventional definition of class in terms of education, income, and occupation, there are abundant data showing the trend in Canada towards a steady increase in those categories traditionally regarded as middle class and a corresponding decrease in lower-class categories (pp. 841-842).

However, social development is not perfect in terms of equally-distributed gains, a fact which brought Vallee and Whyte to discuss the disestablishment. "As the society moves rapidly towards the post-industrial stage, the pace at which skills become obsolete heightens and thousands of people become technologically unemployable . . . [or] downwardly mobile from an already lower-class position" (p. 845). Note that this "process of dislocation and alienation from the larger system" frequently occurs in spite of the fact that standards within groups are improved.

"In the case of the indigenous peoples of Canada, there have been substantial gains in their standards of education, occupation, and income. However, the gains made by the average Canadian have been even greater, so that the socio-economic gap is widening rather than closing" (pp. 845-846).

Finally, Valee and Whyte noted the role of government in the management of resources.

If one characteristic of a developed industrial society is the pervasive role of government, Canada must indeed be highly developed, for there is no doubt that, at provincial and federal levels, there has been a vast expansion in the use of government to define and achieve cultural, economic, and social goals (p. 846). The acceptance of the role of government as the key instrument of society has been one of the most singular social changes to be noted in Quebec, where it has displaced the Church as over-all integrater and regulator of many social functions (pp. 846-847).

Vallee and Whyte thus provided an analysis of Canadian society by examining and interrelating its various structural aspects, especially those aspects concerned with population, values, the division of labor, the structure of class, management and co-ordination. They gave us more than a picture of Canadian society. They were able to summarize varied evidence to explain important dynamic changes which have, or are, taking place in Canadian society. For example, there is the relationship between the changing manpower needs of an advanced industrial society and the apparent inability of the society to upgrade the quality of manpower, thus leading to what the authors refer to as the disestablished, or to what we more commonly refer to as poverty, unemployment, disenfranchisement and the like. This kind of relationship, representing these kinds of social problems, also indicates why it is that societies which are passing through advanced stages of industrialization increasingly focus their attention on social and cultural goals.

Vallee and Whyte concluded their essay with a comment on Canadian social science, almost as if to anticipate comments such as those expressed by Davis, to be discussed shortly. "Our impression is that sociologists are too busy making up for the backlog of sheer information about Canadian society to worry about the enterprise as a whole and to engage in much soul-searching concerning the theoretical and methodological aspects of this enterprise" (p. 849). They continued to suggest that "the [sociological] scene in Canada is so placid that one is tempted to attribute to sociologists the character trait often imputed to the population as a whole: a kind of pragmatic reasonableness which discourages open dispute" (p. 849).

Lively debate on methodological and ideological issues in sociology is most likely to occur in societies where there is a high degree of self-awareness, a clearly established national identity, which makes it possible for social scientists to visualize a total picture of a bounded system with interdependent parts. In other words, it is when sociologists can and do study a population in terms of a 'system-as-a-whole,' when they can adopt what is called a *holistic* perspective, that they are likely to become so aware of their methodological and ideological assumptions that they bother to deliberate about them (p. 849).

Vallee and Whyte argued that sociologists of French-Canadian society have developed a more critical intellectual attitude, largely because they have known a bounded conception of their society. The argument applies equally to the American sociologist studying American society. In other words, sociologists of English-Canadian society do not share to the same degree the social consciousness of their

French counterparts, not because the English are inadept, and not because English Canada and French Canada in point of fact constitute different societies, an observation which may indeed be true; but because Canadian society in its totality, which includes French-Canadian society, is so very much more difficult to comprehend than is French-Canadian society considered alone.

We now turn to an illustration of functional analysis in terms of its more radical variation. Recall that this variation tends to emphasize a number of biases when characterizing the social world and when developing theoretical perspectives concerning it. The radical variation respects the role of man as an agent in social change, viewing social change in terms of a struggle for power and for the control of scarce resources. The radical variation also encourages the perception of social reality in terms of its historical context, usually trying to define the structure of society in terms of antecedent conflicts and compromises and, indeed, always trying to remember that the present structure of society represents but one finite structure in an infinite progression of past, present and future conflicts and compromises.

The material which follows exemplifies the ideological underpinnings of radical functionalism. Davis (1971) argued for historically-relevant theorizing concerning social change and development in Canadian society. He suggested a modified dialectical perspective, Canadian society as metropolis versus hinterland. This can mean urban versus rural areas, but generally it means exploitive versus exploited areas or groups.

Most Canadian and American-trained Anglophone sociologists do not understand either Canadian or American society mainly because they have been trained in the prevailing static, abstract, ideal-typical, structural-functional, ahistorical tradition. Structural-functionalism affords important insights, both segmental and holistic, but it lacks a time dimension and must therefore be supplemented by a historical perspective. Further, this historical dimension must include a dialectical aspect: the viewing of the evolution of a society as a series of oppositions (p. 12).

Thus a metropolis-hinterland perspective is advocated for analyzing Canadian society. Metropolis continuously dominates and exploits hinterland whether in regional, national, class, or ethnic terms. But the forms and terms of domination change as a result of confrontations. Spontaneous and massive social movements in regional hinterlands or urban underclasses may force their way toward an improved status for the colonials within the going system. On the other hand, metropolis-hinterland conflict may be latent for long stretches of time rather than overt. It may be outweighed by conditions of prosperity or by temporary alliances in the face of larger confrontations (p. 12).

Davis used the term "hinterland" to indicate rural areas which export their resources (both goods and migrating labour to larger centres of economic activity, but the term also indicates such groups as urban underclasses, or any group which is the object of control as exercised by an upper-class elite. The term "metropolis" indicates the centres of economic and political power, where power suggests the ability of one group to influence the behaviour of another group, even if that other group should resist (see pp. 12-13).

It is acknowledged that the metropolis-hinterland perspective is a "variation of the dialectical approach stemming from the Marxian tradition of social thought. The dialectical premise is that major long-run changes in the socio-economic structure of a society result from oppositions. In the limiting case of major revolutions, . . . a collision of incompatible interests eventually produces a new institutional pattern which is not wholly like either of the original opposing complexes, but which includes significant elements from each" (p. 13).

In a nutshell, for analyzing such cases of modern development as Canadian western settlement, Quebec-in-Canada, [and] Canada-in-North America . . . during the last century of Canadian history, . . . a comparatively short-run metropolis-hinterland variation of the long-run dialectic seems preferable. We need a frame of reference somewhere between the timeless, static and usually non-holistic structural-functional model on the one hand, and the holistic, dynamic, long-run limiting case of the Marxian dialect[ic] on the other hand. It should be essentially dialectical, holistic, and historical, but capable of illuminating those regional and national confrontations which do not evolve into full-fledged structural revolutions. Instead, these colonials seek to improve their status within a modified existing order rather than in a drastically and perhaps violently re-structured system. However modified, the metropolis-hinterland hierarchical and exploitive pattern remains (pp. 13-14).

The modified dialectical approach as outlined is especially valuable in social analysis when the focus is on social change. But Davis failed to utilize his perspective in any systematic analysis of social change in Canadian society. He included many brief references to historical events. For example, a "case of regional mass movements making their way into the national establishment is documented in J. N. McCrorie's history of the Saskatchewan farmer's movement since 1900. Another Canadian example is the slow drift of the Canadian economy vis-à-vis the United States during the last generation from a competitive to a branch-plant status" (p. 14). But, again, careful and systematic analysis does not follow the fleeting reference.

In addition to pointing the way, Davis carefully noted that revolutionary Marxism is a limiting case, just as is conservative functionalism. While he stressed the metropolis-hinterland perspective, he was careful not to discredit conservative functionalism. His comments in this respect suggested a balanced regard for both the radical and conservative variations in functional analysis. "It is time to emphasize the historical, holistic and comparative approach of classic social analysis in our studies of Canadian society. In no way would this detract from the significant and indeed indispensable contributions of orthodox structural-functional analysis to an understanding of Canada in the modern world" (p. 17).

We can learn certain valuable lessons from orthodox structural-functional analysis. First, social systems change unevenly, but they change as whole. In the short-run, one sector of the system may lead at one time, another sector at another time. In the long-run, of course, the system as a whole changes in one direction, until confronted by a major opposition. For example, changes in one institutional area may induce changes in another. One effect of the post-World War II extension of education and family allowances in far Northern Saskatchewan was to tie the formerly semi-nomadic Métis and Indian trapping families more closely to village settlements (p. 18).

In other words, social systems share a property common to systems in general — some degree of interdependence of parts. This also means, in some measure, cohesiveness of the whole, however loose. Hence follows the limited capacity of each component part of the system to continue short-run change that is not paralleled by complementary changes in other components. Thus during the late 1940's and early 1950's, the Saskatchewan CCF Government built a modern elementary school system in the far northern reaches of the province. This well-meaning education effort declined by the middle 1950's, because it was not accompanied by such other changes as greater job opportunities, wider experience, and acceptance by Métis and Indians of modern standards of living or migration to the south (p. 18).

Davis, still in pursuit of balance in social analysis, concluded that "while we suggest that major changes in social structure result from oppositions, this does not mean that all structural changes are explainable in this way" (p. 18).

It is unfortunate that Davis and others have not initiated original sociological studies of Canadian society in general and smaller social units within Canada in particular, in the perspective of metropolis-hinterland. It seems at present that Canadian scholarship of the political left is experiencing a gap between the perspectives of social liberalism, and the detailed studies which are needed of selected regions and communities within Canada; metropolis-hinterland is rich with the imagery of interpretation, but weak on cases. There are, of course, case studies of note. Archibald (1971) analysed regional underdevelopment in the Atlantic Provinces in the context of metropolis-hinterland, while Usher (1971) published a study of Sachs Harbour in the Northwest Territories, using the metropolis-hinterland model to place the developing North in the context of metropolitan dominance and exploitation. But these studies are problematic for they tend not to be *systematic* attempts to analyse their subjects in terms of an explicit theoretical statement of interpretation. They are *sensitizing* studies but they stop short of being definitive. Because the indicators of metropolis-hinterland processes are left vague, and because there tends to be an unusually heavy reliance upon interpretations of selected historical facts and trends, the loose interpretation of society argued by Davis and others is both appealing and difficult to refute.

More than anything else, there is a clear need for an explicit statement of the processes involved in metropolis-hinterland socio-economic relations. For example, Archibald (1971) listed one of the processes as the "expropriation of profits or economic surpluses on the basis of effective monopoly control by the metropolis over the satellite region's development" (p. 106). Statements such as this one must not only be grounded in theory; they must be worded in clear language, permitting the researcher to test their validity in particular situations. While economists are skilled in the tasks of measurement and geographers can plot the patterns of economic interaction on a map, sociologists in Canada seem reluctant to apply the concepts and methods of the related disciplines to analyse important dynamics in society.

Society As Organization In Space

[T]here is scarcely any aspect of Canadian social life that cannot profitably be considered first and fundamentally from the perspective of the space or territory involved (Card, 1968, p. 13).

There are neglected dimensions in social analysis. Loomis (1960) discussed three conditions of social action: territory, size and time. Time is the historical dimension in the study of society, while size can imply the study of the demographic structure of society. Territory is space. To focus on social space is in large part to analyse on the basis of noncontroversial facts, such as the physical distribution of social actors in space. While space is a neglected dimension in social analysis, it is also one which has become the focus of renewed attention, perhaps because its appeal lies apart from the conservative and radical variations of functionalism.

From the start, however, some of the qualifications and criticisms noted earlier with respect to the metropolis-hinterland interpretation must again be stressed. Davies and Herman's edited volume, SOCIAL SPACE: CANADIAN PERSPECTIVES (1971), is chosen to illustrate a theoretical interpretation several steps removed from either the conservative or radical interpretations, not because their work constitutes a systematic analysis of Canadian society, but because the outline of their interpretation offers direction and challenge for continuing analysis.

As editors, Davies and Herman provided a general perspective for the interpretation of research conducted by others. Their general perspective provided an outline of the social organization of space relations. For the most part they *sensitized* their audience by showing the concept of social space to be a convenient and economical tool in social analysis. Our immediate task is to review the essence of their theoretical perspective as it emerged in a number of brief introductory statements. Later, in Chapter 6, a more detailed overview of their approach will be incorporated into a discussion of social participation.

Davies and Herman claimed to be interested in the various sociological interpretations of Canadian society in terms of the "extent to which they are able to make sense, both of the dominant features of a society and of its variations" (p. 246). They claimed, it would seem correctly, that sociological interpretations that view Canada in terms of the functional organization of its institutions or in terms of relations between hinterland and metropolis "make only partial sense, to a very large extent because they are not able to provide a basis for examining how sectors of Canadian society see themselves or each other" (p. 246). Davies and Herman were thus led to search for the "traditions in Canadian social science which might more fruitfully act as the basis of Canadian sociology" (p. 246).

They came to focus on the traditions of political economy and communications research. Any
attempt to come to terms with Canadian society must involve an integration of these approaches: the first because it deals with the foundations of power, and the second because it defines ways of looking at how people make sense of the power-constraints and their relationships with each other. In some of the communications writing — notably that of McLuhan — the emphasis seems to be much more on technology as communication, though as sociologists we not only have to examine technology but human relationships. . . .
[We therefore must] put the Canadian communications arguments in the context of a wider sociological debate on spatial analysis which views relationships at once as social structures, as ecology, as communication and as values. People do not talk to each other simply to have conversation (though they may do so), nor do they talk because they can't make films or hypnotise (though that also may be true). They talk as part of a structure of social relationships: to talk is to establish rapport with other people (or to conflict with them). One of the purposes of organizing this book [SOCIAL SPACE: CANADIAN PERSPECTIVES] according to definitions of space is to suggest how different kinds of relationships and the assumptions lying behind them affect the ways that people communicate with each other and how people make sense of these relationships and use the different modes of communication (p. 246).

Space is not only a physical reality, it is also psychological and sociological. . . . So in order to understand how we distance ourselves from, or are enclosed with, other people we have to be able to know how social relationships are demarcated by physical, social, cultural and technological factors (p. vii).

Davies and Herman then expanded the focus of their book.
[I]t is entirely about Canada, but a Canada which is not seen as testing out theories and frameworks developed elsewhere, but as actively creating its own categories to frame answers to its own problems. The initial task of the reader is therefore to ask what questions have Canadians themselves posed in order to understand their predicament? And in searching for an interpretation it seems clear that there have been three fundamental areas of analysis: the area of dependence-independence; the sphere of communication; and the physical-biological forces of self-realization. In an important sense these areas are interdependent. Canada has always been dependent on other, more prosperous economies and this has had implications for the ways that Canadians have viewed communications and the use of physical and ecological resources. In turn, successions of conquests have provided real problems in the modes of communication between sectors of the population, further complicated by problems of physical distance and ecological determination. Finally physical and ecological space was not simply 'there' to be conquered, the conquest was determined by power relationships and by existing forms of communication. The continuing tradition in Canadian social science research, in political rhetoric, and in journalistic reportage is focused on these problems. How do Canadians take account of the external political and economic control of their society? How do they speak to each other? And how, with the second largest land mass in the world can they actually create something called a society? As Canadian social scientists have long recognized, these issues are crucial for the understanding of Canada and for the development of a critical social science related to its problems, but to date in Canada they have been discussed mainly by people who would not claim to be sociologists, though

23

this may be because the Canadian social science tradition is essentially inter-disciplinary. Outside of Canada, however, similar questions have been central to sociological enquiry. The task of this book is therefore to use this analysis as the basis for a Canadian sociology and also to indicate the ways that non-Canadian sociological theories and methods might be reformulated to take account of the peculiarly Canadian social processes (p. vii).

In order to do this we have everywhere attempted to move from general-ities to specifics, from formal structures to people thinking out their own relationships. The task is not an easy one. With some societies (e.g. Britain, France or China) the definition of what a society is, is largely contained within its own boundaries. Other societies may impinge from time to time, and the country itself may take over other territories with important con-sequences for its own internal development. But, by and large, it is possible to say that certain institutions and processes are unique to that country: in other words it made itself. With Canada this is not possible. Canada did not make itself — it was made by others. When we talk about family patterns in Canada we are talking about English or Scots or American or French or Ukrainian family patterns; and yet not entirely. The subsequent development of imported institutions makes the character of these different from those of their country of origin. The problem is to be able to specify the interconnect-ing structures, values and time sequences which give these institutions their specifically Canadian meaning (p. vii).

Such is the challenge formulated by Davies and Herman. We can regret that their work is just that and little more; we can regret the fact that key concepts and propositions have been identified and discussed, but that the result does not extend far past the goal of sensitizing persons to the perspective of social space. Perhaps their service was in identifying the utility of social space as a concept. Perhaps the chief advantage of social space is that it is, at least in its objective form, a neutral medium, making it possible (but not necessary) for the social analyst to bypass ideological disputes. In many instances, the concept of social space makes it pos-sible to relate observation and description to physical indicators. Some of the meanings of Canadian society can then be found in the historically-changing inter-relationships between actors as they are distributed and forever redistributed in social space.

It is despairing that Canadian sociology is rich with challenge but weak in terms of specific frameworks for analysis. At the same time, it is unfair to under-estimate the difficulties associated with developing explicit theoretical statements, especially those which achieve a systematic organization of testable propositions. A whole society is not an easy thing about which to be theoretical. The crude com-plexity of the task is one of the reasons why Merton (1957) advocated the develop-ment of "theories of the middle range," or theories which focus upon limited subjects rather than theories which seek to encompass the nature and operation of all of society in all of its supposed integrated detail. Could it be that integration is an academic concept of hope, eclipsing the fact that society is beyond integration?

References

Archibald, Bruce, "Atlantic Regional Underdevelopment and Socialism," in Laurier La-Pierre, Jack McLeod, Charles Taylor and Walter Young, eds., ESSAYS ON THE LEFT: ESSAYS IN HONOUR OF T. C. DOUGLAS, Toronto: McClelland and Stewart Limited, 1971, pp. 103-120.

Card, B. Y., TRENDS AND CHANGE IN CANADIAN SOCIETY: THEIR CHALLENGE TO CANADIAN YOUTH, Toronto: Macmillan of Canada, 1968.

Davies, D. I. and Kathleen Herman, eds., SOCIAL SPACE: CANADIAN PERSPECTIVES, Toronto: New Press, 1971.

Davis, Arthur K., "Canadian Society and History as Hinterland Versus Metropolis," in Richard J. Ossenberg, ed., CANADIAN SOCIETY: PLURALISM, CHANGE, AND CONFLICT, Scarborough, Ont.: Prentice-Hall of Canada, Ltd., 1971, pp. 6-32.

Inkeles, Alex, WHAT IS SOCIOLOGY? AN INTRODUCTION TO THE DISCIPLINE AND PROFESSION, Englewood Cliffs, N.J.: Prentice-Hall, Inc., 1964.

Loomis, Charles P., SOCIAL SYSTEMS: ESSAYS ON THEIR PERSISTENCE AND CHANGE, Princeton, N.J.: Van Nostrand Company, 1960.

Merton, Robert K., SOCIAL THEORY AND SOCIAL STRUCTURE, Revised and Enlarged Edition, New York: The Free Press of Glencoe, 1957.

Usher, Peter J., THE BANKSLANDERS: ECONOMY AND ECOLOGY OF A FRONTIER TRAPPING COMMUNITY, Volume 3, Ottawa: Information Canada, 1971.

Vallee, Frank G. and Donald R. Whyte, "Canadian Society: Trends and Perspectives," in Bernard R. Blishen, Frank E. Jones, Kaspar D. Naegele and John Porter, eds., CANADIAN SOCIETY: SOCIOLOGICAL PERSPECTIVES, Third Edition, Toronto: The Macmillan Company of Canada Limited, 1968, pp. 833-852.

For Further Reading

Barker, Graham, Jennifer Penney and Wally Seccombe, "The Developers," CANADIAN DIMENSION, 9 (January, 1973) 19-50.

Frank, Andre Gunder, "Sociology of Development and Underdevelopment of Sociology," CATALYST (Summer, 1967) 20-73.

Hall, Edward T., THE HIDDEN DIMENSION, Garden City, N.Y.: Doubleday & Company, Inc., 1966.

Levitt, Kari, SILENT SURRENDER: THE MULTINATIONAL CORPORATION IN CANADA, Toronto: Macmillan of Canada, 1970.

Lipset, Seymour Martin, "Canada and the United States: A Comparative View," THE CANADIAN REVIEW OF SOCIOLOGY AND ANTHROPOLOGY, 1 (November, 1964) 173-185.

Rostow, W. W., THE STAGES OF ECONOMIC GROWTH: A NON-COMMUNIST MANIFESTO, London: Cambridge University Press, 1967.

Part II
Social Setting

Part II
Social Scoring

Chapter 3

Social Origins

Societies are not easy to define. The task of definition is made difficult because diverse factors contribute to the complexity of a society. Some of these factors, such as the nature of the physical environment, or specific historical events of the past, are fairly easy to comprehend. Many factors, however, are complex in their own right. The type of government and the system of law are examples of complex factors. They are complex because they bring constant pressures to bear upon the day-to-day activity of a society. Their complexity also arises from the fact that they not only have significant influence in the affairs of society, but they also are re-arranged and employed in different ways according to the peculiar pressures of time and space.

The following illustration outlines the organization of subjects within this chapter and in the two chapters which follow it. It is generally argued that conditioning factors (including historical, geographical, demographic and biological factors) set the broadest limits for a society in terms of its social development and potential for change (this chapter). These broad limits are delimited through the influence of social institutions (Chaper 4), and further delimited by the constraining effects of man's comprehension (Chapter 5). The various limits, of course, are subject to modification because of interaction effects. For example, social institutions, in addition to being partially shaped by conditioning factors such as past historical events or accidents of geography, also influence conditioning factors, for example, by regulating biological mating or by charting the limits of future history. The funnel-like design of the illustration represents the movement from what is possible, what is potentially available to a society in terms of biological, social and cultural options, to what is actually selected as symbolized by, in this instance, Canadian society.

The general purpose of this chapter is restricted to the consideration of some of the more important conditioning factors which must be discussed for a sociological analysis of Canadian society. An arbitrary line often separates sociological from other factors; much that is history or geography or demography can be described as sociology if the latter is taken to mean the general study of the phenomena of human society. If, however, we think of sociology more specifically as the examination of the processes whereby social relations between persons develop and change with time, then such subjects as history, geography and demography can be construed as conditioning factors which place important limits upon sociological processes.

The chapter begins with a brief discussion of the world of the possible, and how that world, characterized by infinite variation, comes through selection to eventually constitute a specific society. This is followed by a brief section concerned with geographical and historical foundations. The final section provides an overview of selected population topics.

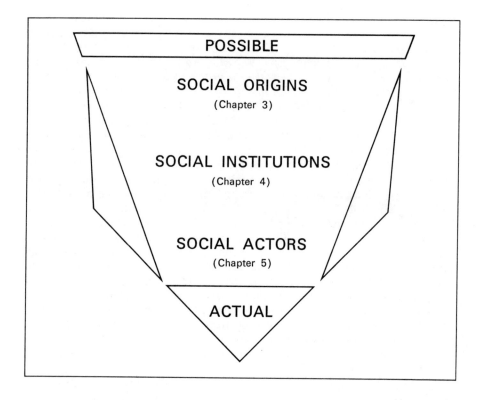

POSSIBLE

SOCIAL ORIGINS
(Chapter 3)

SOCIAL INSTITUTIONS
(Chapter 4)

SOCIAL ACTORS
(Chapter 5)

ACTUAL

The Conceivable and the Actual

Civilization is social order promoting cultural creation. Four elements constitute it: economic provision, political organization, moral traditions, and the pursuit of knowledge and the arts. It begins where chaos and insecurity end. For when fear is overcome, curiosity and constructiveness are free, and man passes by natural impulse towards the understanding and embellishment of life (Durant, 1935, p. 1).

Canadian society is a unique happening. At any given moment in time, our society represents a social organization or social ordering which is a finite selection from the near-infinite world of the possible. Any society can be thought of as a highly selective array of culture themes and behaviour norms which have developed into a unique pattern for that society, such themes and norms having been drawn from a range of culture themes and behaviour norms. Of course, the actual array of themes and norms is constantly changing since no single society is isolated from other societies. The interactions and interdependencies between different societies mean that the world of the actual, so called, cannot in fact be viewed as a finite selection of themes and norms. We only view it this way when, for purposes of analysis, we are forced to make certain simplifying assumptions.

The discussion which follows suggests a number of reasons why selection occurs in the evolution of a specific society. We rely heavily upon the work of Hoebel (1954). He documented the theme that each separate society must indeed be a selection of cultural material. Hoebel cautioned us to avoid assuming that a society is a rigid selection of themes and norms. Williams (1960) went further and suggested that a

norm is a standard (not necessarily explicit) for the course that action *should* follow, not a description of the action that actually occurs (p. 372). An institutional norm is not a point or a line, but a *zone:* typically, a norm is subject to appreciable variations in perception and application, even under highly favorable circumstances. There is usually a 'permissive' zone of variation around even the most specific and strongly supported norms; certain kinds and degrees of overconformity and of underconformity are expected and tolerated. The ambiguities and variability of norms are important but difficult to recognize because of our persistent tendency to think of institutions as solid and well-articulated entities. Even in a highly unified culture, different portions of the normative structure always manifest a wide range of obligatoriness, explicitness, and specificity. Shading off from the level of the most obligatory norms are norms of lesser definiteness held with lesser firmness, as shown for instance by vagueness of definition and by lesser severity of penalties for violations (p. 373).

Hoebel (1954) began with the nature of social order and its relationship to culture. He noted the lesson taught us by anthropologists, that human beings are creatures of "remarkable adaptability . . . as revealed through the wide range of behavior exhibited by men the world over" (p. 10). He went on to quote Benedict (1946; first published 1934) concerning the fact that human cultures are selective symbolic arrangements.

The culture pattern of any civilization makes use of a certain segment of the great arc of potential human purposes and motivations, just as . . . any culture makes use of certain selected material techniques or cultural traits. The great arc along which all the possible human behaviours are distributed is far too immense and too full of contradictions for any one culture to utilize even any considerable portion of it. Selection is the first requirement. Without selection no culture could even achieve intelligibility (p. 207).

Hoebel discussed four factors which impose selection upon culture and society. As already noted by Benedict, the first of these is inherent contradiction or incompatibility. As Hoebel suggested, the people of a culture cannot at the same time cook their meat and yet eat it raw. It must be one or the other. Similarly, the people of a culture cannot practice celibacy while enjoying sexual relations (see p. 10). This, of course, is not to say that people cannot preach celibacy while enjoying sexual relations. Doing one's preaching and doing what one preaches have always been quite different tasks!

Hoebel turned to psychology for the second factor which imposes selection. People learn characteristic ways for satisfying their needs.

Experimental psychology indicates that in animal and self-directed human learning the line of behavior in trial-and-error activity which leads to the drive-reducing goal, since it is the last line of behavior followed before success is attained, tends to be repeated on the next attempt. Repetition reinforces the behavior and, if the stimulus situation is repeated, it tends to become a habit. The pattern of behavior set up in the habit may not be the only one that would lead to gratification of the need; it may not even be the most effective one. But if it is the one first hit upon, it may remain the only one followed. It also tends to be generalized in that it tends to be extended in the form of response patterns evoked by stimuli essentially similar but not identical to the original stimulus. It serves to reduce the drive, relieve the tension, and return the organism to an adequate (if not a complete) state of balance — and that is enough. The other potential lines of behavior are eliminated, at least for the time being (p. 11).

The third factor which imposes selection upon a culture is the very fact of socialization. Children learn selectively, not only because to do so is characteristic of learning, but because they are taught selectively. "What happens between birth and maturation inevitably inhibits the capacity to react in all possible ways" (p. 12).

The final factor noted by Hoebel is the requirement of order (see p. 12). There must be organization so that, to some degree, both other people and situations are predictable for the individual. While there are many steps between social order and chaos, Hoebel and many others have argued that at least a certain level in the development of social organization is prerequisite to anything social. The war of all against all, or something worse, is the alternative!

On these grounds we recognize and accept the proposition that every society must of necessity choose a limited number of behavior possibilities for incorporation in its culture, and it must peremptorily and arbitrarily reject the admissibility for its own members of those lines of behavior which are incompatible with its selected lines as well as many others which are merely different. This does not, however, mean that absolute rigidity is imposed by the nature of things. A measure of permissible leeway exists in most cases, for some deviation is inevitable; and it is in leeway that new modifications find their soil for taking root (p. 12).

Hoebel's comments make good sense. While the beginnings of society are beyond reach, the processes just described show social development to be highly selective. Selectivity is perhaps the best mark of social change. Indeed, social change through selection is the overriding theme of this and the following two chapters. Social change through selection is choice; choice is sometimes consciously made by social actors. While usually there are reasons behind choice, descriptive information concerning the direction of choice is often sufficient if we are to grasp the outline of social change.

Perhaps it should be noted, before continuing, that to talk of changing patterns of social organization is to use a shorthand representing the underlying philosophy, and the development of national and other social goals in Canada through history. To speak of social origins is to plot the evolutionary development of society, but still to do so without any pretense of having reviewed all aspects of social development. As material is considered in succeeding pages, and as the reader takes note of the many important matters which are left unsaid, the focus of the discussion should not be lost from view, namely, that social goals and the philosophies and actions underlying them, together with numerous compositional factors such as the changing distributions of resources, capital and population across time and space, constitute the data in our analysis of Canadian social organization.

Geographical and Historical Foundations

> No study of Canadian history is intelligible without some understanding of Canada's geography. Indeed, geography has been (and still is) one of Canada's chief problems and has, therefore, been a vital factor in determining its history (Lower, 1966, p. 1).

Factors of geography place broad but significant limits upon the structure of Canadian society. It is too easy to forget that such things as the junctions of rivers once provided the strategic reasons for the early social development of Canada's frontier. Similarly, the physical locations of mountain ranges and lakes served almost to dictate patterns of early settlement, systems of transportation and communication.

Lloyd (1968) suggested that the fur traders of old possessed "inherent geographical good sense." In brief, they capitalized upon the relationship between water routes and economic survival. At the same time, the traders and their peers lacked knowledge concerning the shape of the land and the distribution of resources over it. "Canada might well have been a different place if those who directed its destiny in the past century had been trained in the ways of geographers, or even if there had been some simple notions abroad as to the essential physical characteristics of the land mass which was being 'developed.' During much of the period when quite fundamental decisions were being made, for example, the opening up of lands to settlement, or the routing of railways, elementary facts about climate, vegetation, soils, topography and even location were not available. There was no science of geography, and even if there had been there is no evidence to suggest that the Fathers of Confederation, or even the fathers of the Canadian Pacific Railway would have used it" (p. 583).

One of the areas in which geographical factors show their strength is the relationship between different types of land and the social organization which comes to characterize these different land types. While there are no tropical regions in Canada, just about every other type of climatic and geographic region can be found. Canada has its grass prairies and its varied forest covers; there is abundant tundra and in several places desert climate and vegetation can be found. Mixed with towering mountains and rugged coastline, it is no wonder that a framework for settlement patterns is revealed.

A crude measure such as population density reveals different settlement patterns, in that the relationship between land area and population supported suggests the extent to which the population is dispersed, and thus the broad settlement pattern. Table 3.1 indicates that the number of persons per square mile of land is less than one-tenth of one percent in the northern territories, 3.65 in Newfoundland (which includes sparsely-populated Labrador) and less than 7 in each of the western provinces. The table also indicates a more meaningful measure of density by computing it, not in relation to all land, but in relation to the ecumene, or that land which is settled and used for economic gain (see Gajda, 1960, p. 5). The ecumene leaves out some 87.6 percent of Canada's territory. The number of persons per square mile of ecumene for Canada as a whole in 1971 was 49.14. The highest 1971 ecumene densities in decreasing order of magnitude were found in Ontario (117.59), Quebec (98.98), Nova Scotia (76.45) and British Columbia (69.13). A less dispersed population seems to characterize all of the Atlantic Provinces, Quebec, Ontario and British Columbia. A more dispersed settlement pattern characterizes Manitoba and Alberta. And even when taking the ecumene as the reference point, an extremely thin pattern of settlement characterizes the Yukon Territory, Saskatchewan and the Northwest Territories. Not only was the ecumene density slightly greater in the Yukon in 1971 as compared with Saskatchewan, but (and this is not shown in the table) the density increased in the Yukon between 1966 (7.27) and 1971 (9.29), whereas in Saskatchewan it decreased from 1966

TABLE 3.1

Canadian Ecumene and Population Density by Province and Territory, Census Year 1971

	Land Area (sq mi)	Ecumene (sq mi)	Percent Ecumene	Population 1971	Population Density per sq mi land area	Density per sq mi ecumene
Newfoundland	143,045	9,360	6.5	522,104	3.65	55.78
P.E.I.	2,184	2,184	100.0	111,641	51.12	51.12
Nova Scotia	20,402	10,320	49.7	788,960	38.67	76.45
New Brunswick	27,835	16,835	61.3	634,557	22.80	37.69
Quebec	523,860	60,900	11.6	6,027,764	11.51	98.98
Ontario	344,092	65,507	19.6	7,703,106	22.39	117.59
Manitoba	211,775	36,739	17.3	988,247	4.67	26.90
Saskatchewan	220,182	104,610	47.5	926,242	4.21	8.85
Alberta	248,800	74,722	30.0	1,627,874	6.54	21.79
British Columbia	359,279	31,600	14.4	2,184,621	6.08	69.13
Yukon Territory	205,346	1,979	.9	18,388	.09	9.29
N.W.T.	1,253,438	4,144	.3	34,807	.03	8.40
Canada except Territories	2,101,454	432,777	20.7	21,515,116	10.24	49.71
Canada	3,560,238	438,900	12.4	21,568,311	6.06	49.14

Sources: Column 1 from CANADA YEAR BOOK: 1970-71, p.233; columns 2 and 3 from Gajda, 1960, p.8; and column 4 from STATISTICS CANADA DAILY, April 24, 1972.

(9.13) to 1971 (8.85). The ecumene density in Saskatchewan in 1971 approximated what it was in 1961 (8.84).

It should be noted that there is a built-in error contained in the last table in that Gajda's land utilization data are almost fifteen years out of date. Even though the table relates recent population data to land utilization data determined in the late 1950's, it is here assumed that the table's error is not significantly large since changes in land utilization patterns are not of the same magnitude as population changes, and because land losses caused by rural-to-urban migration likely approximate land gains due to hinterland development.

In addition to the factor of population density, it is interesting to note that Canada's industrially and agriculturally developed belt exists south of the forest-tundra transition region of vegetation and, in large part, south of Canada's boreal forests (see Watts, 1968). Two of the country's largest cities (Edmonton and Winnipeg) border on the boreal forests, but the cities of southwestern British Columbia, southern Ontario and southern Quebec extend into different climate and vegetation zones. While this pattern of land settlement and development has persisted right up to the present, there are penetrating signs of movement north. There are the examples of resource towns such as Labrador City, Thompson, Fort McMurray and Whitehorse. And there are the promises for tomorrow as seen, for example, in the concept of Mid-Canada. The Mid-Canada development corridor as proposed overlaps in large part the boreal forests from the Atlantic to the Pacific and north to the Beaufort Sea and Hudson Bay.

Moving on, it is difficult to know where to start and impossible to tell all when the subject is history. There follows a sketch of what are taken to be the most obvious historical events which set the stage for contemporary Canadian society. The sketch is an interpretation to the extent that certain events are selected above others; selection implies interpretation. "History is so indifferently rich that a case for almost any conclusion from it can be made by a selection of instances" (Durant and Durant, 1968, p. 97).

There are several basic interpretations of history which correspond to the institutional resources and commitments of a society. There is legal as well as political and economic history. It is an historical fact of life that Canada is a common law jurisdiction, meaning that Canada's legal institution was born of British common law. But even such fact does not fully support an historical generalization about the institution of law in Canada, for the system of law in the province of Quebec owes its origin to European civil law. In addition, the everyday contacts between the Canadian legal system and those of many countries of the world create a complex pattern of interdependence which prevents making any claim that Canada's legal system is uniquely Canadian. This kind of claim in the area of law as well as in other areas such as government, politics and economics would be dismissed as unrealistic, and perhaps even utopian.

Political history is taken to be the history of Canadian government and politics. The subject of political history is broad for it must deal not only with the development of the Canadian nation as a political system, but also with the political systems of provinces, territories and communities. In addition, there are many political topics of considerable importance for the student of Canadian society. The development of agrarian political movements in the prairie region is every bit as important as the study of changing patterns of political co-operation and conflict between Ottawa and the provinces.

It is economic history which has received widespread attention of Canadian scholars. Canada's economic history began with fish and fur. Documentation became available with the highly regarded studies by Innis: THE FUR TRADE IN CANADA (1930) and THE COD FISHERIES (1940). These and other works form the backbone of what is termed a staple theory of economic history. Watkins (1963) argued that the "fundamental assumption of the staple theory is that staple exports [such as fish and fur, timber and wheat] are the leading sector of the economy and set the pace for economic growth. The limited — at first possibly non-existent — domestic market, and the factor proportions — an abundance of land relative to labour and capital — create a comparative advantage in resource-intensive exports, or staples. Economic development will be a process of diversification around an export base. The central concept of a staple theory, therefore, is the spread effects of the export sector, that is, the impact of export activity on domestic economy and society" (p. 144). Watkins qualified his review by noting that the staple theory is not a "general theory of economic growth, nor even a general theory about the growth of export-oriented economies, but rather as applicable to the atypical case of the new country" (p. 143).

The developing Canadian economy was largely dependent on staples throughout the nineteenth century. The degree to which the economy expanded and diversified from the start of the present century is a function of a vast number of events. The temporal and spatial patterns of economic development, and thus a summary of Canadian economic history, was reviewed by Wolfe (1967) in a marvelously complicated chart covering a period from 1800 to 1967. In brief, the twentieth century brought with it numerous developments, many of which were interdependent, and all of which were consequential for the developing society. A partial list would include the wheat economy, hydro-electric power, the development of oil and gas resources, the extraction of ores and other minerals, the protective tariff, urbanization, the development of communication and transportation links, and the development of a secondary manufacturing and service economy. The staple theory of economic history does not explain urbanization or the development of secondary manufacturing, but it does suggest the nature of the beginning of Canada's economic system.

Historical conditioning factors place broad but highly significant limits upon the structure of contemporary Canadian society. Some of the more obvious factors are listed. First, adoption of the parliamentary form of government and the common system of law were early decisions which continue to influence the nature of decision making and conflict resolution in Canada. Second, Canada's constitutional authority stems from the fact of confederation and the British North America Act of 1867, a document which awarded a division of powers which persists to the present. Third, of great significance is the design for, and actual pattern of, western expansion and settlement, the policies related thereto, and especially the coming of the tides of immigrants at various times since the mid-1800's. Fourth, one of the most significant sociological themes in Canadian history is the "continuity of the French community in Quebec" (Davis, 1971, p. 7). Fifth and sixth, Davis argued further that "urbanization and the rise of urban industries in a capitalist context" and "the key importance of foreign imperialism throughout the entire development of Canadian society" are further themes of importance in any historical review of present-day Canadian society (p. 7). Seventh, the role of the protective tariff in Canada's social development was important for symbolic as well as economic reasons, although Dales (1966) concluded that the "economic evils of protectionism have been particularly virulent in Canada" (p. 1). Finally, continentalism has often been a match for nationalism in Canada, with many federal elections both early and recent hanging in the balance.

These hasty comments should not be taken to reflect a simplified attitude toward history in general, or Canadian history in particular. They are the kinds of summary comments which we all make at one time or another, and in making them we often allow ourselves to be deceived as we try to understand the nature and problems of society. While historians study these factors in great detail, their interpretations are not always passed on to lay audiences, or even to professional audiences. Add to this the fact that many historical interpretations are simply unwelcome news to our minds, and we find some of the reasons why simplification is a habit many of us find easy to embrace.

The whole matter is further complicated by our frequent willingness to accept one interpretation while blocking out others. For example, we may argue that economic development in Canada came about as the resources of the new empire were harnessed through the diligent efforts of workers and good managers. It is a pleasant interpretation; indeed, it may flatter us by pointing to the hard work of our forefathers, the settlers and early developers of the land. This interpretation need not keep us from agreeing with Davis concerning the rise of urban industries in a capitalist context for, after all, capitalism was and is our accepted way of life. Yet, though there are other interpretations consistent with Davis but more detailed and thereby perhaps more threatening to our heritage, we reject them, if indeed we acknowledge their existence. For example, there is a popular interpretation circulating in some parts of the country and among certain groups, that Canadian economic development was and is a brutalizing affair which increasingly concentrates capital in metropolitan locations, and then proceeds to reap the benefits associated with the exploitation of labor and natural resources. The dynamic of capital concentration is seen in the continual movement of capital from hinterland to metropolis, and the tendency to apply that capital in ways which continue the process of exploitation. This, too, is economic development, but an interpretation so blunt as to be often termed controversial, rhetorical and, perhaps because it sounds politically left wing, erroneous. In essence, the interpretation is so described because it is a threat to the individual and corporate members of the economic elite, and because any widespread appreciation of this viewpoint by other than isolated groups in the population might have a revolutionary effect on the present economic organization of society. We will examine the institution of capital in more detail in Chapter 4.

It is difficult to appraise which geographical and historical factors have most influenced the contemporary shape of Canadian society. To so appraise is to judge, and to judge depends very much upon interpretation, as we have just seen. However, there can be no denying the conclusion that Canada's vast hinterland constitutes a major physical reason for the form of settlement and economic development which the land has seen, and that the country's location on the frontier of the United States is a highly related reason for the form of social organization in Canada. It is perhaps noteworthy that most of the historical factors listed earlier relate in some way — usually in a quite direct way — to Canada's perennial national task, namely, to develop patterns of growth in relation to the social interests of other nations, most particularly England, France and the United States. The history of today seems to be no exception.

38

In conclusion, the risks of dealing with history have been noted well by Boulding (1970).

The interpreter of history is in a dangerous occupation. Can he, at the same time, be sensitive to the movements of all social systems, avoid trying to confine history to any particular strait-jacket, beware of giving random events more importance than they deserve, be sensitive to the unnerving complexity both of man and of society, and still avoid the temptation to despair? The interpretation of his own history is for man an intellectual task of the highest practical importance, for only by understanding what is nonrandom in history can man hope to move from the slavery of evolution to the freedom of teleology. It is only as we learn the real processes of society that we can mold the future towards our present ideals. This is a task which requires a strange mixture of humility and boldness — humility to acknowledge that we may be wrong, for without this we cannot learn, and boldness to trust in our present understanding, for without this we cannot act (p. 18).

Overview of the Canadian Population

Measure, by all means, measure, and count, by all means, count. But let us count and measure the things that count (Alpert, 1963, p. 47).

Population data are presented and interpreted from time to time throughout this book. The present section is included so that a more systematic overview of Canada's population is presented from the start, especially with respect to the composition of the population and to selected changes in composition across time. Another reason for including this section is to accent the importance of population studies. Although most social scientists pay lip service to the field of demography and to its indicators, many fail to realize the importance and magnitude of the data available to them through population statistics, and thus many discount population studies as a means for the analysis of society.

The macroscopic importance of population studies is seen in the so-called population transition. The population transition hinges upon the process of industrialization. Pre-industrial society was characterized by slow population growth because limits of agricultural technology limited population growth. In terms of the factors governing population change, migration was relatively unimportant, while birth and death rates were relatively high.

Then came the industrial revolution with all of its implications for social organization. Production moved away from the family and into the factory. Great advances were introduced more quickly than at any other point in human history. "For the first time the world's entire population could be regarded as a single entity responding in varying degrees to one dynamic process" (Davis, 1948, p. 596). The industrial revolution brought with it advances not only in agricultural technology, but also in areas such as medicine and hygiene. Industrialization changed the factors governing population change; migration became much more important, the death rate declined and the birth rate remained relatively high. The result was that industrialization heightened the pace of population growth. Davis calculated that the world's population expanded by .29 percent annually during the period 1650 to 1750, by .51 percent annually during the period 1800 to 1850, and by .75 percent annually during the period 1900 to 1940 (p. 596). The Population Reference Bureau estimated that the world's population is expanding presently by 2 percent annually, this estimate based upon the latest available estimates by the United Nations.

The third phase in population transition is a decline in the rate of population growth, caused primarily by a lower birth rate. This phase has been increasingly operative in western nations; indeed, it is one of the things indicating that certain

TABLE 3.2

Population Information for Selected Countries, Latest Available Year

	Population Mid-1971 (millions)	Annual Births /1000	Annual Deaths /1000	Annual Rate of Growth (%)	Per Capita GNP (1968) (US$)
Seven Countries with Lowest Annual Rate of Growth					
Malta	.3	15.8	9.4	− .8	640
East Germany	16.2	14.0	14.3	.1	1430
Austria	7.5	16.5	13.4	.4	1320
Belgium	9.7	14.6	12.4	.4	1810
Finland	4.7	14.5	9.8	.4	1720
Hungary	10.3	15.0	11.3	.4	980
West Germany	58.9	15.0	12.0	.4	1970
Canada and Five Countries with Annual Rate of Growth within .1 of Canada's Rate					
Canada	21.8	17.6	7.3	1.7	2460
Ryukyu Islands	1.0	22.0	5.0	1.7	580
New Zealand	2.9	22.5	8.7	1.7	2000
China	772.9	33.0	15.0	1.8	90
Lesotho	1.1	40.0	23.0	1.8	80
Trinidad & Tobago	1.1	30.0	7.0	1.8	870
Thirteen Countries with Highest Annual Rate of Growth					
Colombia	22.1	44.0	11.0	3.4	310
Dominican Republic	4.4	48.0	15.0	3.4	290
Ecuador	6.3	45.0	11.0	3.4	220
El Salvador	3.6	47.0	13.0	3.4	280
Honduras	2.8	49.0	16.0	3.4	260
Iraq	10.0	49.0	15.0	3.4	260
Mexico	52.5	42.0	9.0	3.4	530
Paraguay	2.5	45.0	11.0	3.4	230
Philippines	39.4	46.0	12.0	3.4	180
Southern Rhodesia	5.2	48.0	14.0	3.4	220
Venezuela	11.1	41.0	8.0	3.4	950
Costa Rica	1.9	45.0	8.0	3.8	450
Kuwait	.8	43.0	7.0	8.2	3540

Source: Population Reference Bureau, 1971.

areas of the world already have entered a postindustrial era. Table 3.2 suggests divisions between countries classified according to their annual rate of population growth. There is remarkable stability in the death rates across these countries; with only two exceptions, the death rates range from 7 to 16 per 1,000 population. Birth rates are another matter, however, since a country's rate of population growth is clearly associated with its birth rate. The seven countries listed in the table having the lowest annual rate of population growth show an average birth rate of 15.1 per 1,000 population. The six countries listed having an annual rate of growth similar to Canada's show an average birth rate of 27.5 per 1,000 population (note the wide variability of the data). The thirteen countries listed having the highest annual rate of growth show an average birth rate of 45.5 per 1,000 population.

Table 3.2 also suggests that a country's rate of population growth is associated with its per capita gross national product. The seven countries which show the lowest rate of population growth also show the highest average per capita gross national product at $1,410. The six countries which have a rate of growth similar to Canada's show a lower average per capita gross national product at $1,013 (again note the wide variability of the data). The thirteen countries which show the highest rate of growth also show the lowest average per capita gross national product at $594 (although oil-rich Kuwait is a noteworthy exception to the pattern).

Over and above the significant variations and some noteworthy extremes which appear in this table, the data are sufficient to document the importance of the population transition. Like many countries, Canada's rate of population growth has been steadily declining during recent decades. Perhaps Canada has been experiencing the population transition firsthand, and will continue to do so until the birth rate suppresses the rate of population growth even more, to the point where it is less than 1 percent annually.

Population changes are the result of changes in four variables: births, deaths, immigration and emigration. The population equation can be expressed verbally as follows: the population at a given time equals the population at an earlier time plus the number of births minus the number of deaths plus the number of immigrants minus the number of emigrants. Put more simply, the population at a given time equals the population at an earlier time plus the natural increase (births minus deaths) plus net migration (immigrants minus emigrants). Thus, the population of Canada in 1966 (20,014,880) was its population in 1961 (18, 238,247) plus the natural increase between 1961 and 1966 (1,517,893) plus net migration between those same years (258,740).

The magnitude of natural increase is relatively easy to ascertain. Table 3.3 indicates that Canada's birth rate generally has been declining since the mid-1950's. Annual birth rates in Canada since 1921 have generally declined, with only several exceptions, from 29.3 per 1,000 population in 1921 to 20.1 per 1,000 population in 1937, suggesting in part the effects of the depression years (see Kalbach and McVey, 1971, p. 57). From 1937 the rates generally increased, again with only several exceptions, to the post-war year of 1947 when the rate was 28.9 per 1,000 population. There was a certain stability in the rates between 1948 and 1953, and the rate of 28.5 per 1,000 population in 1954 marked the high point at the start of a decline which stretches right up to 1971. While there is a meaningful pattern of variation in the annual birth rates across time, the annual death rates have generally declined since the 1920's, although the magnitude of this decline has been only slight (see Kalbach and McVey, 1971, pp. 46-47). In overall view, natural increase

42

TABLE 3.3

Selected Vital Statistics, Canada, 1941 to 1971

	Births		Deaths		Natural Increase	
	#	Rate	#	Rate	#	Rate
Average 1941 to 1945	277,320	23.5	115,572	9.8	161,748	13.7
Average 1946 to 1950	355,748	27.4	120,438	9.3	235,310	18.1
Average 1951 to 1955	416,334	28.0	126,666	8.5	289,668	19.5
Average 1956 to 1960	469,555	27.6	136,669	8.0	332,886	19.6
Average 1961 to 1965	456,534	24.1	145,368	7.7	311,166	16.4
1966	387,710	19.4	149,863	7.5	237,847	11.9
1967	370,894	18.2	150,283	7.4	220,611	10.8
1968	364,310	17.6	153,196	7.4	211,114	10.2
1969	369,647	17.6	154,477	7.3	215,170	10.3
1970	371,988	17.4	155,961	7.3	216,027	10.1
1971	368,082	17.0	157,164	7.3	210,918	9.7

Sources: CANADA YEAR BOOK: 1970-71, p.286 and p.1380, and Dominion Bureau of Statistics Catalogues 84-001 and 84-201. Rates are per 1,000 population.

in Canada is much more a function of births than of deaths. The excess of births over deaths in 1971 was a sizable 210,918.

The magnitude of net migration is not as easy to ascertain. This is because records on the number of persons emigrating from Canada generally are unavailable. One of the available sources of data is the immigration record in the country to which a person emigrated from Canada. Thus, records in the United States show that 18,582 Canadian-born persons entered the United States in 1969 with the intention of establishing permanent residence in that country (CANADA YEAR BOOK: 1970-71, p. 274). These persons are *some* of the total number of Canadian emigrants in 1969. The only way of counting the number of emigrants from Canada to other countries is the deductive method of applying the demographic equation to solve for the number of emigrants, given all other quantities, including the population at given times known through a national census.

Immigration data are readily available, however. Immigrants have played an impressive part in Canada's population growth. There were several times, for example, when the number of immigrants in a single year exceeded the number of births in 1969. Canada welcomed 375,756 immigrants in 1912 and another 400,870 in 1913 (see Kalbach and McVey, 1971, p. 33). Even in more recent years the immigration tallies have been significant factors in Canada's population growth. For the years 1966 through 1969, respectively, the number of immigrants was 194,743, 222,876, 183,974 and 161,531, compared with the number of births for the same years of 387,710, 370,894, 364,310 and 369,647. The fact that immigration has been so important in Canada's social history was marked in late May of 1972 when the 10 millionth immigrant was greeted after his arrival from London.

Tables 3.4 and 3.5 show changing population totals and percentages for Canada as a whole and for each of the provinces and territories. A declining rate of population growth is documented by these tables. Perhaps more interesting, however, is the fact that growth patterns across the different provinces and territories are far from uniform. There is a strong tendency, with few exceptions, toward a declining rate of growth in the provinces. Looking at the period 1966 to 1971, only four of the twelve jurisdictions showed an increased rate of population growth in comparison with the period 1961 to 1966: Nova Scotia, Alberta, British Columbia and the Yukon Territory. Saskatchewan's rate of growth during the period 1966 to 1971 was negative as the province's population decreased from 955,344 in 1966 to 926,242 in 1971. The other noteworthy change revealed by these tables is the decreasing rate of population growth in the province of Quebec. Ontario had 541,861 more residents in 1951 than did Quebec; by 1971 the population of Ontario was 1,675,342 greater than the population of Quebec. These numbers suggest what analysts have already noted, namely, that Quebec is decreasingly a

TABLE 3.4

Canadian Population by Province, Census Years 1951 to 1971

	1951	1956	1961	1966	1971
Newfoundland	361,416	415,074	457,853	493,396	522,104
P.E.I.	98,429	99,285	104,629	108,535	111,641
Nova Scotia	642,584	694,717	737,007	756,039	788,960
New Brunswick	515,697	554,616	597,936	616,788	634,557
Quebec	4,055,681	4,628,378	5,259,211	5,780,845	6,027,764
Ontario	4,597,542	5,404,933	6,236,092	6,960,870	7,703,106
Manitoba	776,541	850,040	921,686	963,066	988,247
Saskatchewan	831,728	880,665	925,181	955,344	926,242
Alberta	939,501	1,123,116	1,331,944	1,463,203	1,627,874
British Columbia	1,165,210	1,398,464	1,629,082	1,873,674	2,184,621
Yukon Territory	9,096	12,190	14,628	14,382	18,388
N.W.T.	16,004	19,313	22,998	28,738	34,807
Canada	14,009,429	16,080,791	18,238,247	20,014,880	21,568,311

Sources: CANADA YEAR BOOK: 1970-71, p.212, and STATISTICS CANADA DAILY, April 24, 1972.

44

TABLE 3.5

Percentage Change of Canadian Population from Preceding Census by Province, Census Years 1951 to 1971

	1956	1961	1966	1971
Newfoundland	14.8	10.3	7.8	5.8
P.E.I.	.9	5.4	3.7	2.9
Nova Scotia	8.1	6.1	2.6	4.4
New Brunswick	7.5	7.8	3.2	2.9
Quebec	14.1	13.6	9.9	4.3
Ontario	17.6	15.4	11.6	10.7
Manitoba	9.5	8.4	4.5	2.6
Saskatchewan	5.9	5.1	3.3	− 3.0
Alberta	19.5	18.6	9.9	11.3
British Columbia	20.0	16.5	15.0	16.6
Yukon Territory	34.0	20.0	− 1.7	27.9
N.W.T.	20.7	19.1	25.0	21.1
Canada	14.8	13.4	9.7	7.8

Sources: CANADA YEAR BOOK: 1970-71, p.212, and STATISTICS CANADA DAILY, April 24, 1972.

source of new French Canadians, and that French Canada's *la revanche des berceaux* is not well founded in most recent demographic trends (see Joy, 1972, pp. 51-55).

Of related interest is Table 3.6 that reports information on the rural and urban populations. Canada continues to urbanize; the urban population in 1971 accounted for 76.1 percent of Canada's total population (an increase of 2.5 percentage points between 1966 and 1971). The provinces are far from equally urbanized with the range in 1971 defined by Ontario and Quebec (82.4 and 80.6 percent, respectively), and Prince Edward Island (38.3 percent). The only province showing a trend of decreasing urbanization between 1966 and 1971 was Nova Scotia (dropping 1.4 percentage points to 56.7 percent). This drop in Nova Scotia was tied to an increase in that province's rural nonfarm population (from 36.0 to 40.0 percent in the five year period). Nova Scotia, like *all* other provinces, showed a decreasing proportion of its population resident in rural farm areas. Much of the rural farm population appears to be moving to urban areas; and yet, a substantial part of the movement away from the farm is toward rural nonfarm areas (this being especially true between 1966 and 1971 for the provinces of Prince Edward Island and Nova Scotia, and false only in the cases of Newfoundland, New Brunswick, Alberta, the Yukon and Northwest Territories). The overall proportion of the Canadian popula-

TABLE 3.6

Canadian Urban and Rural Population by Province, Census Years 1966 and 1971

| | Census 1971 | | | | | Census 1966 | | | | |
| | | | Rural | | | | | Rural | | |
	Total	Urban	Total	Rural Non-farm	Rural Farm	Total	Urban	Total	Rural Non-farm	Rural Farm
Canada	21,568,310	16,410,780	5,157,525	3,737,730	1,419,795	20,014,880	14,726,759	5,288,121	3,382,910	1,905,211
Newfoundland	522,105	298,800	223,305	218,780	11,525	493,396	266,689	226,707	218,252	8,455
Prince Edward Island	111,645	42,780	68,860	47,730	21,130	108,535	39,747	68,788	37,947	30,841
Nova Scotia	788,960	447,400	341,555	315,290	26,265	756,039	438,907	317,132	271,881	45,251
New Brunswick	634,560	361,145	273,410	247,850	25,560	616,788	312,225	304,563	253,059	51,504
Quebec	6,027,765	4,861,240	1,166,520	861,215	305,300	5,780,845	4,525,114	1,255,731	770,667	485,064
Ontario	7,703,105	6,343,630	1,359,480	995,835	363,635	6,960,870	5,593,440	1,367,430	885,735	481,695
Manitoba	988,245	686,445	301,805	171,390	130,415	963,066	646,048	317,018	157,146	159,872
Saskatchewan	926,245	490,630	435,610	202,275	233,330	955,344	468,327	487,017	207,375	279,642
Alberta	1,627,870	1,196,250	431,620	195,595	236,025	1,463,203	1,007,407	455,796	178,198	277,598
British Columbia	2,184,620	1,654,410	530,215	456,700	73,515	1,873,674	1,410,493	463,181	377,984	85,197
Yukon	18,390	11,215	7,170	7,115	55	14,382	6,828	7,554	7,492	62
Northwest Territories	34,805	16,830	17,980	17,955	25	28,738	11,534	17,204	17,174	30

Percentage distribution

| | Census 1971 | | | | | Census 1966 | | | | |
| | | | Rural | | | | | Rural | | |
	Total	Urban	Total	Rural Non-farm	Rural Farm	Total	Urban	Total	Rural Non-farm	Rural Farm
Canada	100.0	76.1	23.9	17.3	6.6	100.0	73.6	26.4	16.9	9.5
Newfoundland	100.0	57.2	42.8	41.9	0.9	100.0	54.1	45.9	44.2	1.7
Prince Edward Island	100.0	38.3	61.7	42.8	18.9	100.0	36.6	63.4	35.0	28.4
Nova Scotia	100.0	56.7	43.3	40.0	3.3	100.0	58.1	41.9	36.0	5.9
New Brunswick	100.0	56.9	43.1	39.1	4.0	100.0	50.6	49.4	41.0	8.4
Quebec	100.0	80.6	19.4	14.3	5.1	100.0	78.3	21.7	13.3	8.4
Ontario	100.0	82.4	17.6	12.9	4.7	100.0	80.4	19.6	12.7	6.9
Manitoba	100.0	69.5	30.5	17.3	13.2	100.0	67.1	32.9	16.3	16.6
Saskatchewan	100.0	53.0	47.0	21.8	25.2	100.0	49.0	51.0	21.7	29.3
Alberta	100.0	73.5	26.5	12.0	14.5	100.0	68.8	31.2	12.2	19.0
British Columbia	100.0	75.7	24.3	20.9	3.4	100.0	75.3	24.7	20.2	4.5
Yukon	100.0	61.0	39.0	38.7	0.3	100.0	47.5	52.5	52.1	0.4
Northwest Territories	100.0	48.3	51.7	51.6	0.1	100.0	40.1	59.9	59.8	0.1

Source: STATISTICS CANADA DAILY, December 22, 1972.

TABLE 3.7

Canadian Population by Age Groups, Census Years 1966 and 1971

	1966		1971	
0 to 4 years	2,197,387	(11.0%)	1,816,155	(8.4%)
5 to 9 years	2,300,357	(11.5%)	2,254,005	(10.5%)
10 to 14 years	2,093,513	(10.5%)	2,310,738	(10.7%)
15 to 19 years	1,837,725	(9.2%)	2,114,346	(9.8%)
20 to 24 years	1,461,298	(7.3%)	1,889,403	(8.8%)
25 to 34 years	2,483,491	(12.4%)	2,889,545	(13.4%)
35 to 44 years	2,543,172	(12.7%)	2,526,398	(11.7%)
45 to 54 years	2,078,179	(10.4%)	2,291,578	(10.6%)
55 to 64 years	1,479,710	(7.4%)	1,731,738	(8.0%)
65 to 69 years	531,709	(2.7%)	619,958	(2.9%)
70 years and above	1,007,839	(5.0%)	1,124,447	(5.2%)
Total	20,014,880	(100.1%)	21,568,311	(100.0%)

Source: STATISTICS CANADA DAILY, April 26, 1972.

tion resident in rural nonfarm areas in 1971 was 17.3 percent, up .4 percent over 1966. The overall proportion resident in rural farm areas in 1971 was 6.6 percent, down 2.9 percent from 1966 (see STATISTICS CANADA DAILY, December 22, 1972).

So far this section has shown the demographer to be a counter, albeit a counter of large numbers. The tricks of his trade really begin at the point where the study of population and of changes in composition across time and space are analysed in relation to other changes in society. This section concludes with two basic examples of the types of more detailed investigations which are undertaken by demographers: analysis by age groups, and the study of domestic migration.

Table 3.7 indicates the changed distribution of the Canadian population by age between the years 1966 and 1971. Even in so short a period of time noteworthy shifts are revealed. For example, those 9 years of age and below constituted less of the total population in 1971 than they did in 1966 (by 3.6 percentage points). Most of those who were 9 years of age and below in 1966 were five years older in 1971, and so the decline in the number of persons aged 5 to 9 years was less than it was for those aged up to 4 years (by 1.0 percentage point as compared with 2.6 percentage points). Only the latter cohort, those up to 4 years of age, has been subject to the declining birth rate since 1966 (19.4 per 1,000 population in 1966 and 17.0 per 1,000 in 1971).

There were more persons in each of the cohorts between 10 and 34 years of age in 1971 when compared to 1966 (by a total of 3.3 percentage points). On the other hand, there were fewer persons in the age cohort 35 to 44 (by 1.0 percentage point). These were the people born between 1927 and 1936, when the depression

47

helped to push the birth rates lower than their earlier levels. The effect of that phenomenon persists in that there were more persons aged 45 years and above in 1971 than there were in 1966 (by a total of 1.2 percentage points).

The point of all this is that the resources and priorities of society are bent into new shapes as the society's population alters its basic composition. Almost every aspect of social structure is affected by changing population composition. In terms of the above trends, both the absolute size and the experience of the labour force hang in the balance, as do matters like the overhead associated with such things as unused classrooms (built at an earlier period when the rate of growth of school-aged children was higher), or the desirable rate in the expansion of services for those who are aging. Because of the long-range continuity inherent in population analysis by age groups, such a readily available method as the construction of age pyramids suggests much in relation to tasks of social planning. While the data noted above and the discussion have been concerned only with different age levels, the population analyst usually questions in more depth than we have here. For example, data often are analysed across regions. While Canada's death rate in 1970 was 7.3 per 1,000 population, rates by province ranged from a low of 6.3 in Alberta to a high of 9.2 in Prince Edward Island. More significant fluctuations are found in the birth rates across Canada; the lowest rate in 1970 was in the province of Quebec (15.3 per 1,000 population), the highest provincial rate was in Newfoundland (24.2 per 1,000 population), while the highest rate of all was in the Northwest Territories (40.5 per 1,000 population). These compared with Canada's overall birth rate in 1970 of 17.4 per 1,000 population (see Statistics Canada, Catalogue 84-201).

In a similar fashion, data are often analysed across various measuring units such as census tracts. It is common that information concerning sex composition is combined with information on age composition and presented in the form of an age-sex pyramid. A great deal of comparative information is summarized in Figure 3.8 which presents the data on sex and age composition for two Edmonton census tracts for the years 1961 and 1966. Which tract suggests an older area of the city? Which tract includes The University of Alberta within its area? Which tract had the highest proportion of young adults with children in 1966, and how did the composition of that tract's population change between 1961 and 1966? The implications not just for social planning but for *differential* planning in different areas are as numerous as the questions which can be asked of such data.

There is, finally, the subject of domestic or internal migration. There is a constant reshuffling of the population within and between the different provinces and territories of Canada.

Migration is one of the most important topics in the study of any society. The pattern of the movement of people over space and among time periods provides useful reflections of economic and social conditions and changes. Perpetual migrational flows of people seem to be characteristic of the history of Canada (Stone, 1969, p. 21).

The data which follow refer to the period 1956 to 1961. An in-migrant is one enumerated in one province in 1961 but who lived in another province in 1956. An out-migrant is one enumerated in one province in 1956 but who lived in another province in 1961. Specifically, Stone (1969) noted that the in-migration ratio is defined as the in-migration over the reporting population, while the out-migration ratio is defined as the out-migration over the exposed population (see p. 28). The gross migration ratio is a general indicator of the amount of turnover in a given

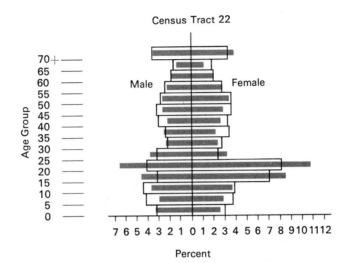

FIGURE 3.8

Age and Sex Distributions in Two Edmonton
Census Tracts, 1961 and 1966

Census Tract 22

Male   Female

Age Group

70+
65
60
55
50
45
40
35
30
25
20
15
10
5
0

7 6 5 4 3 2 1 0 1 2 3 4 5 6 7 8 9 10 11 12

Percent

 1961
1966

Census Tract 42

Male   Female

Age Group

70+
65
60
55
50
45
40
35
30
25
20
15
10
5
0

13 12 11 10 9 8 7 6 5 4 3 2 1 0 1 2 3 4 5 6 7 8 9 10 11

Percent

Source: Unpublished charts. prepared by the Population
Research Laboratory, The University of Alberta.

49

TABLE 3.9

Canadian Interprovincial Five-Year Migration Ratios, 1956 to 1961

	In-Migration Ratio	Out-Migration Ratio	Gross Migration Ratio
Newfoundland	1.6	2.8	4.4
Prince Edward Island	5.6	6.8	12.4
Nova Scotia	4.1	6.5	10.6
New Brunswick	4.9	5.9	10.9
Quebec	1.6	1.7	3.3
Ontario	3.0	2.3	5.3
Manitoba	5.5	7.4	12.9
Saskatchewan	4.2	8.2	12.5
Alberta	7.5	6.0	13.5
British Columbia	6.7	4.2	11.0
Canadian Provinces	3.5	3.5	7.0

Source: Stone, 1969, p. 28.

population; according to Stone it is defined as the in-migrants plus the out-migrants over the average of the reporting and the exposed populations (see p. 28). Stone's monograph should be consulted for detailed definitions of terms.

Table 3.9 shows that domestic migration was relatively unimportant in contributing to the populations of the provinces of Quebec, Newfoundland and Ontario between 1956 and 1961. Migration as a factor determining population composition was at least twice as important in all other provinces, with the greatest population turnover in Alberta. Population instability caused by migration was thus more characteristic of the three maritime provinces and the four western provinces. In percentage terms rather than in terms of absolute numbers, in-migration for the period 1956 to 1961 was greatest in Alberta followed by British Columbia, and least in Newfoundland and Quebec. Out-migration for the same period was greatest in Saskatchewan followed by Manitoba, and least in Quebec followed by Ontario.

Stone qualified his presentation by noting certain problems associated with computing migration ratios across a five-year period (see pp. 329-330). Because the measurement points were fixed at only two points in time, 1956 and 1961, multiple migrations were not included, persons who migrated but returned to their place of origin within the five-year period were not included, and persons who were enumerated, migrated and died, or were enumerated, migrated and then emigrated were not included. Such are the problems of the demographer!

Table 3.10 shows the province moved to by out-migrants between 1956 and 1961. With certain exceptions, there is an obvious contiguity to the pattern; people tended to move to a nearby province rather than to a distant province. British

TABLE 3.10

Provincial Destinations of Out-Migrants from Each Province in Percentages, Canada, 1956 to 1961

To From	Nfld.	P.E.I.	N.S.	N.B.	Que.	Ont.	Man.	Sask.	Alta.	B.C.	Total
Newfoundland		.5	18.2	6.6	13.7	46.9	2.9	2.0	4.3	4.8	99.9
P.E.I.	3.7		17.4	17.9	8.2	40.7	2.0	1.4	5.4	3.4	100.1
Nova Scotia	3.3	4.0		18.5	11.1	46.9	3.3	.9	3.9	8.1	100.0
New Brunswick	2.3	2.8	13.8		30.0	42.2	1.7	.7	3.2	3.2	99.9
Quebec	1.2	.6	4.4	5.8		73.0	3.1	1.2	4.6	6.1	100.0
Ontario	1.8	1.1	8.8	6.6	35.4		13.2	5.2	12.6	15.3	100.0
Manitoba	.5	.3	2.2	2.2	6.0	34.1		15.3	17.8	21.7	100.1
Saskatchewan	.1	.2	.7	.3	1.4	13.7	16.2		39.8	27.5	99.9
Alberta	.4	.3	1.3	1.1	4.8	20.8	9.0	15.9		46.4	100.0
British Columbia	.3	.3	3.8	1.9	5.7	28.7	9.6	11.1	38.6		100.0

Source: Abridged from Stone, 1969, pp. 35-38.

51

Columbia, Alberta and espcially Ontario were the noteworthy exceptions. The centrality of Ontario together with its continued growth along with the provinces of Alberta and British Columbia likely means that the migratory trends reported for the period 1956 to 1961 have continued through the contemporary period. These trends for the most part have persisted since at least 1921 (see Stone, 1969, p. 39).

The promise of this section was to overview the Canadian population in relation to internal composition, changes in composition across time and the broader question of Canada's position within the worldwide context of population transition. Some data already have become available from the last census taken in 1971. The material selected for inclusion in this section only begins to touch upon the many areas of inquiry which mark the work of population analysts.

References

Alpert, Harry, "Some Observations on the State of Sociology," THE PACIFIC SOCIO-LOGICAL REVIEW, 6 (Fall, 1963) 45-48.

Benedict, Ruth, PATTERNS OF CULTURE, New York: Mentor Books, 1946.

Boulding, Kenneth E., A PRIMER ON SOCIAL DYNAMICS: HISTORY AS DIALECTICS AND DEVELOPMENT, New York: The Free Press, 1970.

Dales, J. H., THE PROTECTIVE TARIFF IN CANADA'S DEVELOPMENT, Toronto: University of Toronto Press, 1966.

Davis, Arthur K., "Canadian Society and History as Hinterland Versus Metropolis," in Richard J. Ossenberg, CANADIAN SOCIETY: PLURALISM, CHANGE, AND CONFLICT, Scarborough, Ont.: Prentice-Hall of Canada Ltd., 1971, pp. 6-32.

Davis, Kingsley, HUMAN SOCIETY, New York: The Macmillan Company, 1948.

Durant, Will, THE STORY OF CIVILIZATION: I. OUR ORIENTAL HERITAGE, New York: Simon and Schuster, 1935.

Durant, Will and Ariel Durant, THE LESSONS OF HISTORY, New York: Simon and Schuster, 1968.

Gajda, Roman T., "The Canadian Ecumene: Inhabited and Uninhabited Areas," GEO-GRAPHICAL BULLETIN, 15 (1960) 5-18.

Hoebel, E. Adamson, THE LAW OF PRIMITIVE MAN: A STUDY IN COMPARATIVE LEGAL DYNAMICS, Cambridge, Mass.: Harvard University Press, 1954.

Innis, Harold A., THE FUR TRADE IN CANADA: AN INTRODUCTION TO CANADIAN ECONOMIC HISTORY, New Haven, Conn.: Yale University Press, 1930.

Innis, Harold A., THE COD FISHERIES: THE HISTORY OF AN INTERNATIONAL ECONOMY, New Haven, Conn.: Yale University Press, 1940.

Joy, Richard J., LANGUAGES IN CONFLICT: THE CANADIAN EXPERIENCE, Toronto: McClelland and Stewart Limited, 1972.

Kalbach, Warren E. and Wayne W. McVey, THE DEMOGRAPHIC BASES OF CANADIAN SOCIETY, Toronto: McGraw-Hill Company of Canada Limited, 1971.

Lloyd, Trevor, "Trends," in John Warkentin, ed., CANADA: A GEOGRAPHICAL INTER-PRETATION, Toronto: Methuen Publications, 1968, pp. 583-591.

Lower, J. A., CANADA: AN OUTLINE HISTORY, Toronto: The Ryerson Press, 1966.

Stone, Leroy O., MIGRATION IN CANADA: REGIONAL ASPECTS, Ottawa: Dominion Bureau of Statistics, 1969.

Watkins, Melville H., "A Staple Theory of Economic Growth," THE CANADIAN JOURNAL OF ECONOMICS AND POLITICAL SCIENCE, 29 (May, 1963) 141-158.

Watts, F. B., "Climate, Vegetation, Soil," in John Warkentin, ed., CANADA: A GEOGRAPHICAL INTERPRETATION, Toronto: Methuen Publications, 1968, pp. 78-111.

Williams, Robin M., AMERICAN SOCIETY: A SOCIOLOGICAL INTERPRETATION, Revised Second Edition, New York: Alfred A. Knopf, 1960.

Wolfe, Roy I., "Spatial Interaction in the Economic History of Canada, 1800 to 1967," in John Warkentin, ed., CANADA: A GEOGRAPHICAL INTERPRETATION, Toronto: Methuen Publications, 1968, rear cover insert.

For Further Reading

Clark, S. D., THE DEVELOPING CANADIAN COMMUNITY, Toronto: University of Toronto Press, 1962.

Easterbrook, W. T. and Hugh G. J. Aitken, CANADIAN ECONOMIC HISTORY, Toronto: The Macmillan Company of Canada Limited, 1956.

George, M. V., INTERNAL MIGRATION IN CANADA: DEMOGRAPHIC ANALYSES, Ottawa: Dominion Bureau of Statistics, 1970.

Hughes, Everett C., FRENCH CANADA IN TRANSITION, Chicago: The University of Chicago Press, 1943.

Kalbach, Warren E., THE IMPACT OF IMMIGRATION ON CANADA'S POPULATION, Ottawa: Dominion Bureau of Statistics, 1970.

Lipset, Seymour Martin, AGRARIAN SOCIALISM: THE COOPERATIVE COMMONWEALTH FEDERATION IN SASKATCHEWAN, Revised Edition, Garden City, N.Y.: Anchor Books, 1968.

Robinson, Ira M., NEW INDUSTRIAL TOWNS ON CANADA'S RESOURCE FRONTIER, Chicago: The University of Chicago, 1962.

Wrong, Dennis H., POPULATION AND SOCIETY, Third Edition, New York: Random House, 1967.

Chapter 4

Social Institutions

Sociologists use words such as "norm" and "normative" as routinely as politicians refer to the needs of the people. When something is said to be normative, the implication is that it is the subject of some agreement. The very fact of agreement gives to a norm the nature of an ought or a valid expectation. A social norm is a rule or standard of behaviour defined by the shared expectations of two or more people regarding what behaviour is to be considered socially acceptable. Social norms provide guidelines to the range of behaviour appropriate and applicable to particular social situations. . . . Many sociologists regard society, social institutions, social roles, moral systems, etc., as normative structures based on shared expectations of behaviour (Theodorson and Theodorson, 1969, pp. 276-277).

It follows that a social institution entails the organization of social norms which provide guidance to individuals as they go about the task of achieving institutional goals. It is through social institutions that most people learn what are the appropriate and applicable norms for behaviour in given situations. Some of society's institutions function primarily as socializing and control agencies: education, religion and family. Other institutions help to regulate conduct: law, polity and economy. Still other institutions satisfy the innovative and problem-solving needs of society: science. Social institutions obviously differ in that some have a moral orientation (religion, family, education), or an expedient orientation (economy, polity, science, law). Often there is significant overlap in orientation. For example, while education — a functional need of society — is typically moral in its orientation, the fact that people must be at least minimally socialized in standard ways in order to survive the daily challenges of social living (literacy, for example) means that education as a normative system also has instrumental or expedient purposes. There are, in addition, differing orientations within a single institution. Law as practised by lawyers is concerned with the expedient solution of legal conflicts; law as debated by legal theorists is frequently viewed morally and valuationally rather than instrumentally. The distinction seems to be between the law as *is* (the lawyer's law) and the law as it *ought* to be (the lawyer's conscience).

The study of social institutions is important for at least two reasons. First, institutions are the most common social means by which to satisfy or meet what are often termed the functional prerequisites of society. Functional prerequisites refer simply to the things which must be achieved by a society if it is to survive or persist. Functional prerequisites include such things as role differentiation and role

54

assignment, some means for communication, shared social goals and the normative regulation of means for the achievement of goals, some means for controlling disruptive or deviant behaviour, provision for adequate socialization and shared cognitive orientations (see Aberle, Cohen, Davis, Levy and Sutton, 1950).

Second, institutions are the means whereby a society develops formal commitments to certain social goals and to appropriate means for their achievement. Formal commitments are often expressed through differing degrees of consensus on social norms, the norms being the prescribed (or proscribed) means for goal achievement.

The law is a social institution which deserves careful study. There are a number of reasons for focused attention in this institutional area. The law itself is a significant source of social data because law is promulgated by ordered and recountable procedures, is usually codified and is applied to cases in formal and generally reliable or consistent ways. The law embodies a society's formally-stated normative prescriptions (and proscriptions). It can be assumed that many, if not most, laws are symbolic of the underlying normative structures of a society. To the degree that this last assumption is invalid, it might be expected that social pressures can be observed which push for the re-alignment of law with practice. Finally, the legal institution embodies the most formal statement of sanctions which can be applied to members of a society upon demonstrated violation of normative codes.

To study social institutions, then, is to emphasize the nature of social norms. To study the law as a social institution is to emphasize those norms which are held in such esteem that they can be enforced by legal sanctions. Therefore, the law is of sociological interest in that it broadly represents the normative structure of a social group, and so, the law as an indicator of norms, provides one viable approach to the study of social continuity and social change.

Recall the broad design which ties the present chapter to Chapters 3 and 5. Social institutions are the province of sociology for it is through the influence of institutions that men and women assess and select their options for behaviour. It is also through the influence of institutions that they and their behaviours are evaluated. Social institutions have more of a direct bearing on persons, it is assumed, than do the broad geographical, historical and demographic factors which were discussed in the last chapter.

The present chapter offers an appraisal of capital and property as illustrations of social institutions, followed by a focused discussion of topics which pertain to a Canadian sociology of law. The chapter concludes with a brief comment on social institutions in terms of the concept of authority.

Capital and Property

> [T]he classical theory of natural right [of property] is so deeply embedded in popular thought that the spokesmen of big business sometimes repeat the familiar phrases, although their manner of doing so often betrays that they are not unaware of the contradictions between the classical doctrine and the institutions which they uphold (Schlatter, 1951, p. 280).

Two of the most entrenched social institutions of the western world are capital and property. Capital is that which can be used for investment and economic gain. Capital is currency. It is the distribution of tokens and as such it represents the economic backbone of society. Many persons believe that the ownership of capital, especially when invested in various kinds of property, is the means to most ends.

One of the great difficulties we have in comprehending the importance of the institution of capital lies in our failure to view capital as a social institution. Most of us will quickly acknowledge that our economic system is a capitalistic one, that this means that the ownership of the means of production usually lies in the hands of private individuals and corporate bodies rather than the state, and that free competition in search of profit is the point of the struggle. While we acknowledge these meanings, we often fail to define capital as an institution. We are capable of supplying much more detail, as, for example, was provided in Chapter 3 concerning the developing Canadian economy. We know that the protective tariff played such-and-such a part in development, just as did the expansion of new power sources and the massive movement to urbanize. Despite the detail, despite our awareness of the many factors contributing to that which we term growth, we fail immeasurably when we fail to interpret Canada's social development in terms of the role played by the institution of capital.

It is a well-known thesis that capital is to be welcomed in an underdeveloped area because it alone can stimulate economic growth and development. Thus, the way for the Atlantic Provinces to prosper economically, for example, is to attract investment capital from central Canada and from foreign countries, trying at all times to locate the capital in labour-intensive sectors of the regional economy. Critics of this thesis point to facts which question it, such as there often being net capital outflow rather than inflow, from the underdeveloped to the developed area, or the tendency of developed areas to acquire local enterprises and to finance them with capital raised, for the most part, in the underdeveloped area. After noting several such factors and others (such as the outflow of human capital in the form of a brain drain, or various service charges which the hinterland pays to the sponsoring metropolis), Frank (1967) concluded by asking a fundamental question concerning the institution of capital: might not underdeveloped areas be *less* underdeveloped if they did not receive the supposed benefits of outside capital (see pp. 45-50)?

Notwithstanding such arguments, Canadians seem committed to capital as a social institution. Capital holds both a symbolic and a real value for people; for many, it represents an established social goal or a means to achieve a goal. And yet, many Canadians are troubled concerning the source of capital, or concerning the use of Canadian capital by managers who make their decisions in other lands. The focus recently has been on American investment in Canada.

Institutions such as capital are so entrenched in their own history that interference is usually disavowed. But the broad issue of an American take-over of the Canadian economy demands a certain measure of interference. It is the politician's delicate task to assess appropriate measures.

Politicians know that economies are international affairs. They do what they can to maintain and enhance trade relations with many countries. But they become nervous when economic relations with other countries are dominated by a single relation with one country.

It helps to realize that, in large measure, the dominance of the United States is a function of the dominance of American corporations. We live in the age of the multinational corporation, an entity which is often outside the control of even American politicians. In other words, the multinational corporation is a phenomenon which causes new problems for politicians of all countries, including those countries which dominate in international economic circles. The fact that many Canadians feel that controls must be established for regulating multinational corporations is but a minor issue when compared with the broader adjustment which many countries must make when dealing with corporate bodies which have an extraterritorial voice in the economic operation of states. Multinational corporations are extraterritorial governments of sorts; their base of operation is so diversified that the identity of the country which has jurisdiction over them becomes a matter of some uncertainty.

Sovereignty [as it was once understood] is not compatible with branch-plant status; the greater the degree of foreign ownership and control of Canadian industry, the narrower the freedom of choice in economic as well as political matters (Levitt, 1970, p. 9). Present-day Canada may be described as the world's richest underdeveloped country. Its regression to a state of economic and political dependence cannot possibly be attributed, as is fashionable in some quarters, to an unfavourable endowment of resources. Nor can its present lack of independent dynamic be laid at the door of a traditional culture. Thus we are forced to seek the explanation of underdevelopment and fragmentation in the institutions and processes of modern society. We suggest it is to be found in the dynamics of the New Mercantilism of the American international corporation (Levitt, 1970, p. 25).

The problem is not Canada's alone. Table 4.1 indicates that American corporations acquired 198 companies more than they sold in Canada during the period 1963 to 1967. During the same period American corporations acquired 1,364 companies more than they sold in Europe. These figures, together with the number of acquisitions and sales of foreign companies by American corporations in all other countries of the world for the period 1963 to 1967, suggest that American corporate expansion is first and foremost a European phenomenon.

The capital for American corporate expansion in Canada is for the most part

TABLE 4.1

Acquisitions and Sales by American Companies of Foreign Enterprises, 1963 to 1967

	Acquisitions	Sales	Net Acquisitions
Canada	408	210	198
Europe	1,438	74	1,364
Other Countries	238	281	− 43
Total	2,084	565	1,519

Source: Recalculated from annual data from Levitt, 1970, p.183.

generated or borrowed in Canada. Levitt (1970, p. 180) reported that American foreign subsidiaries in Canada locally borrowed an average of 17.9 percent of their funds during the period 1963 to 1965. An average of 28.3 percent of funds for the same period derived from depreciation, while 42.4 percent derived from retained profits. Net capital inflow from outside Canada amounted to just 11.4 percent of total funds. These percentages suggest that expansion was financed locally. "The effect is to put pressure on the capital markets of the hinterland countries, thus forcing up interest rates, particularly in the Euro-dollar market and in Canada" (Levitt, 1970, p. 179).

The absolute dollar amount of American capital investment in Canada in 1971 was $24.03 billion, up $1.24 billion over 1970. This noteworthy increase in just one year derived primarily from retained profits earned in Canada ($1.04 billion), a continuing trend also suggested by the fact that the net capital outflow from the United States to Canada in 1971 was only $226 million. The American total capital investment of $24.03 billion in Canada in 1971 compared with the American total investment in all of Europe of $27.6 billion. The total American investment abroad in 1971, including the countries of Europe and Canada, was $86 billion (see CANADIAN DIMENSION, January, 1973, p. 65).

It is unlikely that capital will cease to constitute an institution in the years to come, but it is likely that major adjustments will be required as countries try to cope with new concepts of capital utilization. The multinational corporation, for example, is a challenge to conventional wisdom.

At this point, it is appropriate to review the federal government's first major response to the issues of foreign ownership and investment in the Canadian economy. In sum, the government's professed attitude seems to be one of letting well enough alone. Canadian leaders seem to be saying that adjustment to third-world economics, at least through the early 1970's, will be acceptance of the associated realities, and foreign ownership and investment are among the realities.

Tangible legislation was introduced in the House of Commons in May of 1972 under the title of the Foreign Takeovers Review Act. The Act recognized that

the extent to which control of Canadian industry, trade and commerce has become acquired by persons other than Canadians and the effect thereof on the ability of Canadians to maintain effective control over their economic environment is a matter of national concern, and that it is therefore expe-

58

dient to establish a means by which measures may be taken under the authority of Parliament to ensure that, in so far as it is practicable after the enactment of this Act, control of Canadian business enterprises may be acquired by persons other than Canadians only if it has been assessed that the acquisition of such control by those persons is or is likely to be of significant benefit to Canada, having regard to all of the factors to be taken into account under this Act for that purpose (Section 2(1) of the Act).

In assessing, for the purposes of this Act, whether any acquisition of control of a Canadian business enterprise is or is likely to be of significant benefit to Canada, the factors to be taken into account are as follows: (a) the effect of the acquisition on the level and nature of economic activity in Canada, including employment; (b) the degree and significance of participation by Canadians in the business enterprise and in any industry or industries in Canada of which it forms a part; (c) the effect of the acquisition on productivity, industrial efficiency, technological development, product innovation and product variety in Canada; (d) the effect of the acquisition on competition within any industry or industries in Canada; and (e) the compatibility of the acquisition with national industrial and economic policies (Section 2(2) of the Act).

The response to the government's Foreign Takeovers Review Act depends on one's location in social space. The proposed policy is "as different from [Walter] Gordon's economic nationalism as wheat is from oil" (this quotation and those following are from the EDMONTON JOURNAL, May 3, 1972). The Committee for an Independent Canada termed the policy "insufficient in every aspect and having no appreciable effect in checking control of the Canadian economy by foreign investors." The EDMONTON JOURNAL editorialized that the "welcome shingle is as prominently displayed as always," and that all the policy really does is "show up Ottawa's failure to come to grips with an economic development policy for Canadians and Canada for the final third of the twentieth century." Recognizing the policy as a "token show of nationalism," columnist Lynch displayed a middle-of-the-road tone by noting that "foreign investment [as distinct from acquisitions of Canadian business enterprises by foreigners] will continue to play that vital role, provided we can continue to attract it in sufficient quantities and on the right terms." Lynch could not resist adding his judgment that the Foreign Takeovers Review Act reads as a "traditional Canadian solution, designed to give us the maximum of benefits at a minimum of cost, which indicates that we have retained at least a measure of our native ingenuity, and can face the Yankee traders without flinching."

THE GLOBE AND MAIL of Toronto editorialized that the Review Act was "no more than the smallest possible bone the Government could find to throw the nationalists" (May 3, 1972). Columnist Wilson, writing for THE MONTREAL STAR, concluded that the government "has made a minimum decision" (May 3, 1972). In its editorial, THE PROVINCE of Vancouver termed the new policy "utter realism" providing "maximum flexibility." "It can assure ultra-nationalists that Canadian ownership of Canadian resources will not be overlooked. It can offer equally firm assurances that nationalistic considerations will not be allowed to overrule the needs for outside investment" (May 3, 1972).

The Minister of National Revenue, when announcing the review policy in the House of Commons (May 2, 1972), clearly established that the government's intent was not to ban or to severely limit foreign investment.

Foreign investment plays an important role in Canadian development, but it brings with it costs as well as benefits. While there are a variety of opinions among Canadians about the balance of benefits and costs of foreign direct investment, there is certainly no disagreement that foreign investment should work in the interests of this country.

It will be recalled that the Foreign Takeovers Review Act was not legislated in 1972. In the Throne Speech of January, 1973 the government gave notice of re-introducing the legislation, this time revised to include the requirement that a majority of the directors of federally-incorporated companies must be Canadian. The debate continues.

We turn now to property. One of the characteristics of capital is that it is owned. Capital is owned in many forms, from personal savings, to government and other kinds of bonds, to land, real estate and personal possessions. Capital is usually invested in property of one kind or another. Like capital, property is an institution in society for it is symbolic of established claims.

Crimes against property are defined in the Canadian Criminal Code in some detail, suggesting that society places great emphasis on rights of property. Section 292, for example, states that

(1) Every one who (a) breaks and enters a place with intent to commit an indictable offence therein; (b) breaks and enters a place and commits an indictable offence therein; or (c) breaks out of a place after (i) committing an indictable offence therein, or (ii) entering the place with intent to commit an indictable offence therein, is guilty of an indictable offence and is liable (d) to imprisonment for life, if the offence is committed in relation to a dwelling house, or (e) to imprisonment for fourteen years, if the offence is committed in relation to a place other than a dwelling house.

Clearly, the legislation places the emphasis on man's dwelling house. One of the fundamental reasons for the development of law in civilized society was, and continues to be, the protection of rights of property.

Ownership of property has long been a standard of citizenship and, as such, also a standard of voting eligibility. The relationship between the ownership of property and the right to vote on money issues is quite clear in legislation. For example, Alberta's Municipal District Act (1955) legislated that the "owner of a parcel or of any part, share or interest therein is entitled to vote [on a money by-law] in respect of the parcel, share or interest therein" (Section 203(1) of the Act). The Act defined a proprietary elector as "(i) a person who is a resident of the municipal district, and entitled to vote at an election under this Act, and whose name appears on the assessment roll in respect of land liable to assessment and taxation, [and] (ii) a person who is not a resident of the municipal district, but who is entitled to vote at an election under this Act, and whose name appears on the assessment roll in respect of land liable to assessment and taxation" (Section 2(x) of the Act).

The relationship between property and voting, however, has been challenged in recent years. Many jurisdictions have lowered their voting age, thus increasing the pool of eligible electors and, by implication, reducing the proportion of proprietary electors. Such has happened, for example, in Edmonton, where the enumeration of 1971 showed that 127,408 or 46.6 percent of the eligible voters were owners of property, leaving 145,863 or 53.4 percent of the voters without the ownership of property which would enable them to vote on money issues.

These proportions reflect the fact that in Edmonton, just as in most Canadian cities, there has been a gradual re-alignment of demographic factors, such that the renter is beginning to challenge the owner. In certain jurisdictions the challenge to the owner's traditional power has been extended to the point of questioning certain proprietary rights which were previously accepted.

Enabling legislation was passed in 1971 in Alberta's provincial legislature in the form of an amendment to The Municipal Government Act (1968). The addition of Section 311.1 provided that

(1) Notwithstanding the provisions of this or any other Act, the council may, by by-law, authorize all electors of the municipality to vote on a specific by-law or on all by-laws requiring the assent of the proprietary electors. (2) Where a council passes a by-law pursuant to subsection (1), all references to propietary [sic] electors in this or The Municipal Election Act shall, in relation to voting on by-laws, be deemed to refer to and to include all electors.

Edmonton's city government was thus empowered to draft a by-law numbered 3811. On September 27, 1971 the council resolved that a by-law be prepared allowing all electors to vote on money by-laws. Such a by-law was drafted and, after three readings, duly passed on December 23, 1971.

This example of legislative adjustment to changing social conditions is rather remarkable in that majority rights have been maintained (or returned!), even in the face of the historical importance attached to the institution of property. This example of adjustment, however, pertains to the jurisdiction of Alberta. The next illustration shows how adherence to certain property rights complicates democratic government.

The town of Fort Smith in the Northwest Territories held a plebiscite during the spring of 1972 concerning two issues: whether to construct a public works garage and whether to construct a community hall. The decisions of the plebiscite were in support of the garage and against the community hall.

The two construction projects were money issues which meant, of course, that only the proprietary electors of the town were eligible to vote. While the total number of electors eligible to vote in the 1971 town council election was 1,146, the proprietary electors numbered 240 or 20.9 percent of those eligible to vote in the council election. Even more interesting is the fact that only 140 proprietary electors were resident in Fort Smith at the time of the plebiscite, and so just 12.2 percent of those eligible to vote in the council election were eligible to vote on the two money issues.

While the extent of absentee property ownership is a striking observation in the case of Fort Smith, the point for the moment is that a very small proportion of the residents of the town were eligible to vote on a plebiscite which was of general community interest. Many residents supported the construction of a community hall, but most of these people had no voice on the issue because they did not own property.

The community hall project was defeated at the polls by a slight margin of 40 negative votes out of 74 votes cast. It is noted in passing that the total vote represented just 30.8 percent of the eligible proprietary electors, and that the 40 votes which defeated the proposed project represent a microscopic 3.5 percent of the residents of Fort Smith who were eligible to vote, but only on matters other than money issues.

The institution of property seems well entrenched in Fort Smith. Very few people influence the spending patterns of the town's government. At a time when the ownership of property is being questioned as a criterion for the vote, even on money issues, it is interesting to note that situations still exist, such as the one in Fort Smith, where almost all the residents of the town are disenfranchised. Disenfranchisement applies not just to the hundreds of native people who live in the community, but also to hundreds of white government employees and others who reside in government housing. Given that most of the residents of the town are not property owners, it is an anomaly that property continues to be the accepted criterion for defining certain kinds of social participation. It is also surprising that social movements have not developed in communities such as Fort Smith to amend, at the level of the appropriate territorial ordinances, some of the rights associated with the ownership of property. Such a high proportion of northern residents live in government-owned housing that this fact alone constitutes good reason to re-define the rights associated with property.

Fort Smith is not an exception to any rule. The underlying institutional dynamic of property and associated rights and privileges is not apparent to a visitor of the town. Institutional analysis is made difficult because social institutions, being so often hidden or intangible directors of human conduct, persist unquestioned. While their impact is significant, we often remain unaware of the many signs which indicate the force of institutions. The sociological failing in institutional analysis is perhaps the result of sociology's concentration on such institutions as religion and the family, to the relative neglect of other institutions such as those discussed in this chapter. In this context our comments must vary in terms of being analytic at one point and value-intensive at another. The only defence is that some of the core institutions such as capital and property cannot be glanced over without a note of criticism, if society wishes to restructure its institutions once their nature and pervasiveness have been comprehended.

Canadian Society and The Sociology of Law

> That law is valuation . . . implies that law is an on-going process, that the process is meaningful in relation to the solution of social problems, and that legislation and adjudication are ways of discovering and using the ethically valid answers, which it is feasible to implement by force (Hall, 1949, p. 95).

Broom and Selznick's SOCIOLOGY: A TEXT WITH ADAPTED READINGS (1955) is one of the most popular introductory textbooks in sociology. An American text, it has enjoyed numerous adoptions in Canadian colleges and universities. The fourth edition, published in 1968, included a new chapter on the law as a social institution. For Broom and Selznick to have seen fit to include such a chapter is more than happenstance, for not only is the move toward the sociology of law blessed with scholarly precedent, but the subject is most appropriate in this era which seems to be using the law as both agent and controller of social change to an ever increasing extent. In North America especially, sociologists are rediscovering what was common knowledge for their European forefathers: that the law is a significant indicator of institutional dynamics.

The perceptions of individuals are influenced to a significant degree by their value orientations and by communications received through the media. Value orientations include symbolic commitments such as moral and political beliefs which help to channel perceptions and behaviour. For example, a person who is committed to political conservatism will tend to find security in the *status quo* rather than in its change; he or she will become a proponent of the existing social order, and will use these value orientations as a standard against which to compare various communications. Thus, if a political leader strongly advocates socialist control of the national economy, the individual who hears this message will compare its information with a personal value orientation and will react to the message more or less in line with a personal value commitment. The individual will probably reject the politician's communication. There is the further possibility that the person will fail to realize the real import of the communication, simply because he or she and the communicator are so different in their political value orientations that the communication does not, as they say, get through. Selective perception occurs in defence of symbolic commitments.

The tragic death of Pierre Laporte and the incarceration of James R. Cross during the fall of 1970 produced a series of official responses worthy of analysis by social scientists. The events came at a time when Canada seemed to be moving toward constitutional change and possibly toward the entrenchment of a bill of fundamental human rights within a new Canadian constitution. Among other things, entrenchment means a law which is hard to change or amend. The constitutional conference held in early 1971, and many more recent events, seem destined toward these same outcomes. There is little reason to quarrel with the drive toward constitutional revision; there is a definite need to realign the division of powers between the federal and the provincial governments.

The matter of entrenching human rights is noteworthy because its very consideration may indicate either the presence of, or the potential for, a shift in the value orientations of the Canadian people. That shift is seen as away from collectivism and toward individualism. Up to the present, Canada's dominant value orientation with respect to civil rights has been one of collectivism, that is, a value commitment to the whole of Canadian society rather than to constituent individuals. But increasingly, across a number of institutional sectors, there is movement toward a greater expression of legal protection for the individual citizen. Such innovations as the role of the ombudsman and legal aid services are relatively recent in Canada.

While Canada may be moving toward individualism in law and practice, the invocation of the War Measures Act demonstrated that one politically viable response during a time of civil disorder is a return to collectivistic norms. It is for the sake of the whole, so the argument goes, that harsh methods of control are imposed on the few who are associated with the perceived cause of civil disruption. The great majority of Canadians seemed to support the decision taken by the federal government to impose the powers of the War Measures Act. A Toronto research firm conducted a telephone poll of 1,650 respondents in twelve Canadian cities shortly after the imposition of the Act. Eighty percent of those polled agreed with the government's action. The leader of the New Democratic Party, having led his party to vote against the Act in the House of Commons, drew complete approval from just 10 percent of those polled, partial approval from an additional 19 percent and total disapproval from 39 percent (see EDMONTON JOURNAL, November 16, 1970). This margin of support for the government suggests that there was relatively little empathy for those arrested and incarcerated under the authority of the Act, and that there was a mass willingness to sacrifice, as it were, those few persons associated with the illegal Front de Libération du Québec.

Perhaps even more interesting and indicative is the fact that the same man can be quoted in the following contradictory ways. In a speech to the nation, the Prime Minister spoke of his government's reasons for imposing the War Measures Act: its authority "will permit governments to deal effectively with the nebulous yet dangerous *challenge to society* represented by the terrorist organizations. The criminal law as it stands is simply not adequate to deal with systematic terrorism" (EDMONTON JOURNAL, October 17, 1970; emphasis added). Several years earlier, in an address to the Canadian Bar Association, Trudeau stressed that he was "thinking of a Bill of Rights that will be so designed as to limit the exercise of all governmental power, federal and provincial. . . . [T]he power of both the federal government and the provincial governments would be restrained in favour of the Canadian citizen who would, in consequence, be better protected in the exercise of his fundamental rights and freedoms" (Trudeau, 1968, p. 57).

These statements and their contradictory nature can be reconciled in terms of situational factors. The so-called state of insurrection precipitated by the actions of the F.L.Q. had not, after all, been part of history when Trudeau spoke to the Bar Association in 1967, notwithstanding the fact that there had been numerous terrorist hints. It is not so much the contradiction which is of interest here, but the move which takes place from individualistic to collectivistic norms in periods of deemed crisis. This phenomenon is by no means peculiar to Canadian society.

Two questions can be asked of the government's stated intent to entrench a bill of rights in a new Canadian constitution. Specifically, will important unanticipated consequences for individual conduct and for the viability of the social order follow the entrenchment of a bill of rights, particularly consequences such as constraining agencies and agents of enforcement and the administration of justice, solidifying political dissent and providing rationales for criminality? Generally, might not these and other consequences produce a shift in certain of the value orientations of the Canadian people?

To propose some tentative answers, of course consequences would follow, both anticipated and unanticipated, from entrenching a bill of rights. They might include the kind suggested. Both the processes of law enforcement and the administration of justice through the courts likely would be constrained to a significant degree in that such processes would have to comply with the provisions of the bill of rights. Courts would be obliged to safeguard more explicitly than they do at present the legal rights of persons coming before them. They would also have to strike down both laws and legal decisions which contravened the entrenched bill of rights. Provincial courts would be just as responsible for "enforcing" the bill of rights as would the federal courts. In terms of the police, their methods of apprehension and investigation would, in certain areas, be restricted. For both the police and the courts, then, the consequences might certainly include more stringent guidelines of operation which could lessen the effectiveness of law enforcement, and create bottlenecks in the courts in the form of longer dockets, delayed court appearances, longer appeal procedures and the like. If all of these consequences could follow simply from entrenching a bill of rights, who would deny the possibility that certain persons in society might take advantage of the situation (for example, the crime rate might go up or dissent might be encouraged). Such people would perceive that society's laws and agents of law enforcement were formally committed more to the protection of individual rather than collective rights. The thought implicit here is that the protection of individual rights is biassed in favour of the accused, while the protection of collective rights is biassed in favour of those who are threatened.

A number of authors have discussed the role of law in relation to some modal characterization of Canadian society. Wrong (1955) noted that "Canada, except for the province of Quebec, shares with the United States the traditions of British law but without the addition of American constitutionalism and the frontier heritage of antagonism to form law. There appears to be a greater respect for law and legal authority in general in English-speaking Canada. This is indicated very well by the contrast between the popular culture-heroes of American and Canadian westward expansion: in the United States it is the cowboy, a rugged individualist whose relationship to the forces of law and order was at least ambiguous, who has become to symbolize the frontier, while in Canada the 'Mountie,' a policeman who clearly stands for law and order and traditional institutional authority, is a corresponding symbol of Canadian westward expansion" (pp. 37-38).

Lipset (1964) reviewed a number of indicators which suggest value differences between Canada and the United States. For example, in 1961 and 1962 the United States supported a ratio of police-to-population which was slightly more than 35 percent greater than a similar ratio for Canada. Other indicators were: proportionately more on-duty policemen were killed in the United States in the years 1961 and 1963; proportionately fewer lawyers practise in Canada; and in 1960 crime rates in the United States for the offences of burglary, homicide, forgery and counterfeiting, fraud and embezzlement, and theft-larceny ranged from two-and-one-half to, in one instance, almost seven times the rates in Canada. Lipset interpreted these and other data to mean that in Canada there is a "greater reliance on informal social controls based on traditional obligations" (pp. 176-177).

Porter (1967) concluded that Canadians "are more conservative and authoritarian and less egalitarian in values than are the people of the United States" (p. 48). This generalization and the more detailed contributions of Wrong, Lipset and Porter are discussed in the next chapter.

The study of law as social institution, then, is a source of information concerning shifting social values in society. The War Measures Act and, indeed, all items of legislation have their place in social analysis. Laws and public policies, and the debates which give rise to both law and policy, must be taken more often as indicators of social processes, and of the forces and contradictions which are embedded in institutional values and associated value conflicts.

There is, nevertheless, need for caution. If Porter's generalization concerning the conservatism and egalitarianism of Canadians is well grounded, then the presumed validity of conservative theses (as, for example, the mere fact of entrenching a bill of rights will have the effect of undermining proven modes of social control is open to question. While such may be the results, there could also be other consequences of note, particularly that those who are innocent in fact might more often be found innocent in law. However, if the fact of entrenchment does not in and of itself suggest that Porter's generalization is less valid today than it was in 1967, it certainly might have the effect of altering the values which represent the symbolic commitments of society.

Finally, rather than beginning with the premise that a judicious balance must be sought and maintained between social order and individual freedom, it is helpful to begin instead with the co-existing and fundamental needs for both order and freedom, and postulate simply that social activity is the product of negotiations between social actors who are oriented to the satisfaction of these needs. It is difficult, if not impossible, to construe the various consequences of entrenchment as anything more than simply alternative ways in which social things happen. Whether or not entrenchment can affect the viability of society remains an important empirical question.

European sociologists of an earlier day were acutely aware of the importance of the role of law in society. Durkheim used law as an indicator of the stage of social evolution. Weber saw the modern positivistic bias of law as but another example of institutions possessing a rationality bias. The lesson for us is to take much more seriously than we have the broad relationships between law and society, and the relationships between processes of social change and legal change. The sociology of law is a vital topic in the study of Canadian society because it offers numerous perspectives which have stood the test of time and comparison, because it forces upon us a more critical orientation to Canadian society as distinct from other societies, and because, to put it simply, the law is a major source of social data.

Social Institutions and Authority

[I]nstitutions provide procedures through which human conduct is patterned, compelled to go, in grooves deemed desirable by society. And this trick is performed by making these grooves appear to the individual as the only possible ones (Berger, 1963, p. 87).

This chapter began by defining a social institution as one which entails the organization of social norms which provide direction for those who try to achieve social goals. There is something more to social institutions; the frequent reference to law and practice throughout the chapter suggests the need for a concluding comment on the concept of authority.

Legislation which is passed by Parliament usually is prefaced by a comment such as "Her Majesty, by and with the advice and consent of the Senate and House of Commons of Canada, enacts" the following legislation. Such a statement indicates that Canada's authority to create legislation derives from the country's historical relationship with the British monarchy, and thus the monarchy is deemed to be the source of absolute power. The specific transfer of authority from the monarchy to Canada is recorded in the British North America Act of 1867. In defining executive power, Section 9 clearly specifies that the "Executive Government and Authority of and over Canada is hereby declared to continue and be vested in the Queen." The institution of law in Canada was made legitimate by this declaration.

The British North America Act authorized the admission of other colonies into the Canadian confederation. Section 146 reads: "It shall be lawful for the Queen, by and with the Advice of Her Majesty's Most Honourable Privy Council, on Addresses from the Houses of the Parliament of Canada, and from the Houses of the respective Legislatures of the Colonies or Provinces of Newfoundland, Prince Edward Island, and British Columbia, to admit those Colonies or Provinces, or any of them, into the Union, and on Address from the Houses of the Parliament of Canada to admit Rupert's Land and the North-western Territory, or either of them, into the Union, on such Terms and Conditions in each Case as are in the Addresses expressed and as the Queen thinks fit to approve, subject to the Provisions of this Act; and the Provisions of any Order in Council in that Behalf shall have effect as if they had been enacted by the Parliament of the United Kingdom of Great Britain and Ireland."

Authority can best be studied by observing its transfer, and the transfer of monarchical authority from Britain to Canada, as seen in Section 9 above, is a case in point. Section 146 does nothing more than to anticipate further transfers of authority. In the case of the Northwest Territories, the actual steps of transfer came about through a series of legal documents, one of which was the Act for the Temporary Government of Rupert's Land and the North-Western Territory when United with Canada, passed in 1869. Later, in 1905, the Northwest Territories Amendment Act provided for the appointment of a commissioner and council. "This territorial government was given authority to pass ordinances for the governing of the Territories under instructions from the Governor-in-Council or from the responsible federal minister" (Rea, 1968, p. 34).

Further amendments were made from time to time, partly for the purpose of enlarging the territorial council. Provision was made in 1951 for three of the eight members of council to be elected representatives. The proportion of elected to appointed council members has reversed to the point that, in 1970, there were four appointed members and ten elected representatives sitting on the territorial council, all in addition to the appointed commissioner. A storm of public pressure has built up in the Northwest Territories, especially during the summer of 1972, in support of full representation through election. The transfer of authority from Canada to the Northwest Territories (anticipated in 1867 and commenced shortly thereafter), and the structure of that authority, remain very much the same up to the present day. A territorial ordinance usually is prefaced by a comment such as the "Commissioner of the Northwest Territories, by and with the advice and consent of the Council of the said Territories, enacts" the following ordinance. All of which says that the commissioner represents legal authority in the Northwest Territories, although such representation is without a mandate from the people resident in northern Canada.

The path of authority usually can be traced. A close analysis of social institutions suggests that their legitimacy derives from the fact that they have been vested with the authority to act. It must be added, however, that many times authority cannot be traced to legal documents. The transfer of authority is often traditional, as in the case of religious customs which are passed from generation to generation and which specify such matters as the rites of marriage or baptism.

The most complex question of all concerns the ultimate source of authority. Some believe it to be the sovereign state, while others believe it to be defined in terms of nature or by some God.

A legal rule is binding only by reference to another, higher, legal rule. But must this legal rule then be based on another, and so on without end? There must, of course, be some stopping point. The regress from legal rule to legal rule must end somewhere upon some ultimate proposition from which a legal system is traced. The initial hypothesis of a legal system is its fundamental norm (*die Grundnorm*). The reasons for accepting the fundamental rule are meta-legal. . . . Thus, at the summit of every legal system there is a rule providing that the final legislative organ in the form it takes from time to time is to have the power of determining the process by which all other rules are maintained. The birth of a legal system is in this 'hypothetical constitution.' It is this hypothesis that transforms might into right, force into law (Martindale, 1960, p. 260).

References

Aberle, D. F., A. K. Cohen, A. K. Davis, M. G. Levy and F. X. Sutton, "The Functional Prerequisites of a Society," ETHICS, 60 (January, 1950) 100-111.

Berger, Peter L., INVITATION TO SOCIOLOGY: A HUMANISTIC PERSPECTIVE, Garden City, N.Y.: Anchor Books, 1963.

Broom, Leonard and Philip Selznick, SOCIOLOGY: A TEXT WITH ADAPTED READINGS, Fourth Edition, New York: Harper & Row, Publishers, 1968.

Frank, Andre Gunder, "Sociology of Development and Underdevelopment of Sociology," CATALYST (Summer, 1967) 20-73.

Hall, Jerome, LIVING LAW OF DEMOCRATIC SOCIETY, Indianapolis: The Bobbs-Merrill Company, Inc., 1949.

Levitt, Kari, SILENT SURRENDER: THE MULTINATIONAL CORPORATION IN CANADA, Toronto: Macmillan of Canada, 1970.

Lipset, Seymour Martin, "Canada and the United States: A Comparative View," THE CANADIAN REVIEW OF SOCIOLOGY AND ANTHROPOLOGY, 1 (November, 1964) 173-185.

Martindale, Don, THE NATURE AND TYPES OF SOCIOLOGICAL THEORY, Boston: Houghton Mifflin Company, 1960.

Porter, John, "Canadian Character in the Twentieth Century," THE ANNALS OF THE AMERICAN ACADEMY OF POLITICAL AND SOCIAL SCIENCE, 370 (March, 1967) 48-56.

Rea, K. J., THE POLITICAL ECONOMY OF THE CANADIAN NORTH: AN INTERPRETATION OF THE COURSE OF DEVELOPMENT IN THE NORTHERN TERRITORIES OF CANADA TO THE EARLY 1960s, Toronto: University of Toronto Press, 1968.

Schlatter, Richard, PRIVATE PROPERTY: THE HISTORY OF AN IDEA, London: George Allen & Unwin Ltd., 1951.

Theodorson, George A. and Achilles G. Theodorson, A MODERN DICTIONARY OF SOCIOLOGY, New York: Thomas Y. Crowell Company, 1969.

Trudeau, Pierre Elliott, FEDERALISM AND THE FRENCH CANADIANS, Toronto: Macmillan of Canada, 1968.

Wrong, Dennis H., AMERICAN AND CANADIAN VIEWPOINTS, Washington, D.C.: American Council on Education, 1955.

For Further Reading

Godfrey, Dave and Mel Watkins, eds., GORDON TO WATKINS TO YOU. DOCUMENTARY: THE BATTLE FOR CONTROL OF OUR ECONOMY, Toronto: New Press, 1970.

Government of Canada, FOREIGN DIRECT INVESTMENT IN CANADA, Ottawa: Information Canada, 1972.

Kelsen, Hans, SOCIETY AND NATURE: A SOCIOLOGICAL INQUIRY, Chicago: University of Chicago Press, 1943.

Laskin, Bora, CANADIAN CONSTITUTIONAL LAW: CASES, TEXT AND NOTES ON DISTRIBUTION OF LEGISLATIVE POWER, Revised Third Edition, Toronto: The Carswell Company Ltd., 1969.

Rheinstein, Max, ed., MAX WEBER ON LAW IN ECONOMY AND SOCIETY, Cambridge, Mass.: Harvard University Press, 1966.

Tarnopolsky, Walter Surma, THE CANADIAN BILL OF RIGHTS, Toronto: The Carswell Company Limited, 1966.

Trudeau, Pierre Elliott, A CANADIAN CHARTER OF HUMAN RIGHTS, Ottawa: Queen's Printer, 1968.

Watkins, Melville H., FOREIGN OWNERSHIP AND THE STRUCTURE OF CANADIAN INDUSTRY: REPORT OF THE TASK FORCE ON THE STRUCTURE OF CANADIAN INDUSTRY, Ottawa: Information Canada, 1970.

Chapter 5

Social Actors

It has been argued that social institutions place more restricted limits upon social development than do the so-called conditioning factors, such as the circumstances of geography and history. In the final analysis, however, the course of social development and, indeed, the perceived nature of social reality are delimited by individuals, and not by groups, as individuals go about the constant business of negotiating personal life styles with their environments and whatever other conditions are placed upon them (biological limits, accidents of birth, unique social opportunities and so forth). The bias of this chapter is that individuals and not groups develop and express opinions, and that individuals and not groups develop and express a sense of identity in relation to various things, such as being a Canadian or living in Canada. The argument is that only individuals can adopt social values.

The sociologist enters the picture because opinions, senses of identity and values are forged to a great extent through social interaction. Also, the sociologist, regardless of whether he accepts the statement that concepts of society and group are individually based, is most concerned with what happens when several people who share the same or similar concepts come together in interaction and discover their consensus. It is possible to talk about opinion, identity or value at the collective level only if there is a certain consensus on the questions of opinion, identity or value within some cross-section of a society's population.

The broad design of the present chapter is to focus upon Canadian social organization from the point of view of concepts constructed by men and women, concepts which give to them their senses of personal relationship to community and society. In actual fact, however, such a framework is only broad design at best. There is a sense in which the present chapter can be concluded before it begins, for there is no such thing as a clear Canadian consensus concerning opinion, identity or value. The simple truth is that there is much variability.

Notwithstanding the bias that social behaviour is individual behaviour, the chapter's focus is the social actor to the degree that the actor can be aggregated with other actors, and thus to the degree that different actors share the same or similar meanings for concepts encountered in their social worlds. To help avoid confusion, a longer, more accurate title for this chapter might have been "The Collective Understandings of Social Actors."

Oversocialized Man

> Society in its full sense . . . is never an entity separable from the individuals who compose it. . . . [N]o civilization has in it any element which in the last analysis is not the contribution of an individual. Where else could any trait come from except from the behaviour of a man or a woman or a child (Benedict, 1946, p. 219).

Man alone is thoughtful. He employs his mental capacities for many purposes, chief among which is the formation of concepts. Concepts are categories which we learn and which help us in observing and in attributing meaning to our experiences. Concepts may be such things as the concept of pain, which helps us experience pain as a fact, or the concept of development, which helps to relate a series of experiences so that processes of change and continuity can be observed. Otherwise, processes might be observed over long periods of time without our grasping the interrelated significance of the experiences. Some concepts are also scientific concepts. For example, the concept of intelligence helps in the quantification of mental ability and of mental differences among people.

A concept is important sociologically only when persons realize that the meanings of their individual concepts are similar to the meanings understood by others. It is not enough for people to hold similar individual concepts; they must realize through communication that similarity exists across some group of people, which is to say, there must be a common consciousness, at least in terms of the concept in question.

Many sociologists have been responsible for advocating an over-socialized conception of man. This viewpoint has a number of dimensions. One is the conviction that man's behaviour, most of which is social behaviour, is determined for the most part by social factors such as status and role. This dimension offers an over-socialized view in that too much importance is given to social factors. A second dimension is of more pointed interest, the conviction that man, although an organic and psychological being, is not susceptible to the effects of interactions between his social behaviours and his individual concepts. Tied to this is the presupposition that man, being socialized in the ways of his group, conducts himself as though his very self embodies in some near perfect way the standards and ideals of the group. Such conviction and presupposition suggest what is meant by oversocialization.

Wrong (1961) argued that sociologists must make assumptions concerning human nature. He placed the concept of oversocialization in the following context. "To Freud man is a *social* animal without being entirely a *socialized* animal. His very social nature is the source of conflicts and antagonisms that create resistance to socialization by the norms of any of the societies which have existed in the course of human history. 'Socialization' may mean two quite distinct things; when they are confused an oversocialized view of man is the result. On the one hand socialization means the 'transmission of the culture,' the particular culture of the society an individual enters at birth; on the other hand the term is used to mean the 'process of becoming human,' of acquiring uniquely human attributes from interaction with others. All men are socialized in the latter sense, but this does not mean that they have been completely molded by the particular norms and values of their culture. All cultures, as Freud contended, do violence to man's socialized bodily drives, but this in no sense means that men could possibly exist without culture or independently of society" (p. 192).

The ideological orientation called social nominalism was introduced in Chapter 1. Homans was suggested as a writer whose bias illustrated this orientation. An interpretation of Homans, however, places his bias squarely at the centre of the present concern, for Homans was trying to remind sociologists and others that man, and not society, is the source of action. His concern was with "the *behavior* of men," not with "the *behavior* of societies," and his justification for pointing to this difference between the behaviour of actors on the one hand, and aggregates of actors on the other, was simply that "propositions about social aggregates . . . have not been shown to be true and general" (1964, p. 815; emphases added). Homans spoke of two types of behaviour, behaviour$_1$ of men and behaviour$_2$ of societies, and he questioned the legitimacy of the concept of behaviour$_2$. While this justification can be debated, it is hard to deny that man, and not society, is the source of action, regardless of the outcome of the debate. The data of sociology are created when a number of persons agree to follow some course of action, or indeed, when they agree or disagree on inaction, or when they agree to follow incompatible courses of action. The data of sociology are created when persons take note of the behaviours of other persons, or act to assist or block those behaviours. This does not mean that sociological data are fictional, created from nothing. Sociological data derive from interactions, from the product of the behaviours of joined individuals.

Canadian National Character

[T]he years of the Laurier regime saw the rise of a Canadian national spirit, neither French nor British but wholly Canadian in sentiment. It was a compromise, but a powerful compromise in that it attempted to reconcile strong extremes, and in that, though powerful, it was essentially moderate. It was, in short, Canadian, the characteristic product of a country resting on paradoxes and anomalies, governed only by compromise and kept strong only by moderation (Morton, 1961, p. 51).

Is Canadian society marked by a collective identity? Can the society be characterized in any brief and accurate way? Of all the questions posed in this book these are the most difficult to answer, perhaps because they are unanswerable, or because they are not valid questions to start with. Accordingly, the strategy is to first re-assert the bias which says that sociology cannot avoid the human factor. The individual is assumed to be central in the study of society, partly because the individual helps to create that society, and partly because its understanding is so much a function of his or her comprehension. Given such a bias, this section includes a brief review of the modal perspective which has been developed to aid us in the study of national character. This is followed by outlines of several commentaries on Canadian character, which in turn are followed by a discussion of Canadian social patterns and norms as viewed in a comparative light. The last section of the chapter offers a summary and critical analysis of the material.

We start with a brief review of theoretical perspectives. While characterizations of man in culture are often made by literary and other writers, Benedict (1946; first published 1934) provided one of the earliest anthropological statements on the subject. "A culture, like an individual, is a more or less consistent pattern of thought and action. Within each culture there come into being characteristic purposes not necessarily shared by other types of society" (p. 53). Benedict thus was led to describe the psychological coherence of given cultures, although Gorer argued that her emphasis was rather on the "psychological coherence of the varied *institutions* which make up a society" (quoted by Inkeles and Levinson, 1969, p. 419). Whichever it is, Benedict characterized such culture groups as the Pueblo Indians of New Mexico as apollonian because of their nonaggressiveness, and their concerted group action and sobriety (see pp. 62-120); she distinguished the Kwakiutl Indians of British Columbia as servants of a will to superiority, especially as evidenced by the distribution of property and by methods for its redistribution (see pp. 156-195).

While Benedict tried to describe aspects of cultural patterning, other social scientists were either embracing or contesting the notion of national character.

Their strong reactions were often a function of their interests: persons with inter-disciplinary, comparative and/or historical interests, for example, have been more concerned with national characterizations, just as persons more challenged by obvious connections between individual and collective character have been. But many scholars have responded to methodological problems, especially those associated with general aggregation. When individuals such as all those in a nation are aggregated into groups for the purpose of description or analysis, there is the risk of failing to note the many variations among individuals. There is also the risk of committing even more serious errors, such as viewing the description of some aggregate as representative of the single actors who comprise the aggregate. For these and other reasons, the study of such things as social values or norms, customs or national character is certainly problematic. When sociologists and others study national character, they are passing far beyond the problems associated with the psychologist's use of the term "personality" in the individual context.

Inkeles and Levinson (1969) credited disciplinary bias as a central reason for many critical reactions to studies of inquiry into national character. Such inquiry "requires a crossing or transcending of disciplinary boundaries and thereby presents a threat to established disciplinary viewpoints and identities" (p. 418). Later, Inkeles and Levinson echoed Wrong's discussion of sociology's oversocialized conception of man when they noted that the "idea of psychological differences in national or other groups was resisted on the grounds that sociological facts must be explained only sociologically" (p. 421). Chances are good that those who study national character with any degree of seriousness must dismiss such bias *as bias*. Questions concerning collective identity are difficult enough to answer in the perspective of multidisciplinary studies; they should not be made impossible to answer because of disciplinary bias.

There are also problems of conceptual confusion. Some writers concern themselves with national identity, others speak of social values, while still others discuss topics as varied as morality and social norms. All of these things — distinctly different — are discussed as aspects of national character. Sometimes they are taken to be synonymous with national character. Such problems serve as criticisms of most of the discussions cited in this section and, indeed, of the very content of the section. The organization of material in this way is an intentional strategy so that the reasons for the critique which follows this section are rendered obvious.

Notwithstanding many difficulties, there remains the perplexing thesis that national characterizations are developed because the common experience of culture and society causes a common core of meanings to be assimilated by each member of that culture and society. Therefore, it should be possible to observe a "category of traits that individuals come to display in national groups" (Martindale, 1967, p. 35). Martindale judged that a "sociology of national character remains to be developed" (p. 35).

Inkeles and Levinson (1969) defined national character in terms of personality patterns (see pp. 423-428). Specifically, they concluded that the concept of national character "ought to be equated with modal personality structure; that is, it should refer to the mode or modes of the distribution of personality variants within a given society" (p. 425). There are three important aspects to this definition which should be stressed: it uses the statistical concept of mode to signify those personality characteristics which are most frequent or most common to a nation; it allows for the possibility of a multimodal structure; and it acknowledges the many less frequent or less common characteristics which exist but which are less noteworthy than the one or more modal personality characteristics.

Inkeles and Levinson suggested that their "general definition of national character does *not* posit a heavily unimodal distribution of personality characteristics. National character can be said to exist to the extent that modal personality traits and syndromes are found. How many modes there are is an important empirical and theoretical matter, but one that is not relevant to the definition of national character" (p. 427). These authors especially supported the multimodal conception of national character, because it can "accommodate the subcultural variations of socioeconomic class, geosocial region, ethnic group, and the like, which appear to exist in all modern nations" (p. 427). In addition to the closer empirical relationship between a pluralistic society and the multimodal conception of national character, Inkeles and Levinson noted other advantages of the multimodal conception. It tends to "counteract the inclination toward stereotyping and spurious homogenizing in our descriptions," it reminds us of variability, and it provides a "more adequate psychological basis for understanding the internal dynamics of the society, such as political cleavages, shifts in educational, industrial, or foreign policy, and conflicting elites in various institutional structures" (pp. 427-428).

There are many other theoretical statements on national character, but its definition and elaboration in terms of modal and multimodal personality structures is accepted for present purposes, especially since the modal viewpoint suggests a number of criteria which will be stated and applied later in this chapter to evaluate selected attempts at observing characterizations of Canada's collective identity.

Given what has been said, we now turn to outline four of the most basic sociological references on the subject of Canadian national character. Selectivity requires that many contributions be omitted, although a number of additional references are noted elsewhere in this chapter. The four papers chosen for more detailed outline were first published in the years 1955, 1961, 1963 and 1967.

We begin with a monograph by Wrong (1955) which was published at the request of the Canada-United States Committee on Education, a committee of the American Council on Education. Wrong pointed out in his preface how difficult an assignment it was to describe and to compare the value systems of two nations; and yet Wrong was qualified for such a task, having been born a Canadian and having received his high school and undergraduate training in Canada, and also having lived for well over a decade in the United States.

In the perspective of the early 1950's, Wrong described the similarities and differences in American and Canadian outlooks, taking three nationality groups (Americans, Anglophone Canadians and Francophone Canadians) and one broad aggregate of residents (urban, middle class) as his references (see pp. 3-5). His treatment followed the analyses available in the published literature plus his own observations, and his format followed an outline of social institutions. In the present review of Wrong's monograph, we are concerned primarily with a selection of his descriptions of Canadian national character. As a result, most of his comparative observations are not emphasized.

The family is perhaps the most important transmission line of culture. Wrong recognized that the "transition from traditional values to a greater amount of individualism and free choice in family matters" has taken place in English-speaking Canada, especially in urban areas (p. 9). Wrong identified a different pattern in

Quebec where "even in large urban areas . . . French-speaking Canadian families retain many of the features of the traditional rural family and differ markedly from the independent and loosely organized family of the rest of urban North America" (p. 11). "The individualism with which French Canadians are often credited is really an individualism of families rather than of single persons, for the kinship group tends to be the center of the French Canadian's universe" (p. 12).

Wrong concluded that religious loyalties are stronger in Canada than they are in the United States, and that the force of religious affiliation is such in Quebec that "the Catholic Church is the dominant institutional authority" (p. 15). "Religion is but one web — albeit probably the most important one next to language — of the network of ideals, attitudes, and customs that the French Canadian values as his 'way of life' and wishes to protect against outside influences" (p. 16). Wrong followed this statement with a prediction that religious elements will probably become distinct from other aspects of ethnicity and nationality as Quebec continues to industrialize and to urbanize (see p. 17).

Wrong claimed that English Canadians share with Americans a "technocratic approach to [solving] social and political problems," and that mass education is believed in and justified largely because of this commitment (p. 19). However, Wrong noted that American education seemed to be oriented and more accessible to the masses, while its orientation is more vocational and less classical than Canadian education (see pp. 19-20). "Quebec education remains inseparable from religious instruction and its approach to knowledge tends to be doctrinal, laying stress on intellectual discipline as opposed to providing instruction of a more immediately practical nature or promoting the self-expression valued by American progressive educators" (p. 22).

Such things as equality of opportunity and competition for rewards are values in English Canada as they are in America, accorded Wrong, although there is a "greater acceptance of the fact of class differences in Canada" (p. 24). He suggested that in English Canada the monarchy justifies or at least is seen to justify the pattern of authority, while hierarchical differences in Quebec are more entrenched and have long been legitimized by the church (see p. 25). Wrong anticipated the importance of the development of more purely economic interests in Quebec for the eventual redefinition of class relations in French Canada.

Wrong viewed economic activities in English Canada as oriented to private enterprise, although he characterized Canadians as "more conservative in their individual economic objectives" (p. 29). Their conservatism is indicated at least in part by the facts that there is less resistance to public ownership in Canada, and social welfare measures are more a part of Canadian public life (see p. 29). Francophone Canada is another matter, however, and Wrong concluded that in many ways "the economic ethic of Quebec is still that of an agrarian and small-town society" (p. 30).

Wrong noted the differences between Canada and the United States in terms of the formal organization of government and in terms of differences in symbols such as American constitutionalism compared with Canadian parliamentary process (see p. 33). But political democracy is the state system in both countries, and this system is regulated for the most part by a common legal heritage which is British common law (see p. 36). Political democracy is Quebec's means of preserving its "minority rights and interests within the Canadian confederation" (p. 35). Wrong indicated several reasons why legal authority is respected more in Canada than in the United States, and concluded that Canadians are "more prone to identify liberty and democracy with legal traditions and procedures rather than with freedom of business enterprise or with opportunities for individual economic advancement" (p. 38).

Without saying it in so many words, Wrong argued that English Canadians are cosmopolitans while French Canadians are isolationists, more like the Americans (see pp. 43-46). "Canada's dependence on trade for economic survival has produced a livelier consciousness of the interdependence of the nations of the world than is usually evident in the United States with its vast national markets and its greater economic self-sufficiency" (p. 43). Within the Canadian context, "French-speaking Canadians have mainly desired to be left alone to live their own lives in their beloved homeland of Quebec" (p. 45).

Canada has valued cultural pluralism as a model of ethnic social organization. Wrong pointed out that the melting-pot concept which is a popular model of ethnic social organization in the United States cannot so easily be applied to Canada, where the diverse meanings associated with many cultural heritages have emerged as a value in its own right (see p. 49). In the United States, the melting-pot concept implies "the necessity of 'melting,' of becoming Americanized, and this carries the suggestion that ethnic differences are undesirable and efforts to maintain them un-American" (p. 47).

Wrong concluded that America's mass culture is imported into Canada to such a degree that the United States and English Canada are a "cultural unity." Quebec has been insulated in large measure from this importation because of the language barrier. "Fear of cultural swamping by the United States rather than any fear of possible political or economic domination is the main source of the resistance of many educated Canadians to American influences" (pp. 53-54).

These many observations and conclusions cannot be distilled into one or several main themes. Wrong documented the thesis that many differences of value, attitude and behaviour exist between French Canada, English Canada and the United States. He also documented the subthesis that the greatest of these differences, generally speaking, are found between French Canada and English Canada, rather than between English Canada and the United States. Wrong viewed English Canada, across many sectors of activity, in terms of it being a pluralistic mosaic which values diversity but which also cherishes the collective whole. English Canada tends to be a state-centred technocracy which values free enterprise in a social-democratic context. French Canada, on the other hand, is more like a traditional group in democracy and is church-centred and classical, where a monolithic minority may, with time, become organized along economic and class lines. Thus, the two Canadas have distinctive subcharacters which cannot easily be blended into a larger national character.

We should remember that Wrong's comments are almost two decades out of date. Significant changes have developed in the interim. For the present, Wrong's comments serve us as a baseline for estimating at least some of the shifts which have taken place since his monograph was researched in the early 1950's.

We now turn to a paper by Naegele (1961; references are to the editorially revised statement, 1964), especially to that part of the paper which is concerned with characteristics of Canadian society. Naegele's approach is scholarly by being both historical and comparative. His observations are acknowledged as speculations, and his speculations concern the "main elements of a general Canadian consensus" as revealed through comparison with the "major ends and norms of United States society" (p. 498).

Naegele generalized that the English Canadian

seems guided by two models. . . . He feels in the middle between the United States and England. (The French Canadian feels more on his own: he can claim a more distinct culture as his resource and accomplishment; but that culture is relatively local.) (p. 501). The English model stands for stable political forms, for public dignity, and for social orderliness. Its literature, and up to a point its diction, stand in continuity with past accomplishments and with the promise of new departures. . . . Yet England is to be outgrown, not rejected (p. 502).

England is no model, however, with regard to the facilities of daily living or the constraints of social stratification. In these matters Canada is part of a new world. . . . The Canadian wants to be part of an open society, even if he submits more willingly than the American to the facts of inequality. The United States, then, is a model with regard to opportunities and amenities, risks taken, and facts admitted. It is the source, as well, of a great deal of the intellectual and aesthetic [and economic] 'income' of Canada (p. 502).

Thus we have Naegele's thesis of the intermediate character of the Canadian consensus. It is almost as if Canadians *think* of their heritage while they *do* materialism. While there are many symbolic ties with that heritage, such as through the parliamentary process of government, there are many contemporary pressures toward the adoption of a new life in a new world. The realities of the present together with the material aspirations of so many for the future suggest, as Naegele implied, that the dynamics of the Canadian-American relationship are a most important subject for careful study. At the start of the 1960's, Naegele concluded that "cultural values and social patterns in Canada, in comparison to those in the United States, seem muted. The same values are held — but with much more hesitancy. Excess itself is disvalued" (p. 501).

Naegele rendered at least four services to the student of Canadian society. First of all, he carefully described the variations and contradictions which make characterizations oversimplified by definition. He constantly pointed to the many layers of complexity, as the following citation suggests. "The contrast between French and English is not all of a piece. It is compounded by religion: not all French Canadians are Catholics and quite a few non-French Canadians are. It is compounded by place: many French Canadians live outside Quebec. It is compounded by the slow and fast drift of industrialization: for all the rural heritage that fills out part of the substance of the French-Canadian tradition, that tradition contains, as well, important urban, professional, and trading patterns — this, of course, is increasingly true. The contrast is further compounded by various forms of ignorance, defensive beliefs, and other kinds of patterned avoidance that generally accompany the reciprocities sustained by minorities and majorities" (p. 505). Naegele elsewhere noted many other wrinkles, such as patterning by age and sex, and by region and political culture.

Secondly, Naegele reminded us of the difference between stereotype (in this case, that which we are told or we think we are) and sentiment (that which we feel but which remains private because we also feel constrained from its expression). He claimed, for example, that in Canada we "shy away from coining terms that stand for 'Canadianization' or from accusations of 'un-Canadian' activities. The absence of terms, however, need not stand for an absence of corresponding sentiments.

Rather, the general constraint, within which ethnic and other diversities are in fact contained, is itself a quiet, half self-effacing affair — marked alike by English restraint in contrast to American abandon and by American convictions about the perfectibility of the conditions of life" (p. 504).

Thirdly, Naegele like many other persons stressed the nature of the vitality, to use his word, of Quebec (see pp. 505-506). By so doing, he showed the academic importance of French-Canadian society as a real-life laboratory for developing and solving social issues. In terms of Canadian national character, Naegele speculated that Quebec is a "configuration of values constituting a partial alternative especially to the Anglo-Saxon traditions within Canada, while being contained within a wider Canadian consensus. In addition to allowing for the greater proximity of the disparate spheres of industrial society, these values enhance a greater intensity of social relations, a greater concern for the cultivation of family ties, and a greater desire to align the demands of a modern industrial society with the resources — intellectual, religious, and other — of older social patterns" (p. 506). Implicit in this statement is the implication that French-Canadian consensus may be developing in a direction which will allow French-Canadian society to cope with selected aspects of Toffler's future shock (1971), and to do so more successfully than will the rest of North America.

Finally, Naegele provided an outline of research questions in response to his own plea for further research (see p. 506). His service in doing so, of course, is by forcing recognition of the fact that systematic collection of social facts, and not just casual or informed speculation, is required to reveal the structure of Canadian national character, and to reveal changes in that structure with passing time and across the many layers of social patterning.

Lipset (1963) called Naegele's paper the "best effort to sum up the general value system of Canada" (p. 252). That complimentary judgment must now be reviewed within the context of more recent contributions, including several from Lipset himself. Lipset's main references include THE FIRST NEW NATION (1963) and REVOLUTION AND COUNTERREVOLUTION (1970; first published 1968), together with a paper which appeared in THE CANADIAN REVIEW OF SOCIOLOGY AND ANTHROPOLOGY (1964). There is a considerable common core of data and argument across these publications. Also, a critical literature in response to Lipset's various contributions has been emerging during recent years.

Chart 5.1 summarizes Lipset's discussion. He revised the list of pattern variables as established by Parsons (1951; see pp. 58-67) to assist in the task of comparing the value systems of selected countries. These variables are qualitative and dichotomous in their nature, and their very statement has been hailed as the "most important single theoretical formulation" in Parsonian social theory (Devereux, 1961, p. 39). Unlike many aspects of Parsonian theory, the pattern variables are not difficult to understand, for they represent fundamental choices which must be made by individuals before meaningful action can occur.

Lipset employed the pattern variables as means of noting the value choices which seem to have been made in selected societies, and thus as means for characterizing the value structures of those societies. He defined the elitism-equalitarianism variable to mean that a "society's values may stress that all persons must be given respect simply because they are human beings, or it may stress the general superiority of those who hold positions of power and privilege" (1963, p. 211). He defined the other three variables in the following terms. "According to the achieve-

CHART 5.1

Estimates of Relative Rankings of Great Britain, Canada and the United States by Strength of Certain Pattern Variables

	Great Britain	Canada	United States
Elitism (1) — Equalitarianism (3)	1	2	3
Ascription (1) — Achievement (3)	1	2	3
Particularism (1) — Universalism (3)	1	2	3
Diffuseness (1) — Specificity (3)	1	2	3

Source: Lipset, 1963, p.249. Lipset's chart included rankings for Australia.

ment-ascription distinction, a society's value system may emphasize individual ability or performance or it may emphasize ascribed or inherited qualities (such as race or high birth) in judging individuals and placing them in various roles. According to the universalism-particularism distinction, it may emphasize that all people shall be treated according to the same standard (*e.g.,* equality before the law), or that individuals shall be treated differently according to their personal qualities or their particular membership in a class or group. Specificity-diffuseness refers to the difference between treating individuals in terms of the specific positions which they happen to occupy, rather than diffusely as individual members of the collectivity" (1963, pp. 209-210).

Lipset carefully noted that his estimates of relative rankings are charted as just that and nothing more, and he further noted that a society cannot be fully described in terms of the pattern variables or of any other conceptual framework (see 1963, pp. 211-212).

It seems that Lipset's rankings are such as to support Naegele's thesis concerning the intermediate character of the Canadian consensus. Lipset estimated this thesis to be true on each of the four pattern variables. Note that he did not prove the validity of Naegele's thesis; rather he *estimated* its validity. Lipset acknowledged his method when he noted that to "demonstrate that such differences really exist would involve a considerable research program. However, I have drawn on a considerable number of writings which have argued and given some evidence that these differences are as they are presented here and, for the time being, we must depend on such impressionistic evidence to support the discussion" (1963, pp. 249-250). Suffice it to say that Lipset's method in relation to his broad subject has all but forced his critics to examine his work with unusual scrutiny.

In addition to the so-called impressionistic evidence, Lipset brought some quantitative data to bear on the rankings reported in Chart 5.1. In THE FIRST NEW NATION (1963), he employed statistics on the number of persons attending institutions of higher education to indicate a society's orientation to achievement and, to a lesser extent, equalitarianism (see pp. 259-261). Educational statistics cannot be described as direct evidence; a theoretical argument must be supplied. For example, one can argue that more of a value emphasis on achievement or equalitarianism is indicated by relatively more persons in attendance at institutions of higher education, because a society considers that higher education is a means to success, or because the greater the number of people taking advantage of higher education, the more the society must value such things as equality of opportunity. Lipset argued that because England and Wales had 3.7 percent and Scotland had 5.1 percent of their populations aged 20 to 24 years attending institutions of higher education "about 1956," and because the comparable percentage figures for Canada and the United States were 8.0 and 27.2, respectively, therefore such data support the rankings contained in Chart 5.1 (see p. 260). Lipset defended his estimates with further "proof that these differences reflect variation in values" by noting that comparable participation percentages for the Philippines and Puerto Rico were 14.5 and 11.9, respectively, noting that both countries have imported American values; the participation percentage for colonial Jamaica, on the other hand, was 0.7, more in line with the low participation percentage in the case of England (see pp. 259-261).

Lipset used other quantitative data to support his conclusions. For example, given that in 1955 there was in England, Canada and the United States one lawyer for every 2,222, 1,630 and 868 members of the population, respectively, there is support, said Lipset, for the argument that a society such as the United States, which values equalitarianism, has need for the services of more lawyers because the more traditional mechanisms of social control are less effective (see p. 264). Lipset utilized other quantitative evidence in other writings. For example, the conclusion that Canadians hold more respect for law and public authority than do Americans was documented by the fact that the ratio of police to population in 1962 in the United States was greater at 193.8 than was the comparable ratio in 1961 in Canada at 143.2 (see 1964, p. 176; 1970, p. 45). Lipset similarly noted various crime statistics for Canada and the United States, making the point that Canadians are more obedient to the rule of social order (see 1964, p. 177; 1970, pp. 46-47). Lipset even noted that relatively lower divorce rates in Canada suggest the "strength of collectivity-orientation," or the "weakness in Canada of the sort of rugged individualism (self-orientation) and emphasis on achievement so characteristic" of the United States (1964, pp. 178-179). This last reference is to another of the Parsonian pattern variables, self-orientation versus collectivity-orientation, which Lipset omitted from his charted rankings (see 1963, pp. 270-271).

Lipset's overall theme concerning the national characters of the United States and Canada pertained to the historical roots of each, the first through revolution, the other through counterrevolution (see 1964, pp. 181-183; 1970, pp. 55-75). It is not so much that Canada did not have a revolution and America did, but that many aspects of Canada's early development as a nation were defined in reaction to the American Revolution. In this regard, Lower noted that "colonial Toryism made its second attempt to erect on American soil a copy of the English social edifice. From one point of view this is the most significant thing about the Loyalist movement: it withdrew a class concept of life from the south, moved it up north and gave it a second chance" (1964, p. 114). Lipset saw in this statement a "clue to the continuance of British ascriptive and elitist value patterns" in Canadian society, or at least in certain sectors of Canadian society (1970, p. 56).

Davis (1971) questioned Lipset's various analyses on two grounds. He questioned the conception of the United States as an equalitarian, achievement-oriented and universalistic society (see Chart 5.1) because, given "historical fact rather than . . . liberal rhetoric, the United States is a hierarchical, racist society — contrary to the long-nourished American middle-class, 'liberal' self-image" (p. 16). Davis also questioned the conception of Canada as counterrevolutionary. His reason for questioning in this instance, however, does not stand the test of time. Davis failed to acknowledge historical roots while noting the familiar theme that Canada as a hinterland society "*should* have considerably more revolutionary *potential* than the United States" (p. 16; emphases added). Davis neglected to acknowledge that Canada has yet to fight back against its metropolitan exploiters; until the fight develops, this line of argument does not of its own weight negate the revolutionary-counterrevolutionary theme. The comments by Davis do suggest some important research questions, especially when we remember that fighting need not be of the military variety. It is in this broad context of action that such things as continental resources policy, still to be developed between Canada and the United States, can influence Canada's identity as a nation as well as the country's political and economic relationship with the United States.

Perhaps the most severe criticism of Lipset's work is a recent paper by Truman (1971). He began by noting the dubiousness of Lipset's use of secondary sources: "he creates rankings which are *his* estimate of *their* estimate" (p. 498). But Truman developed his most important objections to Lipset's effort by re-analyzing Lipset's statistical interpretations and by re-interpreting many of his historical observations. Truman's critique cannot be reviewed in detail; it is highly recommended for reading. It must be noted, however, that Truman made much of the relative positions of Canada and Australia in terms of the Parsonian pattern variables, and by doing so he documented alternative interpretations. Lipset included Australia in his discussion, but that aspect of his work was purposely omitted from the previous review. The fact that Truman found cause to question Lipset in this regard raises the possibility that at least some of Lipset's statistical evidence may indeed not be valid evidence. To cite but one example, Truman noted several types of statistical data which suggest that Canada not only leads Australia in terms of the equality of educational opportunity — an observation opposite to Lipset's evidence — but that on certain measures Canada leads the United States as well (see pp. 498-501). For example, Canada, at least during the first half of the 1960's, led the Americans in the percentage of national income spent on education (8.5 percent in Canada in 1965 compared to 6.5 percent in the United States in the same year).

Finally, we must turn to Porter and his discussion of Canadian character (1967). To review Porter's contributions is a difficult challenge; his analyses as contained in THE VERTICAL MOSAIC (1965) are comprehensive and demanding.

Porter (1967) argued that "[i]deology did not end in Canada. It simply did not begin" (p. 54). Canada's nonrevolutionary history helped to create the nation's identity confusion. A strong emphasis upon ethnic pluralism helped to create the confusion too, along with other factors such as the relative linguistic and cultural exclusiveness maintained by the French and English, massive immigration, the close proximity to the United States and the high rate of consumption of American mass culture (see pp. 49-56). Because of Canada's cultural orientation to differences rather than to similarities, especially in the spheres of language, ethnicity and regions, Porter observed an "assumed fragility of Canadian society. National unity is best safeguarded by not disturbing the present" (p. 54). Basing himself in part upon the writings of Wrong, Naegele and Lipset, Porter concluded what has already been noted in Chapter 4, that Canadians are "more conservative and authoritarian and less egalitarian in values than are the people of the United States" (p. 48).

The characterization supplied by Porter is buttressed by his lengthy study of social stratification in Canadian society (1965). The various influences noted above are made all the more potent in Canada by a power structure which is both concentrated in space and selective in origin. Porter defined a group of 760 persons as constituting Canada's economic elite, and he noted that these persons accounted for 82 percent of the directorships and 95.4 percent of the bank directorships held by Canadian residents, and 65.6 percent of all directorships in the ten largest Canadian life insurance companies (see p. 274). Porter found that "economic power belongs almost exclusively to those of British origin" (p. 286). Only 6.7 percent of the 760 persons in the economic elite were French in origin, while other ethnic groups "were hardly represented at all" (p. 286). Porter's analysis broadened as other facts were revealed, such as his conclusion that "more than one in three of the economic elite came from families already well established in the upper classes" (p. 291). Indeed, of the 611 Canadian-born members of the economic elite, only 108 or almost 18 percent began in a class position below middle class (see p. 292). Dramatic upward social mobility is not the norm in Canada, at least insofar as Porter's economic elite is concerned. This and much additional evidence brought Porter to conclude that "class differences act as barriers to individual achievement" (p. 557), and that the "inequalities that exist in the social class system arise in part from the inadequacy of educational institutions" (p. 293).

More than any of the authors reviewed in this section, Porter reminds us of the discussion in Chapter 3 on the necessity of selectivity in the development of single societies and cultures. By selecting one social pattern or value, a society is blocked from selecting many other patterns and values. It seems that for many reasons Canada has opted for ethnic diversity, and because of this fact institutional patterns have developed in certain conservative directions. Porter concluded his study of Canadian stratification with the following statement.

Ethnic and religious affiliation in Canadian society have always had an effect on the life chances of the individual. If not its one distinctive value, that of the mosaic is Canada's most cherished. Legitimatization for the mosaic is sought in the notion of collective or group rights which becomes confused with the legal foundation of individual rights. It seems inescapable that the strong emphasis on ethnic differentiation can result only in those continuing dual loyalties which prevent the emergence of any clear Canadian identity. From the point of view of our study of social class and power, it is likely that the historical pattern of class and ethnicity will be perpetuated as long as ethnic differentiation is so highly valued (p. 558).

There is a sense in which Porter cherishes ethnic diversity. But he also quoted classical theory (see pp. 552-554) in resigning himself to the impossibility of true democratic participation and rule. Much of Porter's contribution in pointing to inequities seems to be directed toward the practical goal of erasing restrictions which control access to positions of power. "If power and decision-making must always rest with elite groups, there can at least be open recruitment from all classes into the elites" (p. 558).

There is one final theme in Porter's work which is as important as the role of ethnicity when trying to understand Canadian national character. Porter concluded that Canada lacked a creative politics as a result of the fact that the traditional parties at the federal level are both conservative in their orientations (see pp. 368-379). As a consequence, political dialogue in Canada has been "between unity and discord rather than progressive and conservative forces" (p. 369). Also as a consequence, political dialogue can avoid the gut social and economic issues which would be involved in any political decision to more fully utilize human resources in the service of goals and values. Horowitz (1972) provided an expanded discussion of Porter's creative politics theme on the occasion of reviewing THE VERTICAL MOSAIC.

Many other commentaries have appeared over the years on the subject of Canadian national character, or on one or more of the topics which pertain to national character. Many statements are journalistic, and many of them seek to describe Canada in the negative, in terms of what it is not, or where there has been a failing. For example, Conway (1964) argued that Canada and its citizens have "failed to vest sovereignty where it properly belongs — in the Canadian people. Instead, we have allowed it to remain in the British monarchy, and in doing so we have divided our country and inhibited our emotional and creative development as a people. A nation, like an individual, can achieve integrity and identity only out of its own experience and not derivatively from a parent. This, and not French-Canadian particularism, is at the root of our present difficulties" (p. 101).

Other commentaries describe Canada's meandering search for identity (Fraser, 1967), and still others lament the passing of Canada as a nation-state (Grant, 1965). Many recently published works seek to give coherence and tangibility, and thus meaning and identity, to Canadian society. Different authors view it in different ways. There are the economic nationalists, for example, who argue that Canadian identity will emerge as Canada's economic system is repatriated from the United States. And there are still others — and most who search their souls may find themselves in this category — who feel, as Kilbourn did, that "Canada is a different kind of American society, an American alternative" (1970, p. xiii). Kilbourn argued that national identity does not have to be packaged in a neat, consistent and well-worked-through bundle of meanings; but rather, that there are sufficient meanings to be celebrated in the fact that Canada is a "cultural freeport" where no single ideology or vision predominates, and the judgment that Canadians "have been better interpreters and critics of culture than creators of it" (pp. xv-xvi). Kilbourn celebrated Canada, the "peaceable kingdom," in the following reflective way.

In a world where independence often arrives with swift violence, it may be good to have one nation where it has matured slowly: in a world of fierce national prides, to have a state about which it is hard to be solemn and religious without being ridiculous, and impossible to be dogmatic. In a world with tendencies to political division and cultural homogeneity, Canada is a country that still stands for the alternative of political federation and cultural and regional variety. In a world that strives for absolute freedom and often gains only oppressive power, Canada presents a tradition that sees freedom in a subtle creative tension with authority. . . . In a world of ideological battles, it is good to have a place where the quantity and quality of potential being in a person means more than what he believes: in a masculine world of the assertive will and the cutting edge of intellect, a certain Canadian tendency to the amorphous permissive feminine principle of openness and tolerance and acceptance offers the possibility of healing (pp. xvii-xviii).

In an attempt to follow the reviews of these authors with empirical evidence which speaks to the broad subject of national character, a pilot study was undertaken and some tentative results are reported here prior to the general critique which follows in the next section. The study utilized Miller's Scale Battery of International Patterns and Norms (1970). Miller's instrument was designed to gain an indication of the social patterns and norms of national cultures, and as such it was adopted to study these topics as they pertain to Canadian society. An additional bonus is the fact that Miller already has used the instrument with a number of different national samples, including samples from England and the United States.

Miller published mean scores on each of twenty scales for England and the United States in 1968. His judges were nationals of the country in question. The judges who supplied the Canadian data in December of 1971 resided across all of the Canadian regions and represented different ethnic and linguistic groups. Judges were selected by research associates who were asked to distribute questionnaires to persons known to be informed residents of Canada, and known to have been residents of their particular region for at least two years. Residence was used as a criterion rather than citizenship. Research associates were also asked to select judges of diverse ethnic and linguistic backgrounds.

In all, two hundred questionnaires were sent to twenty-two research associates for distribution. Twenty-five questionnaires were distributed within each of six regions, including northern Canada. Twenty-five questionnaires were directed to persons of German background with a further twenty-five directed to persons of Polish background living in Alberta, Saskatchewan and Manitoba. A total of 118 completed questionnaires were returned for analysis, representing a return of 59 percent. The distribution of respondents varied both by region of residence and by ethnic and linguistic background, with the noteworthy exception that very few French-speaking persons were sampled.

For the sake of information, the distribution of respondents by regional identification was Atlantic (17), Quebec and Ontario (14), Prairie (52), British Columbia (21) and the Northwest Territories (11). Three respondents failed to specify regional identification. The distribution of respondents by language spoken in the home was English (90), German and Polish (22), French (2) and other languages (4).

The mean scale scores for three countries, and twenty scales are reported in Table 5.2. If the numbers are examined with Naegele's thesis concerning Canada's intermediate character in mind, only limited support is evidenced. In a similar vein, limited support appears for some of Lipset's estimates. Canada most clearly is intermediate between England and the United States in terms of social acceptance, degree of confidence in personal security and in protection of property, family solidarity, class structure and class consciousness, and in its definition of the role of private and public ownership of property. England generally defines the conservative position, although the United States places the highest emphasis upon the right of private property.

The normative structure indicated for Canadian society, however, shows many variations which are exceptions to the general thesis of Canada's intermediacy. Respondents indicated the following: that there is less concern for and trust of others in Canada than in England or the United States; that children in Canada have less independence; that in Canada and England the sexes are distinguished more than they are in the United States concerning the matter of moral code and role definition; that Canada leans slightly away from a secular interpretation of existence and thus toward a sacred interpretation; that there is slightly less

TABLE 5.2

English, Canadian and American Social Patterns and Norms

Scale (Six Points of Judgment)	England 1968 N = 15	Canada 1971 N = 118	United States 1968 N = 32
1. Social Acceptance (1 = high)	4.0	3.0	1.6
2. Standards of Personal and Community Health (1 = high)	3.1	3.0	1.9
3. Concern for and Trust of Others (1 = high)	2.0	3.4	2.7
4. Confidence in Personal Security and Protection of Property (1 = high)	2.1	2.9	3.7
5. Family Solidarity (1 = high)	2.9	3.5	4.0
6. Independence of the Child (1 = high)	2.1	2.7	2.1
7. Moral Code and Role Definitions of Men and Women (1 = single code prevails across the sexes)	3.4	3.5	2.3
8. Definition of Religion and Moral Conduct (1 = sacred interpretation and 6 = secular interpretation)	4.6	4.1	4.3
9. Class Structure and Class Consciousness (1 = high)	3.1	3.9	4.9
10. Consensus on Philosophy and Social Objectives (1 = high)	2.1	2.5	2.1
11. Labour's Orientation to Economic and Social System (1 = alienated)	4.0	4.0	5.4
12. Belief in Democratic Political System (1 = high)	2.1	2.7	1.8
13. Definition of Work and Individual Achievement (1 = work and achievement obligatory)	3.1	3.2	2.1
14. Civic Participation and Voluntary Activity (1 = high)	3.1	3.4	1.9
15. Definition of Role of Private and Public Ownership of Property (1 = belief in right of private property)	3.3	2.5	1.7
16. Honesty and Integrity of Government Officials (1 = high)	1.3	3.5	1.8
17. Political Influence of Foreign Enterprise on Host Government (1 = high)	5.3	2.7	5.2
18. Encouragement of Foreign Enterprise (1 = high)	2.3	2.8	2.2
19. Degree of Nepotism in Organizational Life (1 = high)	4.0	3.2	4.8
20. Degree of Expected Reciprocity in Favours and Rewards (1 = high)	5.0	3.0	3.9

Source: Data for England and the United States from Miller, 1970, p.331.

consensus on social philosophy and objectives in Canada; that labour is slightly more alienated in Canada and England in comparison with labour's position in the United States; that Canadians believe less in the democratic political system; that Canada, like England, is less committed to the ethic which says that work and achievement are obligatory; that there is less emphasis on civic and voluntary participation in Canada, especially in comparison with the United States; that Canada far more than both England and the United States questions the honesty and integrity of government officials; that Canada far more than both England and the United States is subject to political influence from foreign enterprises; that Canada does encourage more foreign enterprise; that nepotism in organizational life is greatest in Canada; and that Canada is more oriented to a norm which calls for reciprocity in favours and rewards. Finally, respondents indicated that standards of personal and community health are similar in Canada and England, but lower than are such standards in the United States.

Analyses were undertaken by regional identification and by language spoken in the home. The data are not reported here, although it is noteworthy that in both instances remarkably little variation was revealed. The fact of little observed variation is not the reason for omitting the data and their interpretations; given a well-executed research design, such a finding is as important as any other finding. In the case of the present research, however, problems of incomplete data and problems of measurement make further analysis of questionable value. Even as it stands, the nonsystematic sampling method alone suggests that the Canadian scores reported in Table 5.2 and any interpretations which arise from their analysis must be qualified as tentative and suggestive at the very most. Perhaps the most important implication is in the reminder that the national characterizations provided by various authors tend themselves to be nonsystematic, or without regard for the systematic study of the underlying structure of Canadian national character. The following section outlines minimally sufficient criteria for both doing and evaluating work in this regard.

Summary and Critique

> How stiff should our criteria be? The ideal of science prescribes standards that few, if any, concrete research projects ever meet. The surest way of damning any research report is to compare it with the ideals of science (Zetterberg, 1965, p. 151).

Many persons argue that the tone of sociological investigation has been changing recently, especially in terms of an emerging tendency to examine sociology and its activities in the manner of a critical outsider. The development of the sociology of sociology as a branch of the sociology of knowledge signifies a growing consciousness among sociologists concerning their contributions to social analysis, and especially in terms of the adequacy of their contributions. In one sense, the youth culture which demands relevance has worked itself up to professional and academic organizations and subjects, and we are finding that the relevance of these organizations and subjects is being challenged. Gouldner (1970) suggested that "their mounting awareness of the ways in which their sociology is becoming inextricably integrated into . . . society" is perhaps the central reason why sociologists are becoming more conscious of their mission (p. 511). Gouldner, it must be noted, suggested much more than this, for he argued that the "sociologists' task today is not only to see people as they see themselves, nor to see themselves as others see them; it is also to see *themselves* as they see other people" (p. 25). The goal of the sociology of sociology, or of reflexive sociology as Gouldner called it, is to "*transform* the sociologist, to penetrate deeply into his daily life and work, enriching them with new sensitivities, and to raise the sociologist's self-awareness to a new historical level" (p. 489).

It is noteworthy that not one example exists in all of the reviewed literature in the previous section where data were specifically gathered to examine even the most general assertions. We cannot say that writers in the arts and letters have failed to document their assertions since they abide by no clear and agreed-upon criteria. But underlying a great deal of that which is written in the name of social science is the judgment that Canada's collective identity has been described at best through inference, usually quite indirectly. This is an area waiting to be researched by persons who use methods designed to maximize the validity of inferences drawn directly from data.

Given such sentiment, we should observe first that the commentaries on Canadian character as discussed in the previous section appear to portray the following things in common, or, if not in common, that certain of them comment in ways which should be noted in summary.

First of all, there is much evidence in support of the theme that selective processes occur during the course of social and cultural development. Related to this theme is the determinacy of history, which is to say that many happenings and trends of days past have clearly defined significant aspects of the present structure of Canadian national character. Such facts as the movement and settlement of tens of thousands of United Empire Loyalists of an earlier day seem in retrospect as important as the migration of hundreds of thousands of immigrants during the past century. In their different ways, it is as if such groups stamped the contours of the Canadian nation as it would forever be.

Those stamped contours have persisted in two central respects: the conservative tone of things and persons Canadian, and the cherished mosaic. While these respects have taken on slightly different tones with each new generation, their great importance has been noted by most who write concerning the Canadian scene. The fact of conservatism is always relative to other comparison points. The mosaic, on the other hand, is a distinctly Canadian social pattern which may be sufficiently powerful to keep Canada in the twentieth century long after the century has passed. The very existence of the mosaic has been viewed as a mandate for elite members of the society — persons who are "above" the mosaic — to govern with traditional impunity. And yet, there are very few who suggest that the mosaic must be cracked.

The decline of the importance of the monarchy in Canada indicated the modern transition from postcolonialism to North American continentalism. The developing transition has meant many shifts, such as a steady movement toward a moderate (one dares to say liberal!) individualism. In the abstract, the transition is part of the classic movement from *gemeinschaft* to *gesellschaft*. But the transition is more than the movement from social organization based upon primary relations to organization based upon the synchronization of impersonal relations, for the transition may yet lead to a radical breakdown of *gesellschaft* as members of society seek more meaningful social relations and activities as their society enters its postindustrial phase of development. In any event, the transition of society raises the old question of relativity, and many persons have used relative comparisons as a method for studying Canadian social patterns. In this regard, a great deal has been published concerning the theme of intermediacy, where Canada is viewed as between England and the United States on a variety of indicators.

The transition of society takes different forms in different places at different times. There is much agreement on the unique circumstances which have helped to define the modern province of Quebec, although not all agree concerning the future path of development for French Canada. There are mounting signs in certain circles that the transition of French-Canadian society, as it continues to unfold, may serve more as an answer to some of Canada's identity problems, rather than as a continuing national problem.

Toward the end of the 1960's and during the early 1970's, problems of national identity were made more complicated by various forms of nationalism. While many believe that nationalism is Canada's insurance against a bellowing neighbor to the south, others argue that nationalistic furor avoids the real problems of Canadian survival. While not always of one mind, the nonnationalists point toward such things as the need in Canada for social goals and for an accounting procedure to assess progress with respect to goals (see Hauser, 1965). Others argue for a creative politics to help bring public debate to a point where real political alternatives are discussed in the light of social goals. Underlying much of the debate are principles of social democracy, including a principle which supports the opening up of opportunities for all people with regard only for their achieved abilities.

Such are the generalizations contained in the previous section of this chapter. The total picture obviously is a most complex one, and that fact alone directs us in the following manner. In anticipation of what follows, we must observe that the commentaries which have been reviewed, and other material contained in this chapter, do not hold up very well *if* their content is evaluated according to even the most minimal criteria of adequacy. The criteria which are specified in the following discussion are alike in the sense that they seek to make observations and analyses more systematic, and in doing so they aim for more valid descriptions of Canadian character and consciousness.

It was noted earlier that Inkeles and Levinson's treatment of national character as modal personality structure suggested criteria which might be applied as the bases for a critique of the literature. There are, of course, other criteria, several of which centre upon the problems of, and need for, doing research on such topics as collective values and norms. Card (1968) argued that the deficiency in "definite and reliable knowledge about Canadian values is one of the handicaps with which Canadians enter their second generation" (p. 142). Porter (1967) tied the deficiency to the slow development of the social sciences in Canada, especially in the universities (see pp. 51-52). Whatever the causes and consequences, the following criteria have been framed as a result of directions revealed in the work of these and other authors to allow us to appraise the significance of selected contributions. Three criteria are discussed.

The first of the criteria concerns the definitional explicitness of the object of study. Researchers and commentators should proceed with their research and commentary only after they have clearly specified what it is they aim to study and report upon. This sounds like a basic requirement of any investigation, scientific or otherwise. But there is too much evidence suggesting that this is the criterion which most often is transgressed. This chapter alone has included discussions of many possibly different things: national character, consensus, modal personality structure and national identity. Many more might have been added such as collective conscience or collective morality or public opinion. To clearly define what one intends to study is a basic requisite for doing anything in a systematic fashion. The present judgment is that most, if not all, of the authors noted or reviewed in this chapter have violated this basic requirement, either because they employed different terms to indicate the same thing, or because they used one term to suggest different things at the same or at different points in time.

The second of the criteria concerns the adequacy of theoretical models. A theoretical model which is adequate should explicitly acknowledge various aspects of diversity. For example, the model by definition should force its user to make statements concerning, and to observe patterns of, variability, and to search out and interpret distributions which are not homogeneous in terms of one or more variables. The modal or multimodal model is one which requires its user to beware of such aspects of the real world. Next to the deliberate use of language, this requirement is basic because to know how something varies is to know other things such as its structure of interrelations with still other things. The simple diversity in things can be missed altogether if inadequate models are employed. Indeed, a great many aspects of one's subject can be overlooked by using a wrong model or by not using a model at all. In this regard, few of the authors noted or reviewed in this chapter supplied even a most general model to underlie their study. This fact alone is the reason behind many nonsystematic investigations. To fail to employ an explicit model defining the parameters of study is one reason why so much of the literature on national character is of the narrative, free-flowing variety. We must hasten to note that any model is not necessarily an adequate model in terms of this criterion. Lipset's adoption of some of the Parsonian pattern variables illustrates the fact that models are not guarantees of adequacy. Lipset's failing is very much associated with a related problem, namely, that once a model has been selected to guide observations and analyses, its user ought to specify with utmost care the logic which ties permissible kinds of research evidence to the theoretical content of the model. This requirement reflects the spirit of Truman's critique of some of Lipset's contributions.

The last of the criteria has to do with the actual conduct of research. Even in a difficult area such as the study of national character, researchers should employ methods which enable them to record all important patterns of variation. The purely narrative approach should be used more sparingly, and there should be more empirical research efforts which utilize the most appropriate methods relative to the purpose of study. While methods employed might include carefully sampled surveys or comparative analysis or longitudinal analysis, findings ought to be validated against independent observations or other independent criteria. The criteria which are selected for validation studies ought to match the purpose of the research. For example, the narrative comments of historians or anthropologists are adequate for some purposes, but other documents such as laws and records of legislative debates ought to be used more often as independent checks on research observations and findings. The material noted or reviewed in this chapter is consistently weak with respect to this criterion.

Somehow the circle must be broken, the circle which shows that author$_1$ uses author$_2$ as an informational and/or validational source, while author$_2$ uses author$_3$ and so on. Sooner or later, the circle closes tight when author$_3$ uses author$_1$ as a main source. Such is the deficiency in the study of Canadian national character. It makes a mockery of one of the most important functions of science, namely, to *replicate* earlier findings. Replication is out of the question if the criteria discussed above are left violated because of meandering descriptions and nonsystematic research efforts.

It is noted, in conclusion, that the chosen content of this chapter has been, for the most part, sociological. Its content has been such notwithstanding the fact that the chapter is broadly concerned with social actors, and the fact that the expressed bias of the chapter, as was said in its introduction, is men and women constructing concepts of their society as well as their own social activities within it, and thereby achieving their senses of relationship to community and society. We conclude with a challenge concerning the vast amount of information which is available within the various specialties of social psychology. The field of public opinion offers a rich source of information for questions concerning national character or identity (see Schwartz, 1967). Still more basic are studies which deal with topics such as child-rearing values (see Lambert, Yackley and Hein, 1971), the learning of self-other orientations (see Henderson, Long and Gantcheff, 1970) and identification (see Taylor, Simard and About, 1972). There are studies concerning patterns of ethnic stereotypes (see Gardner and Taylor, 1969). Each of the referenced studies has researched a different question concerning comparisons of French-Canadian and English-Canadian subjects. Still other studies have examined cognitive topics such as English-Canadian attitudes toward French-Canadians (see Dutta, Norman and Kanungo, 1969). The interplays between social actors and their social actions are many and diverse.

References

Benedict, Ruth, PATTERNS OF CULTURE, New York: Mentor Books, 1946.

Card, B. Y., TRENDS AND CHANGE IN CANADIAN SOCIETY: THEIR CHALLENGE TO CANADIAN YOUTH, Toronto: Macmillan of Canada, 1968.

Conway, John, "What Is Canada?" THE ATLANTIC MONTHLY, 214 (November, 1964) 100-105.

Davis, Arthur K., "Canadian Society and History as Hinterland Versus Metropolis," in Richard J. Ossenberg, ed., CANADIAN SOCIETY: PLURALISM, CHANGE, AND CONFLICT, Scarborough, Ont.: Prentice-Hall of Canada Ltd., 1971, pp. 6-32.

Devereux, Edward C., "Parsons' Sociological Theory," in Max Black, ed., THE SOCIAL THEORIES OF TALCOTT PARSONS, Englewood Cliffs, N.J.: Prentice-Hall, Inc., 1961, pp. 1-63.

Dutta, Satrajit, Leonard Norman and Rabindra N. Kanungo, "A Scale for the Measurement of Attitudes toward French Canadians," CANADIAN JOURNAL OF BEHAVIOURAL SCIENCE, 1 (July, 1969) 156-166.

Fraser, Blair, THE SEARCH FOR IDENTITY: CANADA, 1945-1967, Garden City, N.Y.: Doubleday & Company, Inc., 1967.

Gardner, R. C. and D. M. Taylor, "Ethnic Stereotypes: Meaningfulness in Ethnic-Group Labels," CANADIAN JOURNAL OF BEHAVIOURAL SCIENCE, 1 (July, 1969) 182-192.

Gouldner, Alvin W., THE COMING CRISIS OF WESTERN SOCIOLOGY, New York: Basic Books, Inc., 1970.

Grant, George, LAMENT FOR A NATION: THE DEFEAT OF CANADIAN NATIONAL-ISM, Toronto: McClelland and Stewart Limited, 1965.

Hauser, Philip M., "Social Accounting," in Paul F. Lazarsfeld, William H. Sewell and Harold L. Wilensky, eds., THE USES OF SOCIOLOGY, New York: Basic Books, Inc., 1967, pp. 839-875.

Henderson, Edmund H., Barbara H. Long and Helene Gantcheff, "Self-Other Orientations of French- and English-Canadian Adolescents," CANADIAN JOURNAL OF PSYCHOLOGY, 24 (June, 1970) 142-152.

Homans, George C., "Bringing Men Back In," AMERICAN SOCIOLOGICAL REVIEW, 29 (December, 1964) 809-818.

Horowitz, Gad, "Mosaics and Identity," in Bryan Finnigan and Cy Gonick, eds., MAKING IT: THE CANADIAN DREAM, Toronto: McClelland and Stewart Limited, 1972, pp. 465-473.

Inkeles, Alex and Daniel J. Levinson, "National Character: The Study of Modal Personality and Sociocultural Systems," in Gardner Lindzey and Elliot Aronson, ed., THE HANDBOOK OF SOCIAL PSYCHOLOGY, Volume 4, Second Edition, Reading, Mass.: Addison-Wesley Publishing Company, 1969, pp. 418-506.

Kilbourn, William, ed., CANADA: A GUIDE TO THE PEACEABLE KINGDOM, Toronto: Macmillan of Canada, 1970.

Lambert, W. E., A. Yackley and R. N. Hein, "Child Training Values of English Canadian and French Canadian Parents," CANADIAN JOURNAL OF BEHAVIOURAL SCIENCE, 3 (July, 1971) 217-236.

Lipset, Seymour Martin, THE FIRST NEW NATION: THE UNITED STATES IN HISTORICAL AND COMPARATIVE PERSPECTIVE, New York: Basic Books, Inc., 1963.

Lipset, Seymour Martin, "Canada and the United States: A Comparative View," THE CANADIAN REVIEW OF SOCIOLOGY AND ANTHROPOLOGY, 1 (November, 1964) 173-185.

Lipset, Seymour Martin, REVOLUTION AND COUNTERREVOLUTION: CHANGE AND PERSISTENCE IN SOCIAL STRUCTURES, Revised Edition, Garden City, N.Y.: Anchor Books, 1970.

Lower, Arthur R. M., COLONY TO NATION: A HISTORY OF CANADA, Toronto: Longmans, Green & Company, 1946.

Martindale, Don, "The Sociology of National Character," THE ANNALS OF THE AMERICAN ACADEMY OF POLITICAL AND SOCIAL SCIENCE, 370 (March, 1967) 30-35.

Miller, Delbert C., HANDBOOK OF RESEARCH DESIGN AND SOCIAL MEASUREMENT, Second Edition, New York: David McKay Company, Inc., 1970.

Morton, W. L., THE CANADIAN IDENTITY, Toronto: University of Toronto Press, 1961.

Naegele, Kaspar D., "Canadian Society: Some Reflections," in Bernard R. Blishen, Frank E. Jones, Kaspar D. Naegele and John Porter, eds., CANADIAN SOCIETY: SOCIOLOGICAL PERSPECTIVES, Toronto: The Macmillan Company of Canada Limited, 1961, pp. 1-53; 1965, pp. 1-19 and pp. 497-522.

Parsons, Talcott, THE SOCIAL SYSTEM, New York: The Free Press of Glencoe, 1951.

Porter, John, THE VERTICAL MOSAIC: AN ANALYSIS OF SOCIAL CLASS AND POWER IN CANADA, Toronto: University of Toronto Press, 1965.

Porter, John, "Canadian Character in the Twentieth Century," THE ANNALS OF THE AMERICAN ACADEMY OF POLITICAL AND SOCIAL SCIENCE, 370 (March, 1967) 48-56.

Schwartz, Mildred A., PUBLIC OPINION AND CANADIAN IDENTITY, Scarborough, Ont.: Fitzhenry and Whiteside Limited, 1967.

Taylor, Donald M., Lise M. Simard and Frances E. About, "Ethnic Identification in Canada: A Cross-Cultural Investigation," CANADIAN JOURNAL OF BEHAVIOURAL SCIENCE, 4 (January, 1972) 13-20.

Toffler, Alvin, FUTURE SHOCK, Toronto: Bantam Books of Canada Ltd., 1971.

Truman, Tom, "A Critique of Seymour M. Lipset's Article 'Value Differences, Absolute or Relative: The English-Speaking Democracies,' " CANADIAN JOURNAL OF POLITICAL SCIENCE, 4 (December, 1971) 497-525.

Wrong, Dennis H., AMERICAN AND CANADIAN VIEWPOINTS, Washington, D.C.: American Council on Education, 1955.

Wrong, Dennis H., "The Oversocialized Conception of Man in Modern Sociology," AMERICAN SOCIOLOGICAL REVIEW, 26 (April, 1961) 183-193.

Zetterberg, Hans L., ON THEORY AND VERIFICATION IN SOCIOLOGY, Third Enlarged Edition, Totowa, N.J.: The Bedminster Press, 1965.

For Further Reading

Berry, J. W. and G. J. S. Wilde, eds., SOCIAL PSYCHOLOGY: THE CANADIAN CONTEXT, Toronto: McClelland and Stewart Limited, 1972.

Clark, Gerald, CANADA: THE UNEASY NEIGHBOUR, Toronto: McClelland and Stewart Limited, 1965.

Clark, S. D., "Canada and Her Great Neighbour," THE CANADIAN REVIEW OF SOCIOLOGY AND ANTHROPOLOGY, 1 (November, 1964) 193-201.

Clarkson, Stephen, ed., VISIONS 2020: FIFTY CANADIANS IN SEARCH OF A FUTURE, Edmonton: M. G. Hurtig Ltd., 1970.

Cook, Ramsay, THE MAPLE LEAF FOREVER: ESSAYS ON NATIONALISM AND POLITICS IN CANADA, Toronto: Macmillan of Canada, 1971.

Oliver, Michael, ed., SOCIAL PURPOSE FOR CANADA, Toronto: University of Toronto Press, 1961.

Park, Julian, ed., THE CULTURE OF CONTEMPORARY CANADA, Ithaca, N.Y.: Cornell University Press, 1957.

Royal Commission on Bilingualism and Biculturalism, THE CULTURAL CONTRIBUTION OF THE OTHER ETHNIC GROUPS, Book IV, Ottawa: Queen's Printer, 1970.

Part III
Social Dynamics

Chapter 6

Social Microdynamics

The subject of the present chapter is social microdynamics. The chapters which follow it are devoted to social macrodynamics. Our first concern, therefore, must be with the nature of social dynamics.

Societies are dynamic rather than static; they are forever changing. At the same time, societies are not liquid in the sense that there are no patterns of order within them, or in the sense that they take the shape of their historical or geographical containers. There is a structure to every society. They have this structure, however, only if structure is thought of in terms of developed or developing social arrangements which assist persons to cope with their social situations. The concept of structure will be discussed in Chapter 8.

To study social dynamics is to study those forces which produce motion in social structures. The structures in question may be organizations such as a business corporation, or they may be communities or some set of communities within a social region. The social structure may be all of a sovereign region such as Canadian society. In any event, the distinction between *microdynamics* and *macrodynamics* is taken to be the distinction between those social dynamics which are closely related to individual or small group behaviour, on the one hand, and those social dynamics which rarely, if ever, are related to individual or group behaviour, but which are the product of extra-individual conditions which prevail in a society. These conditions may be the broad ones discussed in Chapter 3 such as historical, geographical and demographic conditioners, or they may be more specific conditioners such as macro-economic or political policies which govern the associations of minorities. However approached, the study of social macrodynamics is taken as the study of those forces which produce motion in the social structure of Canadian society as a totality, while the study of social microdynamics is taken as the study of those forces which have more of a direct relationship to individual behaviour.

It should be obvious that this distinction is introduced by definition, and that in practice it is a difficult exercise to distinguish between various social dynamics at different levels of analysis. Some dynamics are appropriate to one level or another, while others operate at some or all levels. These are qualifications which limit the present and following chapters. At the same time, the discussions contained in these chapters are framed with purpose and intent. The three sections which follow in this chapter all deal with rural Canada. One of these offers a case study on the development of local community government in a northern settlement. The second deals with the emergence of hope in an island community off the north-east coast of Newfoundland. The third section is brief and offers a comment interrelating the first two sections. These subjects are introduced within the context of social micro-dynamics because the social development of communities seems primarily to be the effort of small groups of people whose conduct is sometimes the product of government policies, and at other times the product of individual or small group initiative.

Notwithstanding a certain arbitrariness in the distinction between micro-dynamics and macrodynamics, to make the distinction provides a heuristic frame of reference for approaching the intricate subjects of social organization and social change. No doubt, a case can easily be made for examining the various examples of microdynamics as macrodynamics, and vice versa. Just as important, however, is the realization that all social processes must be viewed from both the perspective of the whole (society and other aggregates) and the perspective of its parts (social actors and small social groups).

The final section of this chapter introduces the concept of social participation and suggests why the concept is an important one in social studies, especially when viewed in terms of the social organization of space relations.

Microdynamic: Settlement To Hamlet

The history of the fur trade in North America has been shown as a retreat in the face of settlement. . . . The place of the beaver in Canadian life has been fittingly noted [by white men] in the coat of arms. We have given to the maple a prominence which was due to the birch. We have not yet realized that the Indian and his culture were fundamental to the growth of Canadian institutions (Innis, 1956, p. 386 and p. 392).

The social organization of communities in the Northwest Territories is easily comprehensible, because northern society remains quite simple in comparison to even rural social organization on the Prairies or in Quebec. There are a limited number of communities across all of northern Canada. Most of these are small, and at the beginning stages in terms of local government development; so most continue to be subjects of the central authorities in Yellowknife, Whitehorse (in the case of the Yukon Territory) or Ottawa. Sociologists would say that as a society northern Canada is not as highly differentiated as are other parts of Canadian society, meaning that such things as the division of labour and patterns of specialization are uncomplicated when compared to the patterns of organization which exist in other areas of the country.

All this is changing, of course, as northern Canada experiences economic and social development. In past years, social differentiation in the North came about through the activities of agents of southern organizations, most especially the Hudson's Bay Company, the North West (later the Royal Canadian) Mounted Police and the various church missions. During the last decade government activities have greatly increased across the North. Therefore, it is probably accurate to say that the shaping of a modern society in the North continues to be primarily the task of agents of government or of corporate establishments, such as oil and gas companies. Historically speaking, there are many precedents for this colonial development. However, according to 1971 statistics, 17,339 or 49.8 percent of the population of the Northwest Territories spoke a mother-tongue language other than French or English. So, although development will likely proceed as planned in the conference rooms of corporations and governments, the indigenous minority, with some organization of its own, may retard or somewhat alter the course of development.

That northern Canada has been, and largely continues to be, a colonial outpost of Canadian society — perhaps of American society also — cannot be overemphasized. Social development often follows on the heels of colonial settlement, even though colonial involvement in the North has tended to be a function of those special social interests known as economic interests. Economic and territorial expansion created the first colonial outposts in North America; it can be argued that Canada and the United States would not have achieved relative self-sufficiency without their periods of incubation under the tutelage of countries such as England and France. So colonialism has pros as well as cons! The often-used method now being repeated in the North is clear: a territory is claimed and developed primarily for its resource value, which in turn provides the incentive for developers from territories already developed to risk their surplus capital in new ventures. The challenge, then, is to encourage economic development in ways which protect the interests of all who live in the North, and to see to it that social development creates viable communities which will have reason to live on after the resources which were attractive in the beginning have been depleted, or after those same resources become less attractive because of shifting world economic markets. Not all communities will survive, but development in principle means that in time the colonial ties will be replaced by local initiative and management.

This section, although rooted in government policy, is concerned with the first groping steps toward local initiative and management. The section includes a general overview of local government development in the Northwest Territories, followed by a more intimate look at one small community as it wrestles with the challenge of local government. The broad subject is considered to be a social micro-dynamic for it is tied to individual will and effort. Those responsible for government in the North have been informing the inhabitants that their fate is within their control. The subject of political autonomy for the Northwest Territories in relation to Ottawa and the provinces is not discussed in this section.

There are at least fifty-nine settlements of varying size in the Northwest Territories. Settlement density is therefore very low, particularly when we recall that we are speaking of approximately one-third of Canada's total land area. Great distances separate settlements, especially in the eastern Arctic.

Fifteen of the fifty-nine settlements are small, with a population of less than 100 persons. Another thirty-five settlements are somewhat larger, having populations that usually fall in the range of 250 to 750. This group of settlements is distinct from the first group of fifteen primarily because the development of local government is further advanced; all of these communities have settlement councils which are largely responsible for the conduct of public business. Government in the first group of fifteen settlements is usually through a band council or community association.

There are five communities which have advanced to hamlet status in the Northwest Territories. A hamlet is incorporated and thus has status as a legal entity. Accordingly, a hamlet council has much greater autonomy over the public affairs of the hamlet. Chart 6.1 indicates the extent of local government development in the Northwest Territories in recent years. For example, twenty-three communities have become settlements with elected settlement councils since the beginning of 1970, and twelve of these communities became settlements in 1971 alone. Rae-Edzo became a hamlet in 1971 as did Frobisher Bay. The chart does not indicate that Rae-Edzo became a hamlet only one year after becoming a settlement, a fact which suggests that local government has been developed as quickly in Rae-Edzo as in any other community in the Territories. It should be noted that the swiftness of development may not be a good thing; as in communities elsewhere, many northern communities have experienced, and continue to experience, severe growing pains.

102

CHART 6.1

Development of Local Government in the Northwest Territories

	Existed before 1970	New in 1970	New in 1971
Settlements	Aklavik	Baker Lake	Arctic Bay
	Broughton Island	Belcher Islands	Cambridge Bay
	Fort Franklin	Coral Harbour	Cape Dorset
	Fort Good Hope	Eskimo Point	Chesterfield Inlet
	Fort McPherson	Hall Beach	Clyde River
	Fort Norman	Lac La Martre	Coppermine
	Fort Providence	Norman Wells	Gjoa Haven
	Fort Resolution	Pangnirtung	Grise Fiord
	Igloolik	Pelly Bay	Lake Harbour
	Port Burwell	Rankin Inlet	Pond Inlet
	Resolute Bay	Repulse Bay	Snowdrift
	Whale Cove		Spence Bay
Hamlets	Fort Simpson	Tuktoyaktuk	Frobisher Bay
	Pine Point		Rae-Edzo

Source: ANNUAL REPORT OF THE COMMISSIONER OF THE NORTHWEST
TERRITORIES, 1970, p.86 and 1971, p.101.

There are four additional communities in the Northwest Territories. The largest of these is the capital city of Yellowknife. According to Statistics Canada, Yellowknife's 1971 population was 6,122, or almost 64 percent greater than its 1966 population of 3,741 (although the city's boundaries have expanded in the interim). The three towns in the Territories are Fort Smith, Hay River and Inuvik. Their combined 1971 population was 7,439, or almost 21 percent greater than their combined 1966 population of 6,162. These communities have assumed distinctive tasks within the Territories; their growth is thus an indication of developing social differentiation and specialization in northern Canada. Fort Smith and Inuvik are regional centres of government, while Yellowknife expands as the territorial centre of government. While all of these communities are transportation and communication centres, the role of Hay River is vitally important in this regard for it is a transfer point between its railhead and the barge transportation system of the Mackenzie River. And while Fort Smith is expanding as an education centre, Inuvik is becoming the hub of oil and gas exploration in the western Arctic.

Ever since title to the land now known as the Northwest Territories first passed to Canada in 1870, there have been communities in transition. But the problems of transition have been most marked since the influx of the white man and his methods of administration (see Jenness, 1964). The transition of culture and society has a marked effect on a community.

On the one hand, transition creates victims of change, especially as persons once free become the subject of somebody else's jurisdiction. Thus, the Advisory Commission on the Development of Government in the Northwest Territories noted that the "process of transition and the problems that go with it dominate the lives of the native peoples in all parts of the Northwest Territories. The older generation cling to their traditional pursuits and values. Their children, particularly the young settlement people with some education, have accepted the values, and to some degree the culture, of southern white society. Too often they do not have the opportunity, training or ability to gain acceptance or recognition in the white culture group and remain stranded in a middle position" (1965, p. 67).

On the other hand, transition requires a mixture of determination and vision in people. While the territorial government has strongly encouraged communities to become increasingly autonomous as governing entities, the members of many communities, and often the members of community councils, are reluctant to accept the additional responsibilities which accompany local autonomy.

Such reluctance derives from two facts of life in northern society. The first of these is economic insufficiency. Price fluctuations in the fur market are part of the problem; Wolforth (1971) noted that a large muskrat pelt sold for 70 cents in 1935, $1.10 in 1939, $4.50 in 1945, $3.00 in 1947, returning to 70 cents in 1965 (p. 60). Fluctuating credit is another part of the problem. Stating the obvious, the Advisory Commission noted that the "future development of municipal government, and territorial government as well, depend to a large measure on the degree of economic self-sufficiency which can be developed in the Territories" (1965, p. 90). The people of Aklavik, for instance, seem to be aware of the submarginal nature of the community's economic base. The Fur Garment Co-operative, and seasonal employment in such areas as public works, oil and gas exploration and trapping, do not offer sufficient justification for a prospering Aklavik. Residents have become accustomed to the fact that government expenditures of all sorts are the "principal force sustaining the northern economy" (p. 46). Social assistance is one of those expenditures; during 1970, the proportion of persons in Aklavik receiving social assistance ranged from one-in-five to one-in-three, depending upon the season. Assuming that economic prosperity will not befriend most of the communities in the North for many years to come, if then, and given the widespread attitude of economic pessimism, is it any wonder that local residents fail to want to accept more responsibility for governing themselves. To do so might mean disrupting the present economic marketplace. Their attitude thus becomes one of protective maintenance rather than of change.

The second fact of life in northern society is dependence. For many years, northern communities have learned what it means to be dependent upon governmental support in general, and local area administrators and settlement managers in particular. It is difficult for local residents and their leaders to accept increased responsibilities when, for so long, they have counted on the initiatives of government representatives. Their attitude is often one of complacence rather than of initiative.

Attitudes of maintenance and complacence may change if native Canadians become organized as centres of power, not for the purpose of creating conflict between themselves and governments, but for the purpose of bringing the pressure of organization to bear upon such matters as the resolution of long-standing treaty obligations.

To move on to specifics, the community development movement in the North generally means the orderly progression from settlement status toward that of incorporated hamlets, towns or cities. Not all settlements have such destinies, but those that do find encouragement from Yellowknife. The territorial Department of Local Government is working toward a published goal of "more local autonomy for settlements" in its effort to "involve local residents in the making of decisions affecting the many aspects of living in northern settlements" (ANNUAL REPORT OF THE COMMISSIONER OF THE NORTHWEST TERRITORIES, 1970, p. 85).

Settlement councils generally work to administer an unincorporated settlement. Much of the council's routine pertains to the provision of basic services. Settlement councils are elected by the residents, and although the settlements are unincorporated, they are recognized by the Department of Local Government as being the "representative local body and, as such, it is the policy of the Government of the Northwest Territories to work in consultation with such councils on all matters affecting the community" (p. 85). Settlement councils possess a limited legislative role. To establish a local by-law is possible, but only after a local request is approved by order of the Commissioner of the Territories. In addition, settlement councils possess limited spending authority. Settlements usually receive all of their revenue from territorial and other government grants, including grants for capital projects, and funds for the operation and maintenance of settlement services. In addition to these budget items there is an annual per capita grant, and the settlement council can directly control spending from this grant alone. If a settlement becomes a hamlet, it achieves much greater control over spending, although the source of revenue remains for the most part unchanged. Hamlets have the authority to levy a community service charge or tax, and they control revenue from such sources as licence fees and fines, but most northern communities, except those with municipal status, receive their revenue from central rather than local sources.

Aklavik is a small but famous settlement in the Mackenzie Delta. The Hudson's Bay Company had established a trading post at Pokiak Point in 1912, just across the Peel Channel from what was to become the site of Aklavik. At least one other trader, Northern Traders Limited, also located at Pokiak Point shortly after the Hudson's Bay Company had established itself there. Northern Traders moved across to Aklavik in 1919, while the Hudson's Bay Company moved to its present site in 1924 (see Usher, 1971, p. 89). By 1924 Aklavik as a community had already formed around the Anglican mission which had been founded in 1919, and the police detachment which had arrived in 1922.

Aklavik was by far the "most important single fur trade centre in the entire north, in terms both of the number of traders involved and value of furs traded" (Usher, 1971, p. 83). Indeed, Aklavik has supported twenty-nine fur trading posts since 1912, more than twice the number of its nearest competitor, Fort McPherson, with thirteen posts dating from 1840 (see Usher, 1971, p. 86). "Aklavik of course became the most complex of the settlements . . . both in its external relations and its internal morphology" (Wolforth, 1971, p. 64). Aklavik quickly became a centre for transportation activity, first by steamboat and later by aircraft.

Aklavik's population in 1931 was 411, the largest of any settlement in the lower Mackenzie region. Of that total 180 were Indian, 140 were Eskimo and 91 were white (see Wolforth, 1971, p. 61). In addition to its importance as a trading centre, Aklavik expanded as a government service centre throughout the 1930's.

Wolforth (1971) reviewed the development of the settlement pattern in the Mackenzie Delta. Between 1912 and 1929 the Delta area was a "relatively homogeneous culture region, in which settlements had played an important but not dominant role, [but] then after 1929 their growing dominance was to lead to a transformation of the region's spatial structure into a more nodal configuration" (p. 57). Aklavik was the centre of this configuration, and as specialization increased it became possible for settlements, especially Aklavik, to offer employment in fields other than trapping. "This fact was to lead to the dichotomous society which is found in settlements at present and to the dual allegiance to land and town which characterize the Eskimo and Indian settlement dweller" (p. 58).

While the period 1929 to 1955 saw the continued growth of Aklavik, events of 1953 and 1954 were to restructure the settlement pattern in the entire delta area. A decision was taken by the federal cabinet late in 1953 to establish a new settlement to serve as the centre of administrative activities in the western Arctic. Space and other limitations at the site of Aklavik meant that a new site had to be developed. Inuvik was thus born at a location a score of miles east and slightly north of Aklavik. The development of Inuvik was effected by southerners, even to the extent that concepts of southern planning were adopted from the start. Construction in accordance with the National Building Code and zoning were to be enforced. "The introduction of these concepts was a key element in producing the morphologically segregated settlement that Inuvik was to become" (p. 69). So Inuvik, which at the beginning was planned as a resettled Aklavik, became a settlement established for reasons quite distinct from those which underscored the emergence of other communities in the region. Inuvik was to be a rationally planned and developed centre where wage employment would be more important than the fur economy, and where the life styles of the local people would be shaped by a new form of social organization. "The form of preceding settlements had been largely conditioned by the needs of the people they served. . . . Inuvik, in contrast, came into being largely through decision-making processes which went on outside the North, and from the first it was a planned settlement in which facilities were designed to be similar to those in the South" (p. 67). Inuvik was more than a partial solution to the economic problems of the Mackenzie Delta; it was to stimulate a reshaping of the area's economy. Wolforth noted that the fact that the chosen site for Inuvik was more distant from proven trapping areas "showed either a disregard for or a conscious break with a hunting, trapping and fishing economy" (p. 71).

Aklavik persisted as a community. It is said to have had approximately 550 permanent residents in 1961, although the census of that year showed a population of 711. The settlement's population in 1966 was reported to be 629. More interesting is the fact that, while white residents constituted about one-half of Aklavik's population prior to the move to Inuvik, they constituted approximately 15 percent of the population in 1961. The development of Inuvik changed the composition of Aklavik's population in such a way that the settlement became again what it was in the beginning, a settlement of native Indian and Eskimo people with some whites.

The Advisory Commission on the Development of Government in the Northwest Territories reported in 1966 that Aklavik "can no longer be considered as an important distributing centre." The Advisory Commission also held that "reconstruction of Aklavik is desirable" (page numbers unavailable). What lies ahead for the settlement remains uncertain, especially since competition continues to increase between the communities in the delta area. The evidence suggests that Aklavik's transition from settlement to hamlet will soon occur. In spite of this development, the core of persistent settlers and the location of Aklavik in the resource-rich Mackenzie Delta suggest that the settlement will continue as one of the next-generation communities of northern Canada. The economic future of the area will be more certain when more is known about the economics of discovering and extracting the mineral resources beneath the Delta. Until that time, it is a fair prospect that Aklavik will continue to be a predominantly native settlement, and that trapping will take second place, as it has for some time now, to wage employment and social assistance.

Chart 6.2 records a number of events and comments selected from public documents. The entries are paraphrased or quoted verbatim. They suggest an increasing community curiosity over a period of more than two years concerning the nature and implications of hamlet status. The entries reflect that a firm decision to apply for hamlet status has been made by the settlement, a fact which implies that the council and the larger community are prepared to follow their initial inquiry through to its logical termination point.

Two brief observations seem appropriate concerning this record. The first is the turnover of administrative personnel. What the record fails to show is the equally extensive turnover of members elected to the settlement council. It is generally acknowledged that frequent personnel changes do not serve the interests of organizational stability and direction.

The second observation which remains uncollaborated is the seeming tendency on the part of certain administrators to report in the minutes, and thereby to their superiors, what they deem to be indications of community maturation. Special care is taken to note such things as community participation in the affairs of council or a change in reporting procedures. While the content of this type of notation is more the norm and expectation in the early 1970's, it should be noted that public records of an earlier year often implied a distinctly different meaning, to wit, paternalism. All of which is to say that public records as here used may be helpful for the purpose of discerning superordinate attitudes, in addition to what they may reveal concerning the real growth of community leadership and responsibility.

Aklavik is not a community in harmony with its destiny. The people in the settlement know from past and present experience that Aklavik and many other small communities in the North and elsewhere are in a turbulent state. They are in turmoil not only because their community governments are learning to administer, but also because individual members of communities — especially persons of Eskimo and Indian descent in northern communities — are learning to cope with rapid social change, and are searching for ways to become selectively involved in Canadian society while preserving the heritage of native cultures. Coping means not mere adjustment to imposed new conditions; coping includes negotiation for new life styles amidst changing social conditions. No doubt, many of the negotiations now going on in northern Canada constitute confrontations between various minority and majority groups, and many of these confrontations will absorb the energies of organizers, governments and citizens in the years to come.

CHART 6.2

Local Government Development in Aklavik

January 1970	Area administrator reported that the settlement's advisory council decided not to request the appointment of a secretary-manager.
June 1970	Area administrator reported that the settlement's advisory council decided to change its name to the Aklavik settlement council. The new name was felt to more adequately describe the council's function and to reflect its increasing acceptance of responsibility.
September 1970	Area administrator reported that the settlement council considered a number of documents, including the new basic constitution for settlement councils, but that the council showed little spontaneous interest in such matters. The council continued to be concerned with daily operations in the settlement.
December 1970	Area administrator reported that the settlement council discussed the matter of hamlet status, and requested additional information.
January 1971	Area administrator reported that the settlement council again discussed the matter of hamlet status and, in addition, discussed the question of legal incorporation. The council passed a motion to request representatives of the territorial government to attend its next meeting for the purpose of explaining and answering questions concerning hamlet status. A large attendance by members of the general public indicated the settlement's growing interest in settlement affairs.
February 1971	Area administrator reported that the settlement council and members of the general public discussed hamlet status with representatives of the territorial government. Discussion focused around the funding of hamlets.
March 1971	Area administrator left Aklavik for a new posting. He was replaced by an acting settlement manager.
May 1971	Acting settlement manager reported the implementation of a change in the source and content of the Aklavik monthly report. The change will allow each department in the settlement the opportunity to express monthly statistics and achievements in an effort to develop an awareness of responsibility and to encourage participation in government goals and community development.

July 1971	Acting settlement manager left Aklavik for a new posting. He was replaced by a new acting settlement manager, a person with graduate training in community development.
August 1971	Acting settlement manager reported that the settlement council began to meet weekly rather than monthly. The acting settlement manager increasingly subordinated himself to the actions and wishes of the settlement council. The settlement council decided to request the appointment of a secretary-manager.
October 1971	Settlement council interviewed five applicants and selected a person to fill the position of secretary-manager.
January 1972	Increasing public interest in settlement affairs requires a larger council hall to accommodate interested participants and observers.
February 1972	Settlement council discussed hamlet status. A public plebiscite was discussed. Council considered visiting other hamlets and the need to scrutinize the hamlet ordinance. At a later meeting in February, council discussed hamlet status with representatives of the territorial government.
June 1972	Settlement council made public a decision, reached with representatives of the territorial government, to phase out the position of settlement manager and to strengthen the position of secretary-manager.
August 1972	Acting settlement manager left Aklavik for a new posting. He was not replaced. The secretary-manager continued to serve the settlement and its council.
October 1972	Settlement council in reacting to a public meeting held earlier expressed its view that the time was right to make the first step towards hamlet status. Council unanimously supported a motion that a petition be drawn up and passed around the settlement, requesting the commissioner to establish Aklavik as a hamlet.
November 1972	Territorial commissioner received a petition asking that Aklavik be designated a hamlet, during a personal visit to the settlement.
January 1973	Territorial commissioner informed the settlement that hamlet status would be awarded January 1, 1974.

Source: Published minutes of the Aklavik Settlement Council, various dates.

Microdynamic: New Life on Fogo Island

Prophecy that failed. By 1955 fishery will have been revolutionized. . . . Fishing will pay our people, and the number of fishermen will have doubled. New and scientific methods will have been completely adopted, with large bodies of capital, much of it from outside sources, and will put new life into this great industry (Smallwood, 1931, p. 251).

Fogo Islanders are a proud people, who have tended to maintain their own traditions and life style. Very little out of the ordinary would have happened on the Island if most of the rest of North America had not entered the twentieth century.

But local situations are often defined by relative measures, and the lack of economic development on the Island became apparent as development was seen to occur elsewhere. Social dynamics led to a developing awareness of the extent and causes of the floundering local situation. Awareness led to remedies, and certain successes achieved by the Islanders now provide hope for long-term economic growth and stability. The sentiment of many of the local people is to preserve Fogo Island as a community.

Fogo Island consists of over 100 square miles of nonfertile land off the northeast coast of Newfoundland. The Island is some 50 miles north and slightly east of Gander. Habitation has continued for more than 250 years, a fact which suggests that there exists a local cultural heritage as rich as any to be found in Canada.

The appropriateness of including a section on Fogo Island is increased by such things as the existence of a limited literature concerning the recent history of social development on the Island, the fact that certain note-worthy advances have been made by the residents, and also because many Canadians have become familiar with the problems of development on Fogo Island through the Challenge for Change program sponsored by the federal government and the National Film Board. This section offers a lesson — some would call it a testimony of faith — on the consequences for a community when its residents take it upon themselves to account for the community's future.

Fogo Island must be viewed, first of all, in the context of community organization in Newfoundland. In years past many hundreds of settlements dotted the coastline of Newfoundland, with relatively few communities found in the interior of the province. When Newfoundland joined confederation in 1949, its rural parts were jolted into a new kind of social existence as the entire province began the extensive process of attempted industrialization. With it came significant migration

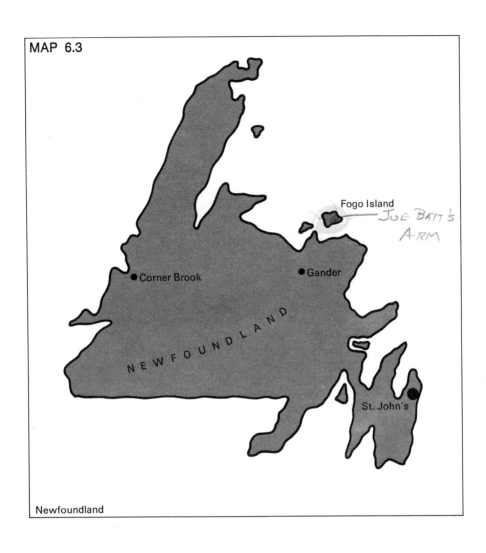

MAP 6.3

Fogo Island

JOE BATT'S ARM

Corner Brook

Gander

NEWFOUNDLAND

St. John's

Newfoundland

and urbanization, and with those trends came the decline of many of Newfoundland's outport communities. The other crucial factor which interacted with the modernizing processes of industrialization, urbanization and migration was the decline of the inshore fishery and thus the decline of the economic base of numerous communities. Newfoundland has experienced more than its share of social change since becoming part of Canada.

Extensive social change also means cultural change, as people come to define differently those things which are meaningful in their daily existence. But rapid social change can also be devastating to communities, especially if the change includes many varied but new influences. These influences in many Newfoundland communities included the construction of roads, the availability of new and diverse consumer goods, the introduction of television and the spread of other media, and the increased mobility of the population.

Literally hundreds of communities throughout Newfoundland have been faced with the prospect of resettlement since the 1950's. Wadel (1969) noted that some 200 settlements (12,000 persons in 2,500 families) had been resettled up to 1969, and that the prospect was for perhaps 400 more settlements to be phased out through to the end of the 1970's (p. 3). The resettlement movement in Newfoundland has favoured centralization for several reasons, including the government's expressed desire to provide better services, and its wish to see Newfoundland's rural areas rise above their subsistence-level economies. Massive resettlement was grasped as the means whereby population concentration might replace population dispersion, and whereby a modern economic system might replace the economic uncertainties of a weather-torn colony.

To review resettlement in Newfoundland is not the purpose of this section. However, a further comment on the resettlement movement is appropriate, given that Fogo Island as an area rejected the option to resettle elsewhere. Laying aside the Island's reasons for rejecting the option for the moment, Wadel argued that up to 1969 the "only apparent plan for rural development in Newfoundland seems to be resettlement" (p. 5). He discussed the basic contradiction between resettlement and the option of "redevelopment or revitalization of the outport economy, carried out simultaneously with a modified and carefully planned form of resettlement" (p. 5). Fogo Island is a case study in successful revitalization of an outport region of communities.

Community development was not the option in the forefront throughout the 1950's and most of the 1960's. The reasons for this oversight, especially on the part of governments, remain couched in speculation. Perhaps a chief reason was the vain belief that the level of economic growth would be sufficient to absorb the labour forces of the larger centres and, in addition, the labour of those leaving the traditional fishery and migrating to growth centres in search of employment. Newfoundland's economic growth has not been rapid enough to absorb its available labour, and so in many respects resettlement has been something less than an ideal experience for thousands of people.

There has been a variation of resettlement on Fogo Island and by Fogo Islanders. DeWitt (1969) reported that at least four small communities had been resettled; their residents moved a short distance to other communities on the Island. More significant, however, was migration to mainland Newfoundland or to other provinces of Canada. Data on migration are hard to come by, but that migration is significant follows from such facts as Newfoundland's rate of natural increase for 1968 being 19.1 (excess of births over deaths per 1,000 population), and Fogo Island's population growth being stable if not on the decline (the largest settlement on Fogo Island is the town of Fogo where the population was 1,152 in 1961 and 1,155 in 1971).

The question was put to the residents of Fogo Island in 1967 by Newfoundland's premier of the day. "Fogo Island has no future unless big changes are made. . . . You have three roads to choose from: (1) drift, where the consequence is death for Fogo Island, (2) resettlement, where the government would have to back you, or (3) development, if you are honest and God-fearing and ready to work. You will have to decide which road to travel" (Smallwood, quoted in DeWitt, 1969, p. 13).

At the time of this challenge in 1967, the residents of the Island were commencing their own debate on the Island's future. It was obvious that it was time for the debate, since economic and other sociological problems were becoming overwhelming. For example, DeWitt (1969) noted the importance of welfare payments to the Island's economy, and he quoted the local welfare officer concerning the last quarter of 1966. "The fall fishery was a failure as was the fishery right through the summer. The employment situation for the next quarter is nil as there is no work whatever during the winter months; . . . the economic potential of the district is at an all time low. There have been no new ventures started . . . and the hopes and outlook for the future is very poor indeed" (p. 16). Had it been possible to have been more pessimistic, the officer would likely have been!

It is of more than passing interest that Fogo Island, although a small island, supported a large number of relatively isolated communities. The situation slowly changed through the late 1950's and early 1960's as road construction advanced. But Newfoundland's communities, with roads or without, have a way of maintaining their independent identities. There is, for example, the story of a man who had lived in Brigus for almost thirty years, since the year when he *migrated* from Cupids. A visitor in his home would not be any the wiser concerning his host's

TABLE 6.4

Percent Population by Community and Religious Denomination, Fogo Island, 1961

	Anglican	Catholic	United	Pentecostal	Other	Total
Shoal Bay	100.0	—	—	—	—	100.0
Deep Bay	97.6	—	.8	—	1.7	100.1
Barr'd Islands	63.1	5.6	31.0	—	.3	100.0
Fogo	50.0	31.1	18.2	.1	.6	100.0
Joe Batt's Arm	49.6	35.8	13.2	.6	.8	100.0
Island Harbour	36.2	61.5	2.1	—	.3	100.1
Seldom	29.5	—	35.7	31.8	2.9	99.9
Stag Harbour	9.9	—	90.1	—	—	100.0
Tilting	.2	99.8	—	—	—	100.0
Little Seldom	—	—	68.6	31.4	—	100.0
Number of Residents	1,814	1,397	1,032	194	33	4,470

Source: Computed from DeWitt, 1969, p.10.

CHART 6.5

Selected Events in the Past of Fogo Island

1738	Population of Fogo was 215.
1874	Population of Fogo was 953.
1908	First telegraph message from Tilting.
1935	Population of Fogo Island was 3,970.
1961	Population of Fogo Island was 4,470.
	Population of Fogo was 1,152.
	Population of Joe Batt's Arm was 1,058.
	Other settlements and their populations were Seldom (484), Tilting (432), Barr'd Islands (358), Stag Harbour (353), Island Harbour (340), Deep Bay (121), Little Seldom (105), and Shoal Bay (67).
	Electricity established at Fogo.
1963	Organization formed earlier to petition for better roads was expanded and renamed the Fogo Island Improvement Committee.
1965	Fogo Island motel opened.
1966	Ferry service established connecting Fogo Island to the mainland.
	Government issued overtures for resettlement.
1967	Smallwood challenged residents to select between resettlement and development.
	Improvement Committee together with Memorial University's Extension Service sponsored a workshop on fisheries and co-operatives.
	Shipbuilding Producers Co-operative established with 125 members and $625 in share capital.
	In November 230 households (25.5 percent of the Island's households) received short-term social assistance.
1968	After 85 years of service Earle & Sons closed its merchant business.
	Fogo Island supported 580 full-time fishermen.
	Shipbuilding Producers Co-operative membership expanded to 575.
	Co-operative launched its first longliners.
	In November 165 households (18.3 percent of the Island's households) received short-term social assistance.
1969	Shipbuilding Producers Co-operative membership expanded to 758 with $40,000 in share capital.
	Residents raised $5,000 toward the cost of a new central school.
	In November 132 households (14.6 percent of the Island's households) received short-term social assistance.
1970	Protestant and Roman Catholic residents held a workshop on integrated education.
1971	Central school opened.

Source: FOGO ISLAND CALENDAR, 1971 (prepared by Ivan F. Jesperson), and other sources referenced in this section.

migratory trek, unless he asked the whereabouts of Cupids. Thirty years ago it was a hard hike those several miles over the hill!

Community isolation in Newfoundland has been traditionally maintained by religious segregation. Table 6.4 tells the story of the distribution of Fogo Island's population by religion. DeWitt (1969) noted that "religion clearly continues to divide the population," even to the extent that fishing crews follow the principle of religious segregation (p. 11). Therefore, if local development were to occur, the residents had to face the fact that their Island was divided by such problems as communication and transportation, and the role of the church.

Chart 6.5 sketches selected aspects of social development on Fogo Island. Early settlement led to significant population growth across the Island. Local expansion and contact with mainland Newfoundland were increasingly important trends throughout the 1950's and 1960's, with such basic services as roads and electric power being provided in the early 1960's. A network of roads joining most of the Island's communities is generally acknowledged as a key factor in bringing modernity to Fogo Island. As time passed, the road network caused a redistribution of social activities on the Island. The construction of a centrally-located motel was the initial impetus, but now there also exists a central school which serves, together with the motel, as a social centre for the Island. In a manner of speaking, where once there were a number of communities with independent and often rival identities, that structure now has been replaced with something approaching an island-wide identity, the result of different communities and people of different religious backgrounds agreeing on co-operative social action. The central school is the prime example of interreligious co-operation.

The Fogo Island Improvement Committee was the product of desperation. It began as an organization to lobby for improved roads, but very quickly the people of the Island realized that roads were secondary to the Island's severe economic difficulties. Pandora's box was now open and the story of social development began. The people of Fogo Island were helped by many outsiders, including members of the Extension Service at Memorial University. The Service's involvement began with the posting of a field representative on the Island. The concern during the mid-1960's was primarily economic, with the problems associated with fisheries development foremost on the agenda. In 1966, however, the people's hope for survival on the Island was shattered.

> The winds of resettlement hit at almost gale force, and in its wake could be seen vacant homes, abandoned fishing boats and gear, and it suddenly became quite obvious that, despite our hard work and planning for the future of our island home, we were slated by some government officials for resettlement. The hand-writing was on the wall. By 1967 the second last fish merchant was preparing to lock its doors. Fishermen were more frustrated than ever, and the morale of the people, in general, was at an all-time low (Kinden, 1971, p. 3).

It has been suggested that such factors as a poor economic outlook, the relative lack of municipal organization and the generally supportive attitudes of the various religious denominations interacted during the period 1966 to 1968 to assist the resettlement movement (see DeWitt, 1969, pp. 31-44). While less than 10 percent of the Island's householders actually applied to resettle during the period, the threat of resettlement was sufficient to dim the hopes of many people. In addition to the factors noted, DeWitt judged that the provincial government's position and actions furthered the sense of anomie or normlessness felt by the Islanders. Fogo Island was not designated a growth centre; nor did the government label the Island as an area to be resettled. To make things worse, the government had "acted in a manner whereby the people of the Island . . . [saw their] choice as either (i) no resettlement and no development, or (ii) resettlement and some chance for development in the new location" (p. 45). During the period 1966 to 1968, religious fractionalism had even defeated the first proposal to construct a central, amalgamated school on the Island. Everything considered, Fogo Island neared rock bottom at about the same time that Canada celebrated its centennial with the glory of Expo.

Then came the Premier's challenge delivered in September of 1967. Earlier that year the Improvement Committee and Memorial University held a workshop on the fisheries and co-operatives. The Shipbuilding Producers Co-operative was established and became the artillery in the battle for economic survival. The Island needed longliners so that fishermen could modernize their industry, and it needed more efficient and varied fish processing and marketing techniques so that economic return would justify investment.

The critical situation on Fogo Island in 1967 was recorded on film by the National Film Board. INTRODUCTION TO FOGO ISLAND tells the general story of the Island's plight. The beginning of the Co-operative was the subject of JIM DECKER BUILDS A LONGLINER. BILLY CRANE MOVES AWAY provided a glimpse at the reasons behind relocation. The very sensitive CHILDREN OF FOGO ISLAND expressed the local cultural heritage to the outside world. Many more films and videotapes were made in, and since, 1967 dealing with such vital subjects as the development of co-operatives, citizen participation, welfare, the role of the Improvement Committee, education and the role of government in local development. The production of all film and videotape materials was partly in the hands of the local people, since the materials were screened for local audiences who in turn could edit them before completion and more general distribution. Film and videotape thus became vehicles of social change (see Gwyn, 1972).

The story of Fogo Island since 1967 is mostly one of toil and effort. Numerous workshops have been held, many longliners have been launched, welfare payments have declined, and there are indications that the Island's economy is successfully adjusting to more modern methods of catching, processing and marketing its fish products. Data gathered by the Improvement Committee and the Shipbuilding Producers Co-operative indicate that fewer men fished in 1970, and that still fewer fishermen operating from longliners were able to catch more than six out of over ten million pounds of fish caught. Fogo Island is now in need of a new and larger fish processing facility, one which will process varied fish products for different markets. Such a multiple-purpose processing plant is the next objective of the Co-operative. Table 6.6 portrays selected aspects of the situation on Fogo Island as of October 15, 1970.

How has the press reacted to new life on Fogo Island? The St. John's EVENING TELEGRAM editorialized that "Fogo seems to keep itself well out in front when it comes to new ideas. For an island which was all set to be deserted under the centralization program it is very much alive and kicking. It is, in fact, living proof that many of the communities wiped out by officially sponsored resettlement could possibly have survived to become prosperous self-sufficient places. . . . [Fogo

TABLE 6.6

Fogo Island Fishery Survey, 1970

	Longliners	Small Boats	Total
Boats fishing in mid-waters	22		22
Boats fishing in mid-waters full season	17		17
Part-time fishermen working on boats	20	137	157
Full-time fishermen working on boats	75	299	374
Fishermen interested in building boats	25		25
Total fish caught between May 1 and October 10, 1970 (in pounds)	6,167,950	4,123,147	10,291,097

Source: Snowden, 1971, p.5.

Island's local development committee represents] the kind of thinking which will help keep Fogo Island alive when other communities will die for want of initiative and the energy to do something for themselves" (March 12, 1971).

The St. John's DAILY NEWS suggested that Fogo Island "lends itself to becoming a pilot plant for experimentation in a comprehensive plan of rural development. There may be limitations to its resources but none to the enthusiasm of its people and their response to community leadership. Because of this Fogo may become an exciting place in which to live and an extremely interesting one for the rest of the province to watch" (March 22, 1971). The NEWS called Fogo an "island bent on survival."

Fogo Island has been recognized outside of Newfoundland for techniques of communication and intervention which were developed there. Film and videotape were used as a means for providing a mirror to the community. The technical process of making films was transformed by a new sensitivity for the uses of the visual media. Traditional film-makers are trained "to think in terms of the product — not of the process or of the effect they are having on subject and audience" (Henaut, 1971-72, p. 3). Film was first used on Fogo Island to facilitate communication. But more basically, film was able to help in the process of community development. Film was perhaps the catalyst the people needed; it displayed objectively themselves and their concerns, it allowed them to focus upon issues, and through communication it helped to create a sense of community on Fogo Island. The first redevelopment successes were enough to reinforce the community's initial efforts, and to give the people more confidence to expand their efforts.

Obviously, film was and is not the whole story. But film has been acknowledged by many as a most important impetus for community development. "One thing we cannot say is: the films did it. Some inspired leadership and hard work on the part of many islanders are factors that still stand out. Certainly film does not loom large in the people's memories as they look back proudly over the accomplishments. I think we *can* say that film broke through the bad habits of non-communication and misunderstanding and liberated the people from apathy. With the fresh film view of themselves, they evaluated their own capacities and energies and put them to work. Essential to the success of film as a catalyst is the manner in which the films were put together. They were not made to sensationalize. They were not made to build confrontations. They were made to build bridges" (Henaut, 1971-72, p. 5).

A lengthy summary seems unnecessary. The survival of Fogo Island and, indeed, its development as an island community, is emerging from the combined efforts of many persons and organizations. The Island's survival chances have been increased, almost in spite of government policy. All has not been won as yet, although the local people have shown themselves ready for the task of modernizing their traditional economy and way of life, rather than abandoning them for the city or for some other adaptation to modern living. We are left with the question of whether Fogo Island's example can serve as a model for the maintenance of more traditional life styles, especially in those areas which rely upon the products of nature for economic functioning.

Delta and Island Communities

> Mesmerized as we are by the idea of change, we must guard against the notion that continuity is a negligible — if not reprehensible — factor in human history. It is a vitally important ingredient in the life of individuals, organizations and societies. Particularly important to a society's continuity are its long-term purposes and values. These purposes and values also evolve in the long run; but by being relatively durable, they enable a society to absorb change without losing its distinctive character and style. They do much to determine the direction of change. They insure that a society will not be buffeted in all directions by every wind that blows (Gardner, 1965, pp. 6-7).

On the occasion of a review of material published by the Institute of Social and Economic Research in Newfoundland, Lotz (1971) was highly critical of selected portions of the Institute's effort. He was especially concerned with the time intervals between fieldwork and publication, and thus with the question of more recent developments. But Lotz also was concerned with the tendency for the Institute's reports to neglect the developmental experiences of other areas of Canada and the world. The effort " 'floats' in insolation, unrelated to the mainstream of social science thought and empirical reality" (p. 55).

His criticisms do not end there. Lotz discredited scholarly attempts to "rationalize the existence of the outports on economic grounds. This is the 'positive thinking' approach to economic development. The 'inertia and political' approach more usually works. People dig their heels in when they see the chaos caused by government 'planning' and start using the political system to get benefits. If the outporters start to organize and demand benefits from the provincial government, this will be a more meaningful strategy for getting opportunities than waiting for a beneficent government to 'help' them by building fish plants or raising the price of fish" (pp. 52-53).

The preceding sections of this chapter dealt with certain of the concerns raised by Lotz. Local situations on Fogo Island and in the Mackenzie Delta have been updated so that more recent developments show the " 'inertia and political' approach" increasingly to be characteristic of local initiatives. It is important to look long enough so that such a tendency is revealed. One of the difficulties inherent in some of the reports of Newfoundland's Institute of Social and Economic Research is that they were conceived, researched and written not only in a short period of time, but also within the broad context of community resettlement. While rural social change in Newfoundland and in other parts of Canada has been associated with community resettlement, the reasons for such change are often made obscure in the debate between the microdynamics of local initiatives and the macrodynamics of such matters as the settlement and migratory patterns of populations.

One other note concerning the preceding sections is their interrelationship. Lotz complained that the studies on Newfoundland outport settlements failed to mention and to gain from, for example, the resettlement experiences in the Mackenzie Delta. Lotz specifically referred to the "famous and extensively documented case of trying to move people from Aklavik to Inuvik, which has resulted in the creation of a mainly native, land-based settlement and a mainly white-dominated government and industrial-based community" (p. 55). This particular northern experience showed that resettlement cannot occur by edict; indeed, resettlement will not occur at all given reasons for continuing attachment to a particular community or area. It is apparently the case that some of Newfoundland's outports which were closed down during the 1950's and 1960's are now being resettled, in part by those who had left earlier.

But the problem of analysis is not an easy one, for social change involves much more than physical relocation. There are the patterns of interaction which reveal a great deal concerning the adjustment of migrants to their new locations. There are new structures of stratification which inevitably form, or structures of stratification which must be breached. Presumably, as a result, there are many academic observations which might be made. It is of more than passing interest, for example, that the Delta experience has shown many native northerners moving from land-based economies to more urban-related fields of employment such as operating heavy equipment and doing construction work. Many employable persons in Newfoundland, in comparison, were unemployed at the time of relocation; considerable evidence suggests that a high proportion of these persons continued to be unemployed after relocation. So it is seen that although economic problems are given to justify resettlement, those same problems are often not diminished by virture of resettlement. If anything, such problems are exacerbated.

This comment and the preceding sections are informative on two counts. The first is that local organization is perhaps the most important weapon when communities are fighting their battles for survival. The second is the need to study community development longitudinally. Short glimpses are inadequate. Only when researchers make their observations over longer periods of time will they be able to effectively supplement the organizational efforts of communities; the longer-term research evaluations are the ones sought by governments when they review the adequacy of their social policies and programs.

Microdynamics of Social Participation

> An individual cannot achieve renewal if he does not believe in the possibility of it. Nor can a society. At all times in history there have been individuals and societies whose attitudes toward the future have been such as to thwart, or at least greatly impede, the processes of renewal (Gardner, 1965, p. 105).

What do people do with their time? By what criteria do they relate to other persons, and in which activities? How do people distribute themselves in social space when they socially participate?

While these questions are of foremost importance in most social studies, they hinge upon a concept — social participation — which is not frequently used in sociology and its related fields. The seventeen-volume INTERNATIONAL ENCYCLOPEDIA OF THE SOCIAL SCIENCES does not list the concept in its index. Standard sociological textbooks and dictionaries tend not to use the concept in any systematic fashion. When it is invoked, it is usually with respect to either political participation (through such behaviour as voting) or participation in voluntary associations (such as community leagues and various service organizations).

There are reasons to begin treating social participation as a systematic sociological concept. It is a concept which focuses upon the life spaces of individual social actors. Social participation as a concept should relate only to voluntary participation. By an odd twist of circumstances, an involuntarily institutionalized prisoner can and does voluntarily participate in various prison activities, even though he may resist certain participations (as all people can) and be coerced into other participations (as all people are).

The main reasons, however, for using social participation as a systematic sociological concept derive from the questions noted at the start. People participate in diverse social activities across time. Because time is always a contingency and always limits choice, various social participations can be ranked on a scale from "possible" to "out of the question," making possible individual decisions concerning how one's time is to be spent. People participate in diverse activities because of felt priorities and needs. These are the criteria behind social participation, the criteria which tell the individual whether or not it is of value to participate. Finally, people participate in different activities because they wish to be associated in both time and space with other persons who share like-minded social interests.

A different kind of reason for developing the concept of social participation concerns its behavioural connotation. The concept must be defined in such a way that it applies to what people actually do and not to what people say they will do or would like to do. Deutscher (1966) reminded us of the difference between word and deed.

The present discussion of social participation comes toward the end of a chapter on social microdynamics. The focus of this chapter has been the contributions of comprehensible actions — of ogranizations as well as individuals — for establishing and changing patterns of social organization. Comprehensible actions are usually small-scale actions, although certainly they may be guided by, or work in spite of, larger-scale policies and programs. To conclude this chapter with a discussion of social participation is meant to suggest that there is a sociological concept which can be formulated to assist observers and analysts alike to more clearly comprehend those social structures and processes which pressure social actions and reactions. In such observation and analysis, it is equally as important to consider how social contingencies and constraints affect patterns of social participation as it is to consider forces in the opposite direction, namely, how patterns of social participation affect the shape and progress of society.

A common-sense proposition to guide the ensuing discussion might be that social participation will generally occur if it is desired and if it is possible in terms of spatial and temporal opportunities. Temporal opportunity is an obvious contingency: whether the person has the time to participate. Spatial opportunity is perhaps not quite so obvious, for it refers to whether or not the person has access to the group or organization in which participation is desired. Access can be blocked or open, or it can be conditionally open (conditional upon the meeting of specified or unspecified requirements). Thus, the whole question of social participation is linked to aspects of spatial organization. It is in this respect that Davies and Herman (1971) studied Canadian society. They concerned themselves with the

distinction between public and private space, which is fundamentally a political distinction. . . . [S]ocial space is bounded by normative constraints, laws, modes of interaction, as well as by physical space and time factors. Central to the whole discussion are the dual concepts of *access* and *control.* Access involves the principle of inclusion-exclusion and that implies boundaries. Control involves the principle of regulation and that implies limitations on freedom. The questions to be asked, then, are: 'Who has access and under what conditions?' and, 'Where is the locus of control?' (p. 50).

The concept of social participation is given life, so to speak, when defined within these terms. The discussion to this point should suggest how *not* to proceed from here. A relatively easy way out would be to list and singly discuss the various dimensions of social participation, for example, the dynamics surrounding individual participation in the occupational sphere, in institutional spheres such as continuing education, religious involvement or leisure activity, or in community activities such as the support of charitable organizations or helping to operate co-operative recreational leagues. Such tales no doubt would be interesting and informative. Alas, perhaps we should move in other directions in the interest of relevance!

Very briefly, Davies and Herman (1971) edited a book of readings which is challenging in its overall scope. After they defined the broad nature of social space, the volume's content was organized according to subheadings suggestive of content: restrictions on public space; the uses of private space; cultural aspects of relationships; private control of public space; private experience and attempts at redefining public relationships; and crises of public relationships. The editors expressed their underlying logic from the beginning. Even public space is often not available to people; they may meet universalistic criteria for participation, but in fact they are excluded from participation on the grounds of "informal, privately defined standards for admission, or because once in they do not conform to the 'private' rules" (p. 94). As it turns out, most social space is private space, and people develop their identities, in large part, through their participations in private space. Davies and Herman noted some of the factors which influence how private, in fact, private space is. A private school, for example, distances itself from the community both physically and socially, thus maximizing its ability to control the activities which go on inside its space (see Maxwell and Maxwell, in Davies and Herman, 1971, pp. 157-164). More generally, the maintenance of private space largely depends upon how closely the location is related to centres of social power (see p. 150).

It should go without saying that relationships in social space are partly the products of a society's cultural heritage. Davies and Herman defined culture in terms of what culture does for people; "it is the way that a group of people make sense of their life-situation in terms of the language, technology, values and codes of behaviour that they inherit and recreate" (p. 166). Furthermore, culture is "how we account for the discrepancies in our daily lives, in the apparent inconsistencies between appearance and experience" (p. 166). In this regard, a paper was reprinted which discounted Canada's "sentimental nationalism" as a revolutionary force because it has failed to "isolate and crystallize the economic contradictions of capitalism" (Drache, in Davies and Herman, 1971, p. 173). Not everyone will agree that Canadian culture will force logical consistency upon Canadians to the extent, as Drache argued, that anti-imperialism is the "only alternative to the policies of the Canadian bourgeoisie," although such a rejection does not necessarily reject Drache's further conclusion that "[a]nti-imperialism, anti-capitalism and Canadian independence are an inseparable unity" (p. 173). Many feel that it is more likely that Canadian culture — or certain powerful Canadian subcultures — will lead Canadians — or Canada as a political state — to accept a little imperialism and a lot of capitalism at the expense of Canadian independence.

Davies and Herman included a section on public space which, in some significant measure, has been transformed into private space. In other words, both access and control have been tightened up. One example is Kelner's study of ethnic access — or lack of access — into the power structure of Toronto (in Davies and Herman, 1971, pp. 186-190). Perlin showed how participation in the public sphere of Newfoundland politics was largely circumscribed throughout the 1950's and for most of the 1960's; it was not until the summer of 1969, some twenty years after confederation, that a local Liberal party organization was created in every constituency (see Perlin, in Davies and Herman, 1971, p. 195).

The intense relationship between social participation and individual conviction was demonstrated by including an extract from WHITE NIGGERS OF AMERICA. As a passionate and perceptive revolutionary, Vallières judged that his "dreams are 'measureless,' and yet I am an ordinary man, I think. I cannot 'live my life' without working to make the revolution. . . . It is not a question of playing at being heroes — besides, who can do that, in the era of the atomic bomb and the agonizing war in Vietnam? — but of getting *together* to build a new world in which ordinary men, like you and me, will no longer be the niggers of the millionaires, the warmongers, and the preachers of passivity, but will be free at last to subject the world to their 'whims': love, scientific curiosity, creation . . . in solidarity and equality, in modesty and pride" (Vallieres, in Davies and Herman, 1971, p. 229). The passion of the argument, nevertheless, is swept aside by those who then ask: who is to be the final arbitrator of the social good, and why is it to be you and not me?

The final section of the volume emphasized the crisis-producing implications of the organization of social space. A prime example is Ossenberg's analysis of French-Canadian society as exhibiting a "double pluralism," a state of affairs in Quebec which finds different socio-economic groups working toward different ends, all in addition to differences created by the two official language groups. Ossenberg speculated that, if lower-class and middle-class French Canadians would join together out of concern for economic deprivation, then "economic deprivation among French Canadians of all social classes could bring about a merger which would virtually guarantee a separatist government in Quebec within the next decade. On the other hand, the absence of such a sense of economic deprivation among the French Canadians generally would tend to perpetuate the double pluralism of Quebec which in many ways has been the most important factor in the preservation of Canadian confederation" (Ossenberg, in Davies and Herman, 1971, p. 250; see Ossenberg, 1971).

Because we are immersed in space we sometimes or often fail to realize the importance of space as a social dimension. Our participations occur in space and thus our social behaviours are in part patterned by spatial factors like access, and at the same time are reflected by our movements in space. Social organization is shaped by individual actors and by small groups of actors according to whether persons act within spatially isolated groups, between spatially contiguous groups, or across groups which are separated by a gulf of social distance. It is hard to be more specific than this for the relationships between social participation and spatial organization remain to be studied in detail.

References

Advisory Commission on the Development of Government in the Northwest Territories, THE NORTHWEST TERRITORIES TODAY, Ottawa: Queen's Printer, 1965.

Advisory Commission on the Development of Government in the Northwest Territories, SETTLEMENTS OF THE NORTHWEST TERRITORIES, Ottawa: Queen's Printer, 1966.

Davies, D. I. and Kathleen Herman, eds., SOCIAL SPACE: CANADIAN PERSPECTIVES, Toronto: New Press, 1971.

Deutscher, Irwin, "Words and Deeds: Social Science and Social Policy," SOCIAL PROBLEMS, 13 (Winter, 1966) 235-254.

DeWitt, Robert L., PUBLIC POLICY AND COMMUNITY PROTEST: THE FOGO CASE, St. John's: Institute of Social and Economic Research, 1969.

Drache, Daniel, "The Canadian Bourgeoisie and Its National Consciousness," in D. I. Davies and Kathleen Herman, eds., SOCIAL SPACE: CANADIAN PERSPECTIVES, Toronto: New Press, 1971, pp. 167-174.

Gardner, John W., SELF-RENEWAL: THE INDIVIDUAL AND THE INNOVATIVE SOCIETY, New York: Harper Colophon Books, 1965.

Gwyn, Sandra, CINEMA AS CATALYST, St. John's: Memorial University of Newfoundland, 1972.

Hénaut, Dorothy Todd, "Powerful Catalyst," CHALLENGE FOR CHANGE NEWSLETTER, No. 7 (Winter, 1971-72) 3-7.

Innis, Harold A., THE FUR TRADE IN CANADA: AN INTRODUCTION TO CANADIAN ECONOMIC HISTORY, Revised Edition, Toronto: University of Toronto Press, 1956.

Jenness, Diamond, ESKIMO ADMINISTRATION: II. CANADA, Montreal: Arctic Institute of North America, 1964.

Kelner, Merrijoy, "Ethnic Penetration into Toronto's Elite Structure," in D. I. Davies and Kathleen Herman, eds., SOCIAL SPACE: CANADIAN PERSPECTIVES, Toronto: New Press, 1971, pp. 186-190.

Kinden, Stan, "Progress Report from Fogo," a speech made in southern Newfoundland, 1971, mimeographed.

Lotz, Jim, "Resettlement and Social Change in Newfoundland," THE CANADIAN REVIEW OF SOCIOLOGY AND ANTHROPOLOGY, 8 (February, 1971) 48-59.

Maxwell, Mary Percival and James D. Maxwell, "Boarding School: Social Control, Space and Identity," in D. I. Davies and Kathleen Herman, eds., SOCIAL SPACE: CANADIAN PERSPECTIVES, Toronto: New Press, 1971, pp. 157-164.

Ossenberg, Richard J., "Social Pluralism in Quebec: Continuity, Change and Conflict," in D. I. Davies and Kathleen Herman, eds., SOCIAL SPACE: CANADIAN PERSPECTIVES, Toronto: New Press, 1971, pp. 247-250.

Ossenberg, Richard J., "Social Pluralism in Quebec: Continuity, Change and Conflict," in Richard J. Ossenberg, ed., CANADIAN SOCIETY: PLURALISM, CHANGE, AND CONFLICT, Scarborough, Ont.: Prentice-Hall of Canada Ltd., 1971, pp. 103-123.

Perlin, George, "Patronage and Paternalism: Politics in Newfoundland," in D. I. Davies and Kathleen Herman, eds., SOCIAL SPACE: CANADIAN PERSPECTIVES, Toronto: New Press, 1971, pp. 190-196.

Smallwood, J. R., THE NEW NEWFOUNDLAND: AN ACCOUNT OF THE REVOLUTIONARY DEVELOPMENTS WHICH ARE TRANSFORMING BRITAIN'S OLDEST COLONY FROM 'THE CINDERELLA OF THE EMPIRE' INTO ONE OF THE GREAT SMALL NATIONS OF THE WORLD, New York: The Macmillan Company, 1931.

Snowden, Donald, "Involvement to Date on Fogo Island," Memorial University of Newfoundland, 1971, mimeographed.

Usher, Peter J., FUR TRADE POSTS OF THE NORTHWEST TERRITORIES: 1870-1970, Ottawa: Information Canada, 1971.

Vallières, Pierre, "Personal Experience and the Redefinition of Power Relationships," in D. I. Davies and Kathleen Herman, eds., SOCIAL SPACE: CANADIAN PERSPECTIVES, Toronto: New Press, 1971, pp. 219-229.

Wadel, Cato, MARGINAL ADAPTATIONS AND MODERNIZATION IN NEWFOUNDLAND: A STUDY OF STRATEGIES AND IMPLICATIONS IN THE RESETTLEMENT AND REDEVELOPMENT OF OUTPORT FISHING COMMUNITIES, St. John's: Institute of Social and Economic Research, 1969.

Wolforth, John, THE EVOLUTION AND ECONOMY OF THE DELTA COMMUNITY, Ottawa: Information Canada, 1971.

For Further Reading

Alinsky, Saul D., REVEILLE FOR RADICALS, New York: Vintage Books, 1969.

Biddle, William W. and Loureide J. Biddle, THE COMMUNITY DEVELOPMENT PROCESS: THE REDISCOVERY OF LOCAL INITIATIVE, New York: Holt, Rinehart and Winston, Inc., 1965.

Brox, Ottar, MAINTENANCE OF ECONOMIC DUALISM IN NEWFOUNDLAND, St. John's: Institute of Social and Economic Research, 1969.

Clark, S. D., THE DEVELOPING CANADIAN COMMUNITY, Toronto: University of Toronto Press, 1962.

Draper, James A., ed., CITIZEN PARTICIPATION: CANADA, Toronto: New Press, 1971.

Gwyn, Richard, SMALLWOOD: THE UNLIKELY REVOLUTIONARY, Toronto: McClelland and Stewart Limited, 1968.

Honigmann, John J. and Irma Honigmann, ESKIMO TOWNSMEN, Ottawa: Canadian Research Centre for Anthropology, 1965.

Iverson, Noel and D. Ralph Matthews, COMMUNITIES IN DECLINE: AN EXAMINATION OF HOUSEHOLD RESETTLEMENT IN NEWFOUNDLAND, St. John's: Institute of Social and Economic Research, 1968.

Lubart, Joseph M., PSYCHODYNAMIC PROBLEMS OF ADAPTATION: MACKENZIE DELTA ESKIMOS, Ottawa: Queen's Printer, 1970.

Mowat, Farley and John de Visser, THIS ROCK WITHIN THE SEA: A HERITAGE LOST, Boston: Little, Brown and Company, 1968.

Parsons, G. F., ARCTIC SUBURB: A LOOK AT THE NORTH'S NEWCOMERS, Ottawa: Queen's Printer, 1970.

Ross, Murray G., COMMUNITY ORGANIZATION: THEORY, PRINCIPLES, AND PRACTICE, Second Edition, New York: Harper & Row, Publishers, 1967.

Chapter 7

Social Macrodynamics I

It was suggested in Chapter 6 that the study of social macrodynamics is the study of those forces which produce motion in the social structure of Canadian society *qua* society. The study of macrodynamics focuses attention upon such things as the processes whereby decisions are taken and the processes of resolving contradictions, and of adjusting to contradictions which seem above resolution. The study of macrodynamics is the study of those broad conditions which prevail in a society and which exert forces that influence the course of change within that society. It goes without saying that these social forces also influence the structure which is a society, or the structure which comes with time to represent the society.

This chapter is the first of two dealing with broad issues which influence the structure of Canadian society. The subjects of the present chapter include a consideration of regionalism in Canada and a discussion of urbanization which provides an appraisal of its impact, not so much for urban dwellers, but for the social organization of rural communities. Chapter 8 will focus upon equally important subjects when it takes up the topics of inequality, language and culture, and social participation. Although most if not all of these subjects can be viewed microdynamically, as that term was used in Chapter 6, the themes of the present and following chapters are generally viewed from the broader perspective of large aggregates of people impersonally organized in society.

Chapters 7 and 8 are notable in terms of the subjects they omit. There are many macrodynamics which might have been included. There are subjects such as ethnicity or minority group relations or relations between Canada and the United States which are not directly considered. At the same time, many of these topics have been noted and discussed elsewhere in this book. Like most things, what we have chosen to consider represents a selection from the possible.

Macrodynamic: Regions and Regionalism

> If the vast lands that edge the polar seas — Scandinavia, Russia, Canada — are to be filled with electric light that dims the aurora, with power that defies the cold, and resources that supply the world, let us see to it that in the new trust of the future of the North we make fewer errors than in the old (Leacock, 1937, p. 254).

The convergence of geography and society in Canada is nowhere more apparent than in the region of the Mackenzie River Valley. The Mackenzie River when linked with the Peace is one of the longest in the world. Its 2,635 miles compares impressively with the Nile (4,145) and the Mississippi-Missouri (3,710). As the St. Lawrence River has opened middle-Canada to the Atlantic, so the Mackenzie may some day open the prairie expanse of western Canada to the Beaufort Sea and the world beyond. The Mackenzie has already played a significant part in opening up the western Canadian Arctic, since river shipping has marked northern expansion from the start. That the economy of the prairie region may be serviced at some point in the future by ocean-going ships utilizing a Mackenzie seaway is a possibility no more outlandish than was the idea of a St. Lawrence seaway in decades past. While such developments are awaited, it is clear that the Mackenzie has stimulated a pattern of settlement which continues to shape the social development of northern Canada.

The Mackenzie River Valley covers a small portion of the District of Mackenzie. The Mackenzie region, as we shall call it, begins at Fort Smith in the southeast and extends west and north of a line connecting Yellowknife and the eastern end of Great Bear Lake with the Mackenzie Delta in the northwest. The region is bounded on the west by the Mackenzie and Richardson Mountains, on the north by the Beaufort Sea and on the south by the provinces of British Columbia and Alberta. The region contains the majority of both persons and settlements — including the largest settlements — in the Northwest Territories. The communities of this region are generally situated near the Mackenzie River or around Great Slave Lake. Some of these communities are, or soon will become, major foci of socio-economic growth and activity in the North.

Table 7.2 indicates that the 1971 census showed more than two-thirds of the population of the Northwest Territories resident in the Mackenzie District. Approximately one in every six residents of the Territories in 1971 lived in Yellowknife. More than one-fifth of the population of the Territories in 1971 lived in Fort Smith, Hay River and Inuvik. On the basis of population concentration, it is obvious that the Mackenzie region is the heartland of a vast Canadian frontier. The

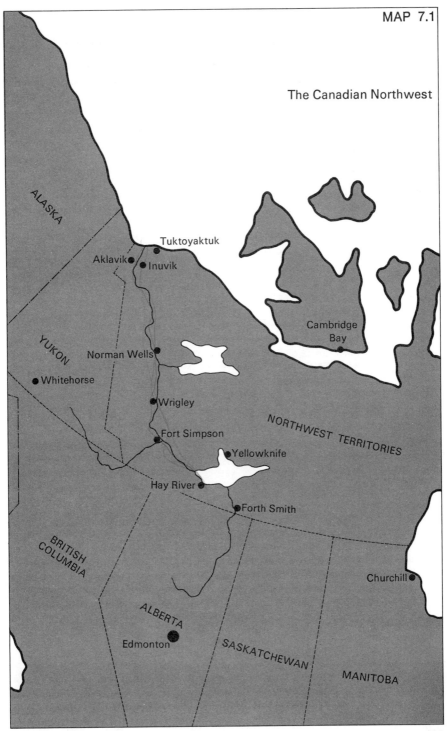

MAP 7.1

The Canadian Northwest

ALASKA

Tuktoyaktuk

Aklavik● ●Inuvik

YUKON

Norman Wells●

Cambridge
Bay

●Whitehorse

●Wrigley

NORTHWEST TERRITORIES

●Fort Simpson

●Yellowknife

Hay River●

●Forth Smith

BRITISH
COLUMBIA

Churchill●

ALBERTA

Edmonton●

SASKATCHEWAN

MANITOBA

TABLE 7.2

Population of the Northwest Territories by District and by Selected Community in the District of Mackenzie, 1961, 1966 and 1971

	1961	1966	1971	Percent 1971 Total
All Districts	22,998	28,738	34,807	100.0
Mackenzie District	14,895	18,685	23,657	68.0
Franklin District	5,758	7,167	7,747	22.2
Keewatin District	2,345	2,886	3,403	9.8
Yellowknife	3,245	3,741	6,122	17.6
Fort Smith	1,681	2,120	2,364	6.8
Inuvik	1,248	2,040	2,669	7.7
Hay River	1,338	2,002	2,406	6.9
Fort Simpson	563	712	747	2.1
Unorganized	6,820	8,070	9,349	26.8

Sources: Dominion Bureau of Statistics, Catalogue No. 92-602 (October, 1967), and Statistics Canada Catalogue No. 92-707 (October, 1972).

concept of Mid-Canada has already recognized this fact since one of its two recommended spurs north of the provinces follows the Mackenzie to Inuvik.

Thus far the argument is essentially that the Mackenzie River is what ties the Mackenzie region together. There are other bases for solidarity within a social region. People identify with one region rather than another because of such factors as a regional political culture and the effects of familiar mass media, and because of established webs of personal interaction and limited physical access to other regions. Most of northern Canada is physically isolated, and therefore its residents are socially and psychologically isolated to a degree unmatched by persons living in other regions of Canada. The indicators of such isolation are many.

For example, the Canadian Broadcasting Corporation provides northern radio and television services, although prior to 1973 television programs came as a frontier package edited in the south for northern telecast one or two weeks after the programs were aired in southern Canada. Radio broadcasts in northern Canada are as anywhere else in the country, although it is of interest to note that in 1971 the C.B.C. station in Yellowknife did not maintain an on-line news teletype. Another general indicator of isolation is the fact that Pacific Western Airlines, the regional carrier which services ten communities in the Northwest Territories (eight of these are in the Mackenzie region), does not offer scheduled air service to or from the Territories on Sundays (this was the case for the system's published schedules for the fall of 1971 and spring of 1972, although one Sunday flight serviced Yellowknife and Hay River during the summer months of 1972). Looking further at the P.W.A. schedule suggests that Edmonton is on the route to and from the Northwest Territories. Flights tend to leave Edmonton and disperse in three directions: to Yellowknife and back via Fort Smith or Hay River, to Yellowknife and beyond to the eastern Arctic, and to Yellowknife and beyond to the western Arctic flying the Mackenzie route. Twice each week P.W.A. flies to Cambridge Bay and Resolute in the eastern Arctic. At least eight times each week the airline connects Edmonton and Yellowknife with Inuvik in the western Arctic, and on most flights stops are made along the river at Norman Wells.

There are other ways to examine Pacific Western's flight schedule. Most of the mainline flights provide jet service. But out-of-the-way communities like Wrigley and Fort Resolution are serviced by smaller aircraft. The argument is not that such places should be serviced by larger aircraft, but that the type of aircraft, the availability of a road to drive out if one wishes and other factors such as the cost of air travel all contribute to social and psychological isolation. The one-way airfare from Inuvik to Edmonton was $150 in 1972; in comparison, the one-way fare from St. John's to Edmonton was $158 (slightly more than twice the distance at approximately the same cost). These indicators are nothing more than suggestive of reasons why the Mackenzie region is developing as a social region.

A social region becomes defined as its boundaries become defined, and as entry to and from the region becomes circumscribed. Also, a social region takes on meaning as movement within the region becomes routinized. Mountains and rivers and man-made creations like political boundaries can become the limits of a region. A mountain pass or a bridge or a highway, not to mention interprovincial commerce, telephone lines, rail and air traffic all are means for crossing boundaries. All other things equal, the man who lives in Saskatchewan but who reads an eastern Canadian newspaper delivered daily by airmail will likely experience a less intense sense of affiliation with his local area. An area takes on the quality of being a social region to the extent that many if not most persons come to identify with a spatial area that they see as circumscribed by boundaries which demarcate what is local from what is foreign or "over the hill". That a social region exists in southwestern British Columbia cannot be denied; physical terrain joins with local culture to form a region felt to be real by residents. Similarly, to the degree that the Peace River area of Alberta or the Cape Breton area of Nova Scotia is demarcated physically and culturally from nearby areas, these areas too can be characterized as social regions. That the process of regionalism is moving forward in the Mackenzie area must now be substantiated and qualified with stronger arguments.

Williamson (1969) argued that the high Arctic prior to 1950 represented a "largely homogeneous cultural area," but that "traditionally, from the indigenous point of view, there was no internal sense of regional pan-Eskimoism" (p. 12). That the situation has changed during the intervening twenty-odd years is an important qualification to the concept of a Mackenzie region. Williamson's arguments brought him to conclude, at least tentatively, that "northern perceptions of northern regionality [are beginning to move] away from the fragmentation of the folk era and the Balkanization of the federal administrative era toward a pan-Eskimoistic, politically broad type of northern regional identity" (p. 17). What are the arguments which support this conclusion?

To begin with, the focus has shifted away from a lament on lost cultural identity, an identity which was never really there because of the absence of east-west communication, and toward the study of developing identity in the modern age. Williamson listed the following developments in support of his conclusion. (1) The construction of the Distant Early Warning (DEW) Line provided the first major east-west contact, enabling the Eskimo to acquire a sense of ethnic identity. Williamson noted that, as white men of varying national and linguistic origins came to work in the Arctic, there emerged an "increasing tendency amongst Eskimo, to minimize the significance of sub-group differences, and to take greater interest in the factors of common identity" (p. 15). (2) The expansion of government services in northern Canada, especially with respect to hostel schooling, had the effect of heightening awareness within Eskimo and other indigenous cultures. Williamson noted the importance of other developments for strengthening cultural awareness, for example, treatment for tuberculosis as well as training in vocational programs brought people of similar cultural but different geographical backgrounds together. (3) The emergence of the media, especially Eskimo language media, provided a vehicle for public communication. (4) The concentration of population in settlements destroyed the impervious isolation of nomadic life. (5) Finally, cultural identity has been stimulated by a developing political culture in northern Canada. Given the right to vote and to hold public office, and given the increasing practice of that right, indigenous people are brought together as a political constituency.

Williamson's discussion forces the qualification that the Mackenzie region, because it does not coincide with a homogeneous culture region, and because it does not parallel such technological roadways as the DEW Line, therefore cannot be considered a social region. Williamson is much concerned with Eskimo culture, which is to say he is concerned with latitudinal contacts. But it would be fallacy to accept his arguments as negating the concept of a Mackenzie region, especially if a culture area is defined as dependent on the satisfaction of economic and communication criteria.

Unlike the wide expanse of northern Canada, from east to west, there exists an historical pattern of economy in the area of the Mackenzie Delta. This pattern has been described by Wolforth (1971). While trapping has declined both in terms of the number of people so occupied and the economic gain achieved, the fact that trapping constituted an industry organized throughout a geographical area is illustrated in Map 7.3 which maps the registered trapping areas in the Mackenzie Delta. Social space is highly differentiated, even above the Arctic Circle.

Relatively speaking, trapping has known its day as the means of survival in northern Canada. Whereas trapping was the economic mainstay in years past, the exploitation of surface animals is giving way to subterranean exploitation. The search for oil and ore requires the development of a surface transportation network which, from one end of the Mackenzie region to the other, will match and surpass the latitudinal ties provided by the construction of the DEW Line.

The DEW Line, of decreasing importance in military technology, served as a model of things to come. It represented an immense construction project, even by tomorrow's standards. Through employment and transport, it linked the North from east to west. It was characteristic of projects in remote areas in that it represented sudden investment over a short period of time. Figure 7.4 indicates that the insured DEW Line payroll jumped from an insignificant $42,000 in 1953 to in excess of $30 million in 1956. History has already shown that the DEW Line was of strategic rather than social or economic importance, and so it is not surprising that its construction did not stimulate a latitudinal social region across the North. It was not meant to so stimulate.

132

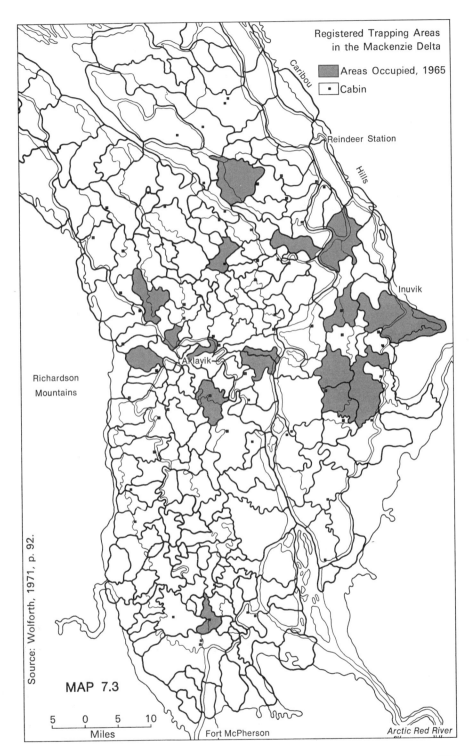

Registered Trapping Areas
in the Mackenzie Delta

Areas Occupied, 1965

Cabin

Caribou

Reindeer Station

Hills

Inuvik

Aklavik

Richardson
Mountains

Source: Wolforth, 1971, p. 92.

MAP 7.3

5   0   5   10
Miles

Fort McPherson

Arctic Red River

133

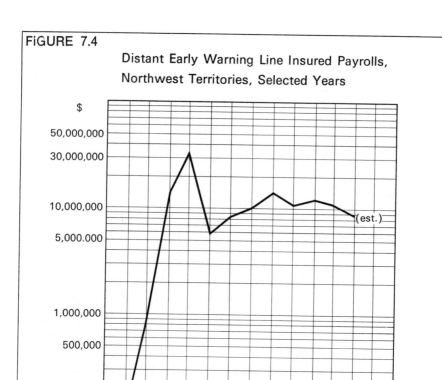

FIGURE 7.4

Distant Early Warning Line Insured Payrolls,
Northwest Territories, Selected Years

Source: Advisory Commission on the Development
of Government in the Northwest Territories, 1965, p.47.

The evolution of the Mackenzie region is on a different footing. The region emerged from diverse beginnings, ranging from the finding of gold at Yellowknife to the already-mentioned fur trade of the Mackenzie Delta. But the evolution of the region is most dramatic today because resource exploration and economic development have, or are about to assume the driver's seat in the management of the North. Exploration and development are the corporate goals of society. In an economic society, exploration and development are the means of applying the society's economic surplus toward the expansion of that surplus.

"Panarctic announces first Arctic islands oil strike!" In the financial newspapers of Canada hardly a day passes when comment cannot be found concerning exploration and development in the North. In recent years, the banner headlines have often been associated with the petroleum industry. While exploitation of Alberta's oil and gas fields now seems to have stabilized with the eventual prospect of decline, corporate industry is looking to the oil-rich areas of the Mackenzie

Delta, the Arctic islands and other northern areas. Alaska's Prudhoe Bay discovery was the first major oil and gas find in the far northern latitudes of North America. Then in the late 1960's the Canadian federal government joined forces with a band of petroleum corporations to form Panarctic Oils Limited. As northern exploration pays off with oil and gas discoveries, the corporate dream of resource exploitation, coupled with profit, nears realization. THE GLOBE AND MAIL printed the terse news: the "Canadian dream of finding oil in the Arctic islands became a reality yesterday with news that Panarctic . . . has found 'clean crude oil' at a well on Ellesmere Island" (February 25, 1972). From such announcements, it is not unrealistic to anticipate the decision to construct one or more pipelines from the Arctic region to southern Canada and beyond. By early in 1972 more than one-half of the necessary gas reserves had been discovered to justify the expenditure of several billions of dollars for constructing a gas pipeline. In anticipation of what is to come, Imperial Oil Limited announced in July of 1972 that it had signed a $4 billion contract to supply ten trillion cubic feet of Mackenzie Delta natural gas to American distributing firms (TIME, July 24, 1972).

An announcement of equal magnitude was made in Edmonton on April 28, 1972. "A new era has dawned for the Canadian North — our last frontier — with Prime Minister Trudeau's stunning announcement . . . that his government is going ahead immediately with construction of an all-weather highway along the Mackenzie Valley to the Arctic Coast. The breathtaking project to cost between $70 and $100 million, promises to mean as much to the North — at least the western side of it — as the building of the Canadian Pacific Railway meant to Western Canada in an earlier era" (EDMONTON JOURNAL, April 29, 1972). Later, in a more detailed assessment, the JOURNAL said that a "Mackenzie Valley highway will be the beginning of the end of a way of life . . .; the highway, followed by two pipelines, will revolutionize the economy of the Western Arctic . . .; [and there will be] enormous upheavals in communities" (May 9, 1972).

As the prospect of highways, gas and oil lines do much to unify the Mackenzie as a social region, pressures grow for latitudinal communication. Only several hours by jet separate Fort Smith and Inuvik, while the trip between Frobisher Bay and Yellowknife can take several days via the airports of southern Canada. The territorial government announced early in 1972 that steps were being taken to establish a scheduled air link between Yellowknife, Churchill and Frobisher Bay. The need for such a service points to the increasing self-sufficiency of the Mackenzie region, and to the need to reduce the difficulties of communicating with areas outside of the circumscribed region. The Mackenzie region becomes metropolis!

Much more can be said concerning the Mackenzie as a region, especially with respect to the structure and services of the territorial government. In lieu of such discussions, which themselves would require considerable space, perhaps it is sufficient to summarize by noting that the Mackenzie lowland area is a social region in that it is a bounded area with a "subnational economy"; it is a "community of interest," especially in terms of existent and proposed transportation and communication networks, and in terms of economic growth prospects (see Nicholson and Sametz, 1970). It is clear that resource exploitation in the North will soon be feasible on a widespread scale. Exploration and extraction will become routinized. With economic development as a certain prospect, attention must now be turned to the impact of economic development on human resource development in the

135

North. While the latter is immensely problematic, it too can be fulfilling in terms of the emergence of identity throughout the Mackenzie region.

Let us now consider regions and regionalism more generally in Canadian society. The study of the Mackenzie as a social region was made in part for the purpose of describing the nature of a social region in the process of its emergence. While regional development is an established fact in southern Canada, the Arctic in general and the Mackenzie area in particular offer a "ring-side seat in watching the processes of region formation" (Card, 1969, p. ix). Returning to the provinces and to their historical situations, the discussion now turns to regionalism, or the organization of society in terms of social regions, and to a brief discussion of some of the ways in which regionalism as social process gives rise to unique conditions and patterns of organization in different social regions.

It is little wonder that regionalism is an important dynamic in Canadian society. Differences of many kinds pervade Canada from coast to coast. Indicators of differences are many. Table 7.5, for example, confirms that seats in the House of Commons are roughly proportioned according to the distribution of population by region. At the same time, the table confirms a political fact of life in Canada, that the provinces of Quebec and Ontario contained 63.8 percent of Canada's population in 1968, and in that year they held 61.3 percent of the federal seats. Regionalism is encouraged by political apportionment.

TABLE 7.5

Estimated Population by Canadian Region and Representation in the House of Commons by Region, 1968

	Seats	Percent	Population	Percent
Atlantic	32	12.1	2,001,000	9.7
Quebec	74	28.0	5,927,000	28.6
Ontario	88	33.3	7,306,000	35.2
Prairie	45	17.0	3,457,000	16.6
British Columbia	23	8.7	2,007,000	9.7
North	2	.8	46,000	.2
Total	264	99.9	20,744,000	100.0

Source: CANADA YEAR BOOK 1970-71, p.89 and p.243.

But more basically, regionalism is encouraged by economic disparities. Table 7.6 shows that in 1969 the per capita income ranged from a high of $3,369 in Ontario to a low of $1,613 in Newfoundland. Because of Ontario's substantial population, estimated at 7,452,000 in 1969, it follows that total personal income in Ontario in 1969 was the highest of all provinces at $25,104,000,000, an amount which was approximately 41 percent of Canada's total personal income for that year. The provinces of Quebec and Ontario reported slightly less than 67 percent of Canada's total personal income in 1969. For political and economic reasons, then, Quebec and Ontario combine to serve as Canada's heartland, and for these reasons regionalism is and will continue to be an undying issue in Canadian society.

TABLE 7.6

Per Capita Income by Canadian Region and by Province, 1969

	Personal Income (millions of $)	Population Estimate	Per Capita Income ($)
Atlantic	4,091	2,012,000	2,033
Newfoundland	829	514,000	1,613
Prince Edward Island	200	110,000	1,818
Nova Scotia	1,760	763,000	2,307
New Brunswick	1,302	625,000	2,083
Quebec	15,718	5,984,000	2,627
Ontario	25,104	7,452,000	3,369
Prairie	9,748	3,499,000	2,786
Manitoba	2,785	979,000	2,845
Saskatchewan	2,413	959,000	2,516
Alberta	4,550	1,561,000	2,915
British Columbia	6,451	2,067,000	3,121
North	122	47,000	2,596
Canada	61,234	21,061,000	2,907

Source: CANADA YEAR BOOK 1970-71, p.243 and p.1181. Per capita income computed by dividing personal income by population estimate for June 1, 1969.

The regions of Canada ranked as follows in terms of per capita income in 1969: Ontario ($3,369), British Columbia ($3,121), the Prairies ($2,786), Quebec ($2,627), the Yukon and Northwest Territories ($2,596) and the Atlantic region ($2,033). This indicator suggests that Quebec is not fully a heartland province, since per capita income in that province in 1969 was 78 percent of what it was in Ontario. More pronounced still is the fact that per capita income in the Atlantic region was approximately 60 percent of what it was in Ontario in 1969, or just over 77 percent of what it was in Quebec. The dynamic of regionalism is disparity, but it is also something more than disparity in that people of different regions come to be aware of their servitude to the unique conditions and patterns of economic organization which characterize their social region. Perhaps it is fortunate that so many are so little bothered by the hard facts.

TABLE 7.7

Percent Distribution of Canadian Interregional Trade in Manufactured Goods, 1967

	Atlantic		Quebec		Ontario		Prairie		British Columbia	
	Exports To	Imports From	Exports To	Imports From	Exports To	Imports From	Exports To	Imports From	Exports To	Imports From
Atlantic	—	—	12	4	12	5	5	1	4	1
Quebec	43	36	—	—	48	81	28	22	13	23
Ontario	44	59	64	88	—	—	37	65	26	60
Prairie	9	3	15	6	26	10	—	—	56	16
British Columbia	3	2	9	2	13	5	29	12	—	—
Total	99	100	100	100	99	101	99	100	99	100

Source: Bank of Montreal BUSINESS REVIEW, December 22, 1971, p.2.

Economic organization can be seen by examining interregional trade patterns. Interregional trade data for manufactured goods are summarized in Table 7.7. These data suggest that there is a great deal of economic interaction between the regions of Canada, although there is a strong tendency for a given region to trade most with its neighboring region. In overall terms, the Bank of Montreal's BUSI-NESS REVIEW noted that Ontario and Quebec "are each other's largest single market." These provinces "absorb 55% and supply 86% of all manufactured goods traded between regions." In 1967 they represented the "first and second most important trading partner of each of the three remaining regions in Canada" (December 22, 1971).

Regionalism as a social macrodynamic stems in large part from attitudes of mind. What would otherwise be undisputed fact becomes redefined by our attitudes. For example, Saskatchewan as a territory is bounded on the west by Alberta, on the east by Manitoba, on the north by the Northwest Territories and on the south by the American states of Montana and North Dakota. Although the boundaries are undisputed, attitudes of mind have us look at Saskatchewan as a province within confederation, as a depressed social area or as an autonomous political state, rather than as part of a larger region, as part of a larger economic system of production and trade or as composed of many differentiated parts such as diverse religious and ethnic groups. Even undisputed facts encourage us to look at things in different ways. The familiar map helps to create an attitude of mind, itself cautioned by another attitude which reminds us that the familiar is not always the best framework for taking thought.

Let us take the example of Quebec. If asked, many Canadians, rightly or wrongly, would probably support the notion that Quebec is Canada's social problem. During the 1960's and early 1970's, such a stereotypical attitude was often felt to be justified. In their words, look at the terrorists, the separatists! It was felt to be justified because many people failed to see the importance of other problems in society, such as regional disparities, the settlement of treaty rights and poverty. After all, Canada was viewed as a happy, prosperous country! Sanguine phrases such as this one serve many people as justifications of their mental attitudes.

The fact of the matter is that a prudent social analysis of Quebec society can be made only if such things as terrorism and separatism are viewed as symbolic of root causes, especially of those which relate to economic and class conditions. Only a superficial examination will suggest that terrorism and separatism are direct functions of religious or ethnic or language conflict. The crux of the issue is an attitude, which many share, of being disadvantaged in the larger sphere of economic activity.

Prudence suggests that the focus should not be the terrorists and their acts, nor should it be the separatists and their ideology, but it should be an examination of the development of economic and political consciousness in Quebec, especially at the level of the provincial government and its relations with other governments of Canada. To define the matter this way means, by implication, that Quebec is not and has not been Canada's social problem, although it has been the scene where many of the recent dramas in Canadian society have been enacted.

Economic conditions in Quebec are frequently comparable with, if not more prosperous than, conditions in other provinces and regions. Podoluk (1968) demonstrated that the average income of males in Quebec for the year ending May 31, 1961 was exceeded by the averages for just four other provinces: Ontario, Alberta, British Columbia and Manitoba (see p. 160). Gosselin's major study of poverty in

Montreal (1966) gave rise to many comparisons using income and other socio-economic data from the 1961 census. Of peripheral interest to his study is the fact that data for Canada and Quebec, although not to the same extent for Montreal, generally exhibited similar values.

Economic conditions in Quebec stimulate social unrest and social action, it is suggested, because many residents of that province experience common identifications through language, ethnic, religious or labour affiliations which support their attitudes, especially those attitudes which label them as members of oppressed minorities. This suggests that regionalism as a social dynamic may be more advanced in Quebec than in any of the other regions of Canada.

Meanwhile the times change, and the attitudes of Canadians change too. In a new introduction to the Carleton Library edition of his book COMMUNITY IN CRISIS: FRENCH-CANADIAN NATIONALISM IN PERSPECTIVE (1972), Jones said of his attitudes in 1966: "I believed in a unique Canadian experience which might serve as a model elsewhere in the world; I hoped for the development of a new federalism which, although bound to encounter perennial difficulties, might reduce the separatist threat; and I attached a high priority to the survival of the French language and culture in Canada, hoping that an ever greater *épanouissement* would be possible" (p. x).

"Five years later, in 1971, this viewpoint has altered radically. I now have great doubts about the success of bilingualism in its coast-to-coast form; my hope of reaching some kind of agreement on the nature of a new federalism that would be likely to satisfy Ottawa, the English provinces and Quebec has all but evaporated; and my fears of Canada's being swallowed up by the giant to the south have greatly increased. On the other hand, the priority which I accorded to the survival and growth of the French language and the French-Canadian culture has not diminished. If anything, my dread of greater cultural uniformity has led me to attach even greater importance to this last priority" (p. xi).

In the other regions of Canada, identities of kind also continue to emerge and to be altered. The Atlantic region, for example, has the Atlantic Provinces Economic Council which has been concerned with the economy of its region in general. The Council's THE ATLANTIC ECONOMY (1971) gave special attention to economic development in the region, and to the role of the federal Department of Regional Economic Expansion (DREE). Two of the three reasons given "for DREE's disappointing record during its first 30 months" included the "government's inept handling of the national economy [which] made significant regional progress extremely difficult," and the "structure and approach of DREE itself" (p. 99). Accordingly, the Council recommended that the "operations of DREE be regionalized as much as possible" (p. 100).

The concerns expressed by people of the Prairie region are many and varied in comparison with the more singular focus on economic development witnessed in the Atlantic region. Historically speaking, the two regions emerged out of quite different circumstances. The core Atlantic provinces of Nova Scotia and New Brunswick were part of Canadian confederation from the start; even Nova Scotia's Joseph Howe, who led a movement against confederation, yielded to pressure from the British and Canadian governments. Western entrance into confederation was quite another matter, promoted by "three major national policies: immigration and western settlement, all-Canadian transcontinental railway transport, and industrialization by means of a protective tariff" (Creighton, 1970, p. 25). During the period of Sir Wilfrid Laurier's term as prime minister, from 1896 to 1911, more than two million people immigrated to Canada (see Kalbach and McVey, 1971, p. 33), and a very large portion of this number settled in the Prairie region. Saskatchewan and Alberta became provinces in 1905. But westward expansion had already encroached upon those who had settled the land west of Ontario. Although Manitoba became a province in 1870, that event lay in the shadow of the 1869 Red River Insurrection under the leadership of Louis Riel. Riel wished to protect the culture of his Métis people from the onslaught of western settlement. While Manitoba became a province before its time was due, it did serve as a foothold for westward expansion. Times were hard in Manitoba in the 1870's and 1880's, and the Métis, finding themselves pursued in their own move westward by the white colonialists, invited Riel to return and to lead them in protest. Meanwhile, the Canadian Pacific Railway was in financial trouble. In Creighton's words, the "crisis of the railway and the crisis of the rebellion [of 1885] coincided. Each solved the other. The rebellion ensured the completion of the railway; the railway accomplished the defeat of the rebellion" (1970, p. 56).

From this brief review of history we come to the modern scene, strangely similar to the past. "The tradition of dissent is as much a part of the Western Canadian heritage as the monarchical tradition is a part of the British heritage" (Anderson, 1971, p. 36). Barr and Anderson, in an introduction to their book THE UNFINISHED REVOLT: SOME VIEWS ON WESTERN INDEPENDENCE (1971), suggested that "no one who is not a Westerner can really understand the kind of helpless anger Westerners have felt for the past decade or so as they have tried, and failed, to get a hearing for their unique regional perspective."

While some talk of revolt, others dream of political unity. On the occasion of a national conference to study the feasibility of the political amalgamation of the Prairie region, Mowers, the editor and publisher of THE LETHBRIDGE HERALD, noted that "[o]ne generation is frightened by the collapse of the old certainties, the other impatient with their persistence. The Western society we have known is tumbling down. . . . No longer can anything be assumed. Whatever belongs to the age now dying must be challenged and proved before it will be accepted by the age now being born" (Elton, 1970, p. 7).

> Uniting the three Prairie provinces into one might not of itself make a profound difference to our country's destiny, but coupled with Maritime Union it could stimulate new purpose. But whether it is found in that direction or not, there must be new purpose, stimulated by change somewhere if Canada is to have the loyalty essential for survival (Elton, 1970, p. 8).

Canada's regional mosaic is constantly changing. Our purpose so far in this chapter has been to emphasize the dynamic of regionalism as a social force in Canada. Students of society cannot avoid the need for careful studies of regions, especially as events peculiar to a region (such as a new provincial government policy or the development of new industry), together with events of national scope (such as the policies and actions of government agencies like DREE), influence regional social development. There also are underlying changes of attitude, for example, the Trudeau government claimed to have changed its attitude toward the western provinces as a result of the federal election in 1972. Detailed assessments of claims and counterclaims, backed by hard evidence of regional consequences, is a continuing requirement of the sociology of Canadian society.

Macrodynamic: Cities and Countryside

> We should not be greatly disturbed by the probability that our civilization will die like any other. . . . Perhaps it is desirable that life should take fresh forms, that new civilizations and centers should have their turn (Durant and Durant, 1968, p. 100).

Statistics Canada uses a concept which indicates the phenomenon of metropolitanization: the census metropolitan area. There were nineteen metropolitan areas in Canada in 1966. It was estimated that as of June 1, 1969 these metropolitan areas boasted a combined population of 10,273,000 persons, or 48.8 percent of Canada's total population. Obviously, to speak of metropolitan areas is to speak of a small number of large cities which support a great many people. Many persons take their first look at Canada and see vast numbers of people inhabiting a relatively small land area in and around a small number of cities. Some persons fail to look any further.

We can look further by examining the distribution of population within these nineteen metropolitan areas. It is found that fourteen of the areas have a population of fewer than 500,000 persons, ten have a population of fewer than 250,000 persons, and three have a population of fewer than 125,000.

We can look beyond these large cities in another direction and ask: what is left after the metropolitan areas and their share of Canada's population are removed from the equation? Table 7.8 does not eliminate the metropolitan areas, but it does manage to convey one answer to the question. What remains is a vast number of communities, most if not almost all of which are incorporated as legal entities. There are many more than 4,276 communities in Canada, but this number at least suggests that the complexity of Canadian social organization exists outside the metropolitan areas as well. The complexity of social organization exists especially in rural Canada. The social dynamic of cities and countryside is manysided, but in large measure it can be viewed as cities versus countryside, as each draws from the other in an attempt to use, if not control the economic surplus of society.

The first task of this section is to examine aspects of the social and economic structure of cities. This examination is followed by a discussion of the often-made distinction between urban and rural areas. Then there is consideration of the fundamental problem of growth and decline in hinterland areas.

Usually the structure of cities is considered to be hidden and impervious to study. Urban structure does not have to remain beyond our grasp; a considerable amount of information is available to help us penetrate the underlying structure of urban areas. The central question concerns the nature of social structure.

TABLE 7.8

Canadian Municipalities by Region, 1970, and by Population Group, 1966

	Atlantic	Quebec	Ontario	Prairie	B.C.	North	Canada
Municipalities							
Cities	12	64	38	29	31	3	177
Towns	139	195	151	268	13	3	769
Villages	117	292	150	569	54	0	1,182
Rural Municipalities	24	1,084	551	449	40	0	2,148
Totals	292	1,635	890	1,315	138	6	4,276
Population							
Over 100,000	1	3	9	5	2	0	20
50,000 to 99,999	4	7	16	1	4	0	32
10,000 to 49,999	26	72	55	24	25	0	202
Under 9,999	261	1,553	810	1,285	107	6	4,022
Totals	292	1,635	890	1,315	138	6	4,276

Source: CANADA YEAR BOOK 1970-71, p.129. Not included are two metropolitan corporations, two regional municipalities and 137 counties and regional districts.

The word "structure" usually refers to form and to the organization of parts. The structure of a building has to do with its architectural design, its height and other dimensions, the organization of rooms, and the location of such things as ventilation and heating equipment. In a similar vein, it is possible to think of the structure of society in terms of such factors as the number of people, the way in which the people are distributed across the land, that is, what proportion live in urban areas in comparison to rural farm and rural nonfarm areas, the availability and type of transportation systems and the consequences associated with the availability of natural resources in given areas. In these contexts, structure appears to be the fixed features of things. Let us look at three examples of urban structure.

Maxwell (1965) classified Canadian cities on the basis of their functional structure. He meant by "functional structure" the activities around which various cities are organized. He recognized that wholesale trade is important for some cities while manufacturing is important for others. He classified Canadian cities according to their degree of specialization, their population and their geographic location. Maxwell found support for two familiar patterns, that "specialization generally increases with increases in the importance of manufacturing, and heartland cities are generally more specialized than the periphery cities" (p. 93).

Maxwell's analysis revealed five distinct groups of cities in Canada. Thirty-one cities are called specialized manufacturing centres. Almost all of these cities are located in the Canadian heartland, that is, in an area inclusive of southern Ontario and the St. Lawrence River Valley of Quebec. The manufacturing function is much more important than the wholesale trade function. Some of the heartland cities in this group are Oshawa, Hamilton, Windsor, Shawinigan and Trois-Rivieres. Trail is

143

an example of a peripheral city in this group. These cities tend to be highly specialized. Populations tend to be small rather than large; only a few of the cities in this
group have more than 100,000 residents. Moving on, eight cities are called special
centres. These are highly specialized locations with both the manufacturing and the
wholesale trade functions of low importance. Special cities include Glace Bay,
Timmins, Sudbury, Ottawa and Victoria. Special cities tend to be highly specialized
government and extraction centres. Seventeen cities form the third group called
regional capitals with manufacturing relatively unimportant. Examples include
North Bay, St. John's, Moncton, Halifax, Brandon, Prince Albert, Penticton, Lethbridge, Calgary and Edmonton. *All* of these seventeen cities are hinterland service
centres outside the Canadian heartland. These centres are oriented to the gathering
and distribution of goods. In several cases, retail trade and transportation are dominant functions. A fourth group of twenty cities is called regional capitals with
manufacturing relatively important. This heterogeneous group includes Trenton,
Sherbrooke, London, Medicine Hat, Kingston, Chicoutimi and Quebec. Maxwell
found that these cities fall midway on most of his measures: specialized but not
overly specialized, with wholesale trade and manufacturing important but not too
important. The final group of four cities includes Montreal, Toronto, Winnipeg and
Vancouver. These major metropolitan centres achieve their position because of
large populations and because of the relatively high importance of both wholesale
trade and manufacturing. There are differences, however, within this last group.
The peripheral cities of Winnipeg and Vancouver are more involved with wholesale
trade activities, while the heartland cities of Toronto and Montreal are the largest in
the country and emphasize manufacturing to a greater extent (see pp. 93-95).

A second discussion of urban structure is found in the 1961 census monograph by Stone entitled URBAN DEVELOPMENT IN CANADA (1967). Stone
suggested that there are four industry groups which contribute most to the performance of metropolitan functions. These groups are wholesale trade, business
services, fabricating industries, and finance, insurance and real estate (see p. 189).
Since the proportion of the labour force active in these four groups is known, it is a
simple matter to determine the orientation of each of Canada's metropolitan areas
toward these groups. One metropolitan area ranks these four industry groups
among its top four industry groups: Toronto. Two metropolitan areas rank at least
three of the four industry groups among their top four: Montreal and London. The
other and most important industry group in London is health and welfare services;
the other and fourth most important industry group in Montreal is transportation.
Seven metropolitan areas rank at least two of the four industry groups among their
top four groups: Vancouver, Windsor, Winnipeg, Kitchener, Calgary, Edmonton and
Ottawa. Four metropolitan areas rank at least one of the four industry groups
among their top four groups: St. John's, Halifax, Saint John and Hamilton. Finally,
three metropolitan areas fail to rank any of the four industry groups among their
top four groups: Quebec, Sudbury and Victoria (see pp. 192-193). The last three
groups of cities show heavy concentrations of their labour forces in the following
industry groups: storage, health and welfare services, education and related services,
transportation, other manufacturing industries, retail trade, public administration
and defence, construction, communication, and mines, quarries and oil wells (see
pp. 190-191).

From these brief reviews, it is obvious that both Maxwell and Stone examined the structure of Canadian cities from the vantage point of economic characteristics. Although both tended to view such things as a city's degree of specialization and its size as dependent upon economic considerations, they were quick to add that broad economic factors are themselves conditioned by geographic location and by the nature and availability of local resources. Thus, while Maxwell and Stone provided information concerning the economic nature of the form of Canadian cities, their work tells us relatively little concerning the organization of economic and social activities within cities. Indeed, census data do not readily provide this type of information. What we see from these studies, then, is a glimpse of the economic underside of Canadian cities. We do not find a direct glimpse of the social underside of cities, especially in terms of the groping nature of urban existence, the process of building institutional permanence and the development of social means for coping with change. The social underside is very much more difficult to describe and comprehend.

Let us consider Edmonton as a third example of urban structure. Edmonton is a large metropolitan area which had 495,702 residents in 1971 and 401,299 residents in 1966. Of this latter number there were 199,945 males and 201,354 females. Certain groups of people were single (205,639), married (177,983), widowed (14,671) and divorced (3,006). There were 105,016 dwellings of all kinds in Edmonton in 1966; 63,319 of these were owned and the remainder were rented. The total number of dwellings included 32,531 apartments or flats and 321 mobile homes. Obviously, there is hardly any end to the wealth of information available concerning the demographic structure of Edmonton.

The demographic structure tells us much about the social structure. For example, in the Edmonton metropolitan area in 1966 there were 123,565 persons between the ages of 5 and 19, inclusive. This total provides us with information concerning the dependent school-aged population. Similarly, there is information on how many persons constituted the potential labour force (101,752 males and 103,741 females aged 20 to 64, inclusive), and how many persons were past retirement age, some of whom constituted the dependent elderly population (23,286 persons aged 65 and above). These numbers reflect social structure to the extent that they suggest such things as: how many schools are required in which areas of the city, what is needed in the way of special medical and service facilities for people of different age groups, and the number of employable persons. Even the number of females of child-bearing age tells us something about the fertility of the area, and thus the need for maternity hospitals, nursery schools and day-care centres.

In case the argument is not obvious, there are, in brief, many social consequences for communities because of their demographic structure. For example, 5.8 percent of the population in the Edmonton metropolitan area in 1966 was aged 65 years and above. The comparable percentage for the Victoria metropolitan area was 15.1. For Kelowna the percentage was 16.8. If the age range were made to extend upward from 55 rather than 65 years, the percentages for Edmonton, Victoria and Kelowna would be 11.8, 24.0 and 26.8, respectively. In comparison to Edmonton, then, both Victoria and Kelowna had higher proportions of older residents in 1966. Also, proportionately, there were many more persons aged 55 to 64 in Victoria and Kelowna than there were in Edmonton. Looking at the other end of the age range, the percentages aged 14 and below in 1966 for Edmonton, Victoria and Kelowna were

34.5, 27.2 and 27.0, respectively. Related to both Victoria and Kelowna, then, Edmonton had the greater proportionate and absolute burden for educating its residents.

There seems to be a good distance between the argument waged to this point and the social underside of cities. The latter can be comprehended only if we carefully study such things as urban stratification, or the causes and consequences of inequalities between people, and the primary relationships between them. To document these things is a major task. For the present, let us return to the word "structure" and emphasize that, in a sociological sense, structure should not be thought to refer to fixed or even relatively fixed features. Social structure is quite different from the physical structure of a building. Sometimes there are fixed features, or relatively fixed features, associated with social structure; for example, family members learn fairly stable ways of relating to one another. But usually social structure is more a long-term exercise in coping which involves, among many other things, the frequent development of standardized ways of acting in particular situations.

The following quotation is adapted for present purposes and comes from a book review by Erikson (1966). Mental hospitals are the subject of the book under review, but Erikson's comment is just as pertinent for urban society. "The authors themselves are committed to the notion that human life is in a continual process of transformation and change, and their view of social structure reflects much the same qualities. [Urban society] . . . is seen here as a scene of restless activity, an arena in which people are constantly negotiating with one another to establish a momentary division of labour which will sooner or later be replaced by another. What most sociologists would call the 'structure' of the [city] . . . is scarcely more than a temporary arrangement built on provisional bargains and transient agreements. Freeze the moving scenery at any given moment in time, as one does with a photograph, and we have an illusion of stability and order; but observe the moving scenery over a period of time, and we discover that today's pattern of stability soon gives way to tomorrow's, as the members of the group go through the exhausting business of forming and reforming the conditions of their work world. Now this does not necessarily mean that the [city] . . . is less structured than other kinds of establishment. It means that one must look for evidence of structure in the ebbs and tides of the negotiation process itself" (pp. 225-226).

Cities, then, are not fixed social structures simply because they exhibit transportation networks, a business core, slums, parks and residential areas. Their social underside is moving and transient. They can be pushed and bent into new forms. They can be left to decay. To analyse their workings is one of the major tasks facing social studies.

The matter is clarified little by moving to the study of rural areas. Whereas cities are concentrated in space and large in population, rural communities are dispersed in space and small in population. Communities of even small size are not always to be found in rural society; across the Prairie region, for example, dozens of miles often separate small communities, with just a small number of farmers' homes sitting on sections or part-sections of land between them. While friends may be just around the corner, as the saying goes, the corner can be one or many sections of land distant. Rural society offers a different setting for social organization.

The words "rural" and "urban" should not pass without comment. By having to use two words we might infer that we are talking about two things. Sometimes we are; sometimes we are not. We are talking about two separate things when we note that the rural dweller in history is the person who continually tries to survive against the challenges of the natural environment, while the urban dweller is the person who tries to adapt to a man-made social environment. But, in some respects, the rural and urban dweller are not separable. Both raise families, both work for production or service, both drive new automobiles, both go on vacations and both vote in elections.

The distinction between "rural" and "urban" is reflected in such things as population statistics. For instance, the density of population — the number of persons per square mile of territory — will usually provide a hint about whether we are speaking of a rural or an urban area. Very high densities suggest cities or large metropolitan areas; very small densities suggest sparsely populated rural areas. Somewhere in between there are rural communities of varying size.

But there are problems. Speaking strictly in terms of numbers, Statistics Canada defines an urban area as one containing more than 1,000 inhabitants. By this standard, many communities which we ordinarily think of as rural are in fact urban, such as Osoyoos, British Columbia, or Mayerthorpe, Alberta, or Montague, Prince Edward Island. Our sense of what is urban is associated with Montreal or Winnipeg, or even Red Deer. The real complication comes when we realize that urbanization as a process signifies not just size, but a complex and interdependent pattern of social relationships within and between persons and organizations. This realization permits the thought that "[b]etween town and country lies a richly variegated social gamma of rural and urban patterns, in which a city may sometimes be rural and a village highly urbanized" (Beijer, quoted by Whyte, 1966, p. 4).

So perhaps we should argue that Osoyoos, Mayerthorpe and Montague are urban centres just like Red Deer and Winnipeg. They all share certain things in common which characterize urban areas. The orientations of the members of these communities are toward diverse rather than common ends. The people in such communities are directed by social rather than natural time; their concept of time is "determined by the need for synchronization of . . . activities with the activities of other men" (Whyte, 1966, p. 6). These communities experience more rapid rates of social change. In comparison, the prairie farmer and the coastal fisherman are oriented to the single objective of extracting a living from nature. Their sense of time is natural, in line with seasonal variations or with the movement of ocean tides. And there is not too much change; it is as though the seasons or the tides guarantee constancy and predictability.

A tentative conclusion can be drawn from this argument: the problems associated with the distinction between what is rural and what is urban are so great that perhaps there is benefit in not using the terms and the distinction at all. Rather, it might be more profitable to apply the term "hinterland" to the region which surrounds the larger urban centre. Thus, Edmonton lies at the centre of a vast hinterland region which stretches from the Rocky Mountains on the west to Saskatchewan on the east, and from Red Deer in the south to the Peace River region in the northwest and to Lake Athabasca in the northeast. Indeed, Edmonton's hinterland region extends far into northern Canada. Edmonton is an urban centre because this vast hinterland area is dependent upon the city for goods and services, and because the city is an economic marketplace for the distribution of the products of the hinterland.

Hinterland areas are more dependent upon the natural resources of the land than are urban areas. Given this fact, there is a much greater likelihood that hinterland communities will experience economic problems, especially those communities which are heavily dependent upon a single resource industry such as farming, lumbering or mining. Markets are distant and sometimes in foreign lands, and usually their operation is far outside the control of local extractors or producers. Hinterland economic problems are sometimes so great that communities are forced to confront the question of community life or death through development or departure. This question is approached here by examining the essentially conservative bias which many people share concerning the subject of social development.

This bias is difficult to discuss because its implications extend beyond the single individual. As persons we realize that we live in a world which is constantly changing. But only infrequently are we willing to take change to its logical conclusion. In brief, both populations and communities rise and fall because the history of mankind is very much the history of the utilization of resources. Since resources rise and fall in the sense that where once they existed they are later depleted, so populations and communities which form to exploit resources must also rise and fall. Since cycles of growth and decay usually occur over many decades or more, the average individual does not participate in more than one full cycle, if that. In addition, the individual is less likely to perceive cycles because of such factors as physical and social mobility. In addition to geographical moves from place to place, the person moves up and down socially in the socio-economic and status hierarchies of communities; perceptions of cycles are blurred all the more. In brief, many things which we experience in the social world keep us from seeing that world as it really exists.

We often express concern when a community is on the decline. The issue of whether to promote local development or to move elsewhere, singly or collectively, emerges for local government and residents. It is hard if not impossible to contemplate the death of one's own home town. We have numerous examples of communities which try to live on after the point of their economic death. The people who remain are not assured of a good life. Indeed, quite the opposite is true. But the realization that communities do in fact die may not even become apparent to people, even though they begin to experience the consequences of impoverishment and sometimes isolation.

There is, then, a conservative bias in human life which pushes people to hold on, often in false hope rather than with any guarantee of improvement. This bias is largely a product of the individual's circumscribed sense of history. After all, if we live and survive in a place for several decades or more, this fact alone gives some reason, we think, for assuming that there is a local future. Errors are frequently made on the basis of such reasoning, especially in instances where the economic utility of a community has dissolved through the migration or the shutting down of industry, or because of the depletion of resources. One of the challenges in applied social science is to learn best how to inform people about historical cycles which seem to all but guarantee, given many circumstances, that after growth there is decay. Communities and their residents must be forewarned of such eventualities in time to allow for adjustment.

This conservative bias is intrinsic to human existence. It constitutes one of the many biases which we learn almost naturally. It is even possible that many learned individuals do not come to grips with the implications of the inevitability of cycles of growth and decay. When the problem is placed in a larger context, as when we think of the process of urbanization, or the process of rural development, it becomes obvious that no single part of society can be analysed in isolation from other parts, especially because of the underlying economic relations between the various parts. Cities, for example, grow within their economic means; they sometimes begin to show signs of deterioration when they grow at a faster rate than is permitted by their economic means. Urban problems develop: unemployment, inadequate and insufficient housing, transportation and the problems associated with a lagging tax base. It is possible to argue that these and other problems arise not just from inadequate planning and management, but also from the unnecessary and unwise push for growth when growth is not in the cards, so to speak. Growth requires an economic surplus which can then be invested in further growth and development. The editor of THE GLOBE AND MAIL once suggested that "urbanization is inflationary;... we are paying a greater price than perhaps we have realized for the growth of our cities" (March 10, 1971).

The conservative bias often appears in such fields as community development. The development worker is concerned with the organization of communities and with the mobilization of community resources toward the achievement of certain goals. The goals are occasionally examples of radical social change, that is, of some major alteration in the organization of social relationships. Community development is noted as an example of the conservative bias because the community development worker often tends, like the rest of us, to assume that intervention is the correct procedure in most if not all situations. The worker may know that intervention does not always bring about the consequences anticipated and planned for. Nonetheless, it is considerably more difficult to realize that, sometimes, not to intervene in situations has more favourable consequences relative to our goals than would have been the case through active intervention. Couple this fact with our general inability to view events over long periods of time and it becomes obvious that sometimes, rather than pushing onward toward further growth and development, we should try to use our knowledge and influence to achieve a levelling off, or even a decline in the complexity of social organization. Given certain objectives, however, the overriding theme persists: "[w]hen to do something and when not to are the major questions of our time" (Rosenberg, 1968, p. viii).

Communities grow, then, because there is an economic surplus to distribute. The surplus creates additional jobs as well as a wider variation of products and an increase in standards of living. The surplus decreases as such things as the demand for public services increase. These and other factors have more intense effects if the resources of a community and its surrounding area have been depleted, or approach being so. Redevelopment is sometimes a possibility; thus governments attempt and often succeed in bringing new industry into economically depressed areas. But redevelopment is not always a viable possibility, especially if the new industry does not extract locally available resources. It is one thing for industry to settle in an area where it can utilize local resources, but quite another for industry to settle there and be dependent, at cost, upon resources only available from distant areas. In brief, there tends to be a relationship between the availability of raw material, the location of its production into marketable products and the market area. It follows, then, that if redevelopment is not a viable alternative for strengthening a community's economic and thus social future, planning to ease that community's death as a social unit is a possible and perhaps preferable course of action.

It seems that we should do everything possible to study the economic and social viability of our hinterland communities and regions. We should encourage planning for development before the need for redevelopment becomes apparent. If for a variety of reasons redevelopment is not a sensible option, then we should plan positively for resettlement in one or more alternative locations. Because we know that resettlement is not an easy task, especially for those persons who are dislocated, perhaps the greatest need is to plan to plan positively when the need for change becomes obvious to local residents.

References

Advisory Commission on the Development of Government in the Northwest Territories, THE NORTHWEST TERRITORIES TODAY, Ottawa: Queen's Printer, 1965.

Anderson, Owen, "The Unfinished Revolt," in John J. Barr and Owen Anderson, eds., THE UNFINISHED REVOLT: SOME VIEWS ON WESTERN INDEPENDENCE, Toronto: McClelland and Stewart Limited, 1971, pp. 35-59.

Atlantic Provinces Economic Council, THE ATLANTIC ECONOMY, 1971.

Barr, John J. and Owen Anderson, eds., THE UNFINISHED REVOLT: SOME VIEWS ON WESTERN INDEPENDENCE, Toronto: McClelland and Stewart Limited, 1971.

Card, B. Y., ed., PERSPECTIVES ON REGIONS AND REGIONALISM, Edmonton: University of Alberta Printing Services, 1969.

Creighton, Donald, CANADA'S FIRST CENTURY: 1867-1967, Toronto: Macmillan of Canada, 1970.

Durant, Will and Ariel Durant, THE LESSONS OF HISTORY, New York: Simon and Schuster, 1968.

Elton, David K., ed., ONE PRAIRIE PROVINCE? Lethbridge, Alta.: Lethbridge Herald, 1970.

Erikson, Kai T., Review of PSYCHIATRIC IDEOLOGIES AND INSTITUTIONS, AMERICAN JOURNAL OF SOCIOLOGY, 72 (September, 1966) 225-226.

Gosselin, Emile, "The Third Solitude," in John Harp and John R. Hofley, eds., POVERTY IN CANADA, Scarborough, Ont.: Prentice-Hall of Canada, Ltd., 1971, pp. 187-212.

Jones, Richard, COMMUNITY IN CRISIS: FRENCH-CANADIAN NATIONALISM IN PERSPECTIVE, Toronto: McClelland and Stewart Limited, 1972.

Kalbach, Warren E. and Wayne W. McVey, THE DEMOGRAPHIC BASES OF CANADIAN SOCIETY, Toronto: McGraw-Hill Company of Canada Limited, 1971.

Leacock, Stephen, MY DISCOVERY OF THE WEST: A DISCUSSION OF EAST AND WEST IN CANADA, Boston: Hale, Cushman & Flint, 1937.

Maxwell, J. W., "The Functional Structure of Canadian Cities: A Classification of Cities," GEOGRAPHICAL BULLETIN, 7 (1965) 79-104.

Nicholson, N. L. and Z. W. Sametz, "Regions of Canada and the Regional Concept," in Ralph R. Krueger, Frederic O. Sargent, Anthony de Vos and Norman Pearson, eds., REGIONAL AND RESOURCE PLANNING IN CANADA, Revised Edition, Toronto: Holt, Rinehart and Winston of Canada, Limited, 1970, pp. 6-23.

Podoluk, Jenny R., INCOMES OF CANADIANS, Ottawa: Dominion Bureau of Statistics, 1968.

Rosenberg, Bernard, "Editor's Forward," in Richard R. Korn, ed., JUVENILE DELIN-QUENCY, New York: Thomas Y. Crowell Company, 1968, pp. vii-viii.

Stone, Leroy O., URBAN DEVELOPMENT IN CANADA, Ottawa: Dominion Bureau of Statistics, 1967.

Whyte, Donald R., "Rural Canada in Transition," in Marc-Adélard Tremblay and Walton J. Anderson, eds., RURAL CANADA IN TRANSITION: A MULTIDIMENSIONAL STUDY OF THE IMPACT OF TECHNOLOGY AND URBANIZATION ON TRADITIONAL SOCIETY, Ottawa: Agricultural Economics Research Council of Canada, 1966, pp. 1-113.

Williamson, R. G., " 'Regions' and Identity in the North: Some Notes," in B.Y. Card, ed., PERSPECTIVES ON REGIONS AND REGIONALISM, Edmonton: University of Alberta Printing Services, 1969, pp. 11-18.

Wolforth, John, THE EVOLUTION AND ECONOMY OF THE DELTA COMMUNITY, Ottawa: Information Canada, 1971.

For Further Reading

Jenness, Diamond, ESKIMO ADMINISTRATION: II. CANADA, Montreal: Arctic Institute of North America, 1964.

Lithwick, N. H., URBAN CANADA: PROBLEMS AND PROSPECTS, Ottawa: Central Mortgage and Housing Corporation, 1970.

Lotz, Jim, NORTHERN REALITIES: THE FUTURE OF NORTHERN DEVELOPMENT IN CANADA, Toronto: New Press, 1970.

Mumford, Lewis, THE URBAN PROSPECT, New York: Harcourt, Brace & World, Inc., 1968.

Rea, K. J., THE POLITICAL ECONOMY OF THE CANADIAN NORTH: AN INTERPRE-TATION OF THE COURSE OF DEVELOPMENT IN THE NORTHERN TERRITORIES OF CANADA TO THE EARLY 1960s, Toronto: University of Toronto Press, 1968.

Robin, Martin, ed., CANADIAN PROVINCIAL POLITICS: THE PARTY SYSTEMS OF THE TEN PROVINCES, Scarborough, Ont.: Prentice-Hall of Canada, Ltd., 1972.

Sjoberg, Gideon, "The Rural-Urban Dimension in Preindustrial, Transitional, and Industrial Societies," in Robert E. L. Faris, ed., HANDBOOK OF MODERN SOCIOLOGY, Chicago: Rand McNally & Company, 1964, pp. 127-159.

Thomlinson, Ralph, URBAN STRUCTURE: THE SOCIAL AND SPATIAL CHARACTER OF CITIES, New York: Random House, 1969.

Wade, Mason, ed., REGIONALISM IN THE CANADIAN COMMUNITY, 1867-1967, Toronto: University of Toronto Press, 1969.

Chapter 8

Social Macrodynamics II

The spirit of Chapter 7 is continued in this chapter as we review subjects which influence, at the broadest level, the shape of Canadian social organization. The first topic discussed in the macrodynamic of inequality where special emphasis is reserved for policies which govern the distribution of valued resources. The discussion of inequality is followed by a section on language and culture, again examining the topic in relation to policy and in the context of actual trends concerning language assimilation.

Social participation is what people differentially do in time and space. The concept was introduced in Chapter 6 as a sociological means for relating that which people do to the contingencies and constraints of their environments, that is, to the things which influence what people do. This chapter concludes with another essay on social participation, except that on this occasion the concept is viewed in the context of social macrodynamics. By so doing, the distinction between micro-dynamics and macrodynamics becomes obvious, for the former implies the social participation of persons in personally meaningful contexts, while social participation at the level of macrodynamics is often an impersonal type of participation.

Macrodynamic: Inequality

> In progressive societies the concentration may reach a point where the strength of number in the many poor rivals the strength of ability in the few rich; then the unstable equilibrium generates a critical situation, which history has diversely met by legislation redistributing wealth or by revolution distributing poverty (Durant and Durant, 1968, p. 55).

Social inequality is ubiquitous. This fact alone is the basis for many of the dynamics in society. Alienation is often the result of a person realizing that he is without power to influence. To be alienated in this sense, accorded Seeman (1959), means the "expectancy or probability held by the individual that his own behavior cannot determine the occurrence of the outcomes, or reinforcements, he seeks" (p. 784).

The study of inequality is the study of how society is stratified, and the study of stratification forces us to deal with the concept of social class. Sociologists have extensively debated the question of whether social classes are real groups or simply statistical aggregates. Warner (1964), for example, argued that "living above, below, and at the common man level" is not indicative of "categories invented by social scientists to help explain what they have to say; they are groups recognized by the people of the community as being higher or lower in the life of the city. . . . The designations of social levels are distinctions made by the people themselves in referring to each other" (p. viii). Porter (1965), on the other hand, qualified his work on the structure of inequality in Canada by saying "we are talking about artificial statistical groups which do not have any life of their own or any coherence" (p. 11). The debate, like most debates, has not been resolved, if only because there are occasional instances of statistical groups which are, or do become real social groups with a coherence and consciousness. In lieu of furthering the traditional debate here, perhaps it is enough to echo the wisdom in Lenski's (1952) conclusion, namely, that people of a community or in a society generally are unable to identify discrete social classes, although they can and do see the class system as a continuum on which is distributed selected commodities of power and prestige. Such a description of the class system allows for the special case of a statistical group which is, or becomes a real social group.

This section does not aim to present a discussion of poverty in Canada; nor does it survey the distribution of wealth. Many volumes have appeared recently on these subjects. Instead, a selected review of Porter's contributions is followed by reporting some objective indicators of inequality in Canada. Then, the White Papers on tax reform (Benson, 1969) and income security (Munro, 1970) are placed in the context of Canadian incomes policy and taxation. The section concludes with a

153

note on the definition of poverty. Throughout, it is assumed that the "primary determinants of social stratification in modern communities are unquestionably economic" (Ginsberg, quoted by Porter, 1965, p. 10).

Porter's analysis of social class and power represents one of the most extensive pieces of social research ever undertaken in Canada. Its extent makes it a difficult contribution to summarize briefly. Porter's discussions of the structure of class suggest that, according to a number of objective criteria, social inequalities are many in Canadian society. It is not so much that social organization is marked by clear and consistent stratification, but that tradition and practice have combined to support inequalities in many of the institutional sectors of society.

To begin with education. Porter, a strict defender of the principle of educational opportunity for all, noted the historical situation whereby Canada imported much of its skilled labour, a fact which "permitted the continuity of class-bound education" (1965, p. 166). Listing income inequality, family size, regional differences in educational facilities and the influence of religion as social factors which have created and which perpetuate inequality of educational opportunity, Porter nevertheless noted that none of these factors "is beyond the control of social policy" (p. 168). More difficult to control are psychological barriers to equality of educational opportunity, the "attitudes and values which individuals have and the motives with which they are either endowed or inculcated to become educated" (p. 168). Porter concluded that policies must be developed to "overcome those [social and] psychological barriers which cut so many young people off from both the material and the spiritual benefits of education. Without such policies inter-generational continuity of class will remain, mobility deprivation will continue, and external recruitment will still be required to meet the needs of a complex occupational structure" (p. 198).

Perhaps Porter's most important analysis concerned ethnicity and social class. His method was twofold: first, to establish the degree to which different ethnic groups are represented in various occupational categories; and second, to examine the data across time and to see whether different ethnic groups changed their levels of representation in different occupational classes. Table 8.1 condenses the census data used in the analysis. The comparison point is always the male labour force. For example, 3.8 percent of the male labour force in 1931 was found in clerical occupations; persons of Italian origin were *under*represented in clerical occupations (3.8 less 2.5 equals 1.3 percent), while persons of Irish origin were *over*represented in this class (3.8 plus 1.0 equals 4.8 percent). The raw data can be found in an appendix supplied by Porter (see pp. 562-564).

Porter was able to demonstrate that the association between ethnic affiliation and occupational distribution in 1931 suggested class distinctions. Using data on ethnic origin and selected occupational classes, he concluded that in 1931 there was "little difference among the three British groups [English, Irish, Scottish], and they and the Jews rank high. French, German, and Dutch would probably be ranked next, followed by Scandinavian, Eastern European, Italian, Japanese, 'Other Central European,' Chinese, and native Indian" (p. 81). Porter noted the importance of the period during which an ethnic group arrived in Canada, since those who arrived earlier (such as German and Dutch immigrants) showed relatively higher occupational status even in 1931 (see p. 82). "This association between time of arrival and movement up to higher occupational levels does not apply to the French who by

154

TABLE 8.1

Percentage of Representation in Canadian Occupational Classes by Ethnic Origin, Male Labor Force, 1931, 1951 and 1961

	British				French	German	Italian	Jewish	Dutch	Scand.	East Euro-pean	Other Euro-pean	Asian	Indian and Eskimo	Total male labour force
	British total	Eng-lish	Irish	Scot-tish											
1931															
Professional and financial	+1.6	+1.6	+1.0	+2.2	−.8	−2.2	−3.3	+2.2	−1.1	−2.9	−3.9	−4.4	−4.3	−4.5	4.8
Clerical	+1.5	+1.8	+1.0	+1.4	−.8	−2.2	−2.5	+.1	−1.9	−2.7	−3.4	−3.5	−3.2	−3.7	3.8
Personal service	−.3	0.0	−.5	−.7	−.3	−1.2	−2.1	−1.2	−1.5	−1.5	−1.1	−1.7	+27.3	−3.1	3.5
Primary and unskilled	−4.6	−4.4	−4.9	−4.8	+3.3	−5.3	+26.1	−14.5	−4.8	+1.4	+12.4	+35.8	+10.2	+45.3	17.7
Agriculture	−3.0	−6.1	+2.7	−1.5	+.1	+21.1	−27.6	−32.4	+18.5	+19.8	+14.5	−5.8	−20.9	−4.9	34.0
All others	+4.8	+7.1	+.7	+3.4	−1.5	−10.2	+5.2	+45.8	−9.2	−14.1	−18.5	−20.4	−9.6	−20.1	36.2
Total	0.0	0.0	0.0	0.0	0.0	0.0	0.0	0.0	0.0	0.0	0.0	0.0	0.0	0.0	100.0
1951															
Professional and financial	+1.6	+1.6	+.9	+2.5	−1.5	−2.2	−3.1	+4.2	−1.7	−2.1	−2.9	−2.4	−2.8	−5.2	5.9
Clerical	+1.6	+1.8	+1.3	+1.4	−.8	−2.5	−1.7	0.0	−2.4	−2.8	−2.8	−2.5	−2.9	−5.2	5.9
Personal service	−.3	−.2	−.4	−.5	−.2	−1.2	−2.0	−1.4	−1.2	−1.0	+.6	+2.0	+23.9	+.6	3.4
Primary and unskilled	−2.2	−1.7	−2.2	−3.2	+3.0	−3.7	+9.6	−11.5	−1.7	+.5	+2.3	+5.7	+1.9	+47.0	13.3
Agriculture	−3.2	−5.5	+.5	−1.6	−.3	+19.1	−14.7	−18.7	+17.3	+14.7	+11.2	+3.4	+8.7	−7.8	19.4
All others	2.5	+4.0	−.1	+1.4	−.2	−9.5	+7.9	+27.4	−10.3	−9.3	−8.4	−6.2	−7.6	−28.2	52.1
Total	0.0	0.0	0.0	0.0	0.0	0.0	0.0	0.0	0.0	0.0	0.0	0.0	0.0	0.0	100.0
1961															
Professional and financial	+2.0				−1.9	−1.8	−5.2	+7.4	−.9	−1.9	−1.2	−1.1	−1.7	−7.5	8.6
Clerical	+1.3				+.2	−1.8	−3.2	+.1	−1.7	−2.4	−1.7	−2.0	−1.5	−5.9	6.9
Personal service	−.9				−.2	+.7	+2.9	−2.4	−.5	−1.1	+.9	+5.1	+19.1	+1.3	4.3
Primary and unskilled	−2.3				+2.8	+2.1	+11.5	−8.9	+2.0	+.2	+0.0	+1.8	+3.6	+34.7	10.0
Agriculture	−1.5				−1.4	+8.8	−9.5	−11.7	+10.3	+10.6	+6.9	+.6	+6.5	−6.9	12.2
All others	+1.4				+.9	+2.4	+3.5	+15.7	−5.2	−5.0	−4.9	−4.4	−9.1	−29.5	58.0
Total	0.0				0.0	0.0	0.0	0.0	0.0	0.0	0.0	0.0	0.0	0.0	100.0

Source: Porter, 1965, p.87.

155

1931 had very clearly lost out in the occupational structure, a situation for which they have frequently blamed the British, but which, no doubt, is as closely related to their own institutions as it is to the political federation which they have always viewed with some suspicion" (p. 82).

Concerning changes in the participation patterns of members of different ethnic groups across time, Porter first compared the years 1931 and 1951; later he updated the comparison to 1961. It is not easy to make such comparisons, especially because of intervening trends such as the decreased proportion of all workers in agriculture (from 34.0 percent in 1931 to 12.2 percent in 1961). Nonetheless, Porter was able to decipher certain trends. "[I]t would seem that over the twenty-year period the British retained their over-representation in the white collar world. Underrepresented at the white collar levels, the French scarcely managed to retain their class position relative to others" (pp. 84-85). Porter especially noted the position of the French. Although their position did not greatly change between the years 1931 and 1951, other ethnic groups improved their representation in the occupational structure during those years. Improvement was especially true of Italians (they were overrepresented in primary and unskilled occupations by 26.1 percent in 1931, but only by 9.6 percent in 1951) and Other Europeans (they were overrepresented in primary and unskilled occupations by 35.8 percent in 1931, but only by 5.7 percent in 1951).

No significant re-alignments took place during the period 1951 to 1961. Porter noted the changing distribution of workers within the professional and financial class of occupations. Jewish, British and Asian groups increased their hold on this class of occupations, which is to say they increased their degree of overrepresentation. Those groups which lost ground in this class included the French, the native Indian and Eskimo, and Italians.

It must be obvious that the subject of ethnicity and social class is a complex one. This brief review of Porter's analysis has perhaps stimulated an awareness of how people with characteristically different social backgrounds are unequally represented within various social categories. It must be obvious, too, that Porter's analysis went much beyond this review, and that there is reason therefore to directly examine his work in more detail.

We turn now to examine some objective indicators of inequality in Canada. The broad subject is income and its unequal distribution across the income-receiving units of society. Like most things, income is hard to define, largely because there are many different types of income, for example, per capita income, personal and family income. Also like most things, the unit of measurement must always be clearly specified. For those who believe that this is not an important point, note that the degree of inequality in the distribution of income is a function of its measurement. Podoluk (1968) concluded that "family income when classified on a per capita basis is more equally distributed than family income measured by size of total income" (p. 273).

It is a difficult task to obtain data concerning the changing distribution of income across time. Table 8.2 suggests that there was a slight trend toward increased income equality between the years 1931 and 1951. The data are interpreted to mean, for example, that the first 20 percent of families earning wages and salaries (or the lowest fifth in terms of dollars) slightly increased their share of all wages and salaries by 2.7 percentage points over a period of twenty years. Their share was increased at the expense (!) of those families earning most in wages and salaries. Podoluk concluded that there was more income inequality in the prewar years than in the postwar years. The specific reasons for this change are unknown, although transfer payments such as family allowances and unemployment insurance were available in 1951 whereas they were not available in 1931. This raises the question of the influence of transfer payments, especially in terms of whether they have the effect of more equally distributing income across the economic strata of society.

TABLE 8.2

Percentage Distributions of Wages and Salaries of Canadian Wage and Salary Earning Families, 1930-31 and 1951

| | Percentage Share of Wages and Salaries | |
	1930-31	1951
Lowest Fifth	5.3	8.0
Second Fifth	11.3	13.9
Third Fifth	17.3	17.9
Fourth Fifth	23.5	22.6
Highest Fifth	42.6	37.5

Source: Podoluk, 1968, p.268.

TABLE 8.3

Percentage Distributions of Canadian Nonfarm Family Income Before Tax, Selected Years

| | Percentage Share of Total Income | | | Average Income per Family ($) |
	1951	1961	1965	1965
Lowest Fifth	6.1	6.6	6.7	2,263
Second Fifth	12.9	13.4	13.4	4,542
Third Fifth	17.4	18.2	18.0	6,102
Fourth Fifth	22.5	23.4	23.5	7,942
Highest Fifth	41.1	38.4	38.4	13,016
All Families	100.0	100.0	100.0	6,669

Source: Economic Council of Canada, 1968, p.107.

The situation since 1951 seems to be relatively stable. Table 8.3 indicates that the lower income groups received but a fraction more in terms of total income between 1951 and 1965. Again, the lower income groups gained — if it can be called that! — from the higher income groups.

Tables 8.2 and 8.3 suggest an astonishing degree of stability in the distribution of income across economic strata. More basic, however, is the judgment that social forces in Canada have worked to establish and then to firmly maintain a high level of income inequality. The inescapable conclusion is that the rich are becoming richer in absolute terms if not in proportionate terms, and that if those who are less rich are to become richer, the economic marketplace must be regulated by government policy which aims to significantly redistribute income along more equitable lines.

Incomes policy generally has to do with national wage policy and with wage-price guidelines. Incomes policy can help to stabilize the domestic economy, to assist in making more accurate economic forecasts, and to serve as an educational device to show the relations between various economic indicators and the merits of moderation (see Smith, 1966). Consider incomes policy in the broad context of the concept of welfare.

Welfare means to be in a state of well-being. The politics of welfare, however, mean much more; it is the latter context which has tinged the concept of welfare with connotations of handout and dole. The intent here is to broaden the concept of welfare to its initial meaning of well-being, and to stress the need for social policy which reduces the objective inequalities found in society. To state such an intent marks it as biased. And so it is. Welfare implies its desirability for all citizens, and that governments are responsible for equalizing those objective inequalities which impair social well-being.

It is not possible to control subjective inequalities. It is possible to influence subjective perceptions of inequality, but the linkage between the type of influence and the perception is beyond the scope of scientific inquiry. Subjective inequalities will always exist because life styles and objective indicators of life styles are correlated imperfectly.

Podoluk (1968) provided evidence suggesting that the "redistribution of income through the imposition of taxes and . . . through transfer payments has a substantial levelling effect on the income distribution" (p. 287). She used a measure of inequality called the gini ratio; the ratio can range from zero (which implies perfect income equality) to one (which implies that all income is received by a single income-receiving unit). The ratios reported in Table 8.4 confirm that gross income (*inclusive* of all sources of income, including transfer payments) was distributed similarly in Canada for the years 1951 and 1961, and that the degree of income inequality was slightly less than a ratio of two-fifths. The ratios approach three-fifths when various transfer payments are *excluded* from gross income, which is to say that income inequality is notably less (by a margin of approximately one-fifth) when governments transfer payments back to the people. Transfer payments thus have been an important means for reducing inequality in Canadian society. It is interesting to note that the ratios for gross income less taxes are slightly less than are the ratios for gross income alone, which is to say that Canada's experience for the years 1951 and 1961 was that taxes slightly *increased* income inequality. The thought which emerges here is that a different taxation system and re-alignments in certain transfer payments are factors which *can* be manipulated to meet the policy goal of more income equality.

TABLE 8.4

Magnitude of Canadian Income Inequality, 1951 and 1961

	Gross Income	Gross Income less Transfer Payments	Gross Income less Taxes
1951	.390	.584	.369
1961	.385	.580	.366

Source: Podoluk, 1968, p.287.

Taxes are usually progressive, proportional or regressive. Progressive taxes such as the income tax increase as a percentage of income as income increases. A person with a higher income thus pays a higher percentage in income tax than a person with a lower income. Proportional taxes are a standard percentage of income notwithstanding the size of income. Regressive taxes are a greater burden for the low-income person. For example, "low-income groups usually spend a higher share of their income than higher income groups which usually save more and a higher proportion of their expenditures is likely to be on commodities subject to sales taxes. Such taxes then may be a higher proportion of low incomes than of high incomes. Another tax that tends to be regressive is the property tax" (Podoluk, 1968, p. 284).

The study carried out for the Royal Commission on Taxation concluded that, for federal taxes in total, the federal tax structure was regressive at the lowest end, that is for family units with money incomes below $2,000, and progressive above this level; provincial and local taxes were also regressive below $3,000 and, on balance, proportionate above this level. For all taxes combined, the tax structure was very regressive for the lowest income groups, proportionate for the middle income ranges and progressive at the highest end. This, however, is balanced by the fact that when benefits from government expenditures, in total, both through direct transfer payments and goods and services, are allocated by income level, the lower the income the greater the benefits relative to income. For family units with incomes below $4,500, a positive redistribution occurs when the value of benefits received is compared with the amount of taxes paid; within the income range $4,500 to $7,000 the redistribution changes from positive to negative and above $7,000 is negative (Podoluk, 1968, p. 285).

Obviously, the policies of governments make a difference. In a manner of speaking, an individual's net income is as much a function of the decisions of various governments concerning incomes policy, sales, property and other taxes such as those on imports, as it is a function of the amount of an individual's gross earnings. This statement is not pure fantasy for it would be true given perfect income equality; as income inequality is reduced in a society, it follows that fantasy becomes fact to an ever-inceasing extent.

There has not been sufficient time to assess the likely impact of several major pieces of federal legislation arising out of the White Papers on tax reform (Benson, 1969) and income security (Munro, 1970). The full impact of the new measures, indeed, will not be thoroughly assessed for many years to come. There are reasons to expect that the tax reform legislation effective for the tax year 1972 will affect the national distribution of personal income after taxes, perhaps even in the direction of reducing the extent of income inequality. The legislation, for example, raises personal exemptions to $1,500 from $1,000 for a single taxpayer, and to $2,850 from $2,000 for a married taxpayer. These facts alone will remove many thousands of lower-income taxpayers from the tax rolls. The legislation also provides for a special exemption of $650 for taxpayers 65 years of age and over, exempts the guaranteed income supplement from tax, makes child care expenses deductible up to $500 per child under 14 with a maximum of $2,000 per family, and allows an employment expense deduction up to $150 per year. There are many other provisions which at least suggest the possibility of some advantage for lower-income persons and families. The verdict, however, must be awaited. There is always the possibility that the gains registered by those of lower income will be less than those registered by those in the higher-income brackets, with the consequence, at least insofar as the tax structure is concerned, that the level of income inequality will be maintained at or above the level of the 1960's.

Given evidence that government transfer payments have had the effect of reducing income inequality at least to some extent, and given the design of the proposed federal legislation on income security, the case can be made that a more equal redistribution of income in Canada during the 1970's will be due to the income security legislation rather than to the tax reform legislation, if a more equal redistribution results at all. Although much of the legislation concerns old age income security, the legislation is illustrated here by the new family income security plan which was designed to replace the Family Allowances Act of 1944. The old plan provided $6 per child per month for every child in Canada under 10 years of age, and $8 per child per month for every child 10 to 15 years of age, inclusive. Family allowances cost Canada $560,049,848 during fiscal year 1970, this amount going to 6,865,302 children at an average allowance of $15.68 per family (CANADA YEAR BOOK 1970-71, p. 382). Youth allowances of $10 per child per month were also paid after 1964 to all persons 16 and 17 years of age; in fiscal 1970 these allowances amounted to $55,101,899 for 484,476 persons (p. 383). The new family income security plan is expected to "double benefits to 1,249,000 families, improve them for 623,000 more families, reduce them for 585,000 families and end them for 1,050,000 families" (EDMONTON JOURNAL, March 25, 1972). The monthly benefits increase as family size increases, although benefits decrease in steps by a certain fixed amount as family income exceeds in steps an established income floor ($4,500 for a family with one child). Legislation such as that outlined to replace the Family Allowances Act had not been passed by the end of 1972.

The White Paper on income security (Munro, 1970), while not a radical social document, did move forward in terms of broadening the concept of social welfare. The paper's theme was action with restraint. "The best approach for overcoming deficiencies of the existing system at this time does not lie in the direction of dismantling the system in favour of one, overall guaranteed income program. The best approach is to revise income security policies to redirect their emphasis and scope, and to seek the combination of programs that will best meet basic income security objectives" (p. 2). This statement from the White Paper suggests a political strategy geared to the national economic situation in 1970; "any new initiatives are necessarily limited by what is economically feasible" (p. 1). Nevertheless, the "economy must be enlisted in support of social objectives " (p. 1). "Income security protects people by giving them additional money when their own resources are not enough to meet the needs regarded by society as being basic. It replaces also the income of people who have lost earning capacity for such reasons as unemployment, maternity, sickness, disability or death of the family income earner. As one component of overall social security policy, income security programs are strengthened by the other parts, such as health insurance and special services for social assistance recipients" (p. 1).

Two brief notes conclude this section. The first of these concerns the definition of poverty. It is common not only for the makers of policy and others to define poverty according to income, but often they proceed to debate the merits and demerits of different income levels below which people live in poverty and above which they do not. The set line, of course, is a function of such factors as family size, the cost of living and residence location. The debate on the line of best fit can be a particularly cruel one for those who fall below it. The Special Senate Committee on Poverty (1971) presented some poverty lines for 1969 which set $5,000 as the defining limit of poverty for a family of four. The Committee compared this amount with the figure supplied by Statistics Canada and the Economic Council of Canada for the same year, which was $4,420, and said the discrepancy "should be taken to mean not that the Committee lines are too high but that those of the E.C.C. are too low" (p. 8). Can the poor afford the debate?

Poverty is not deficiency of income alone. Even if we persist in the debate scorned above, perhaps the line which is established can be defined in part as follows. Poverty is not a family of four earning $4,999 in 1970; rather, poverty is the multiple consequences of earning that amount. At or below some dividing line, a family finds it continually impossible to move ahead of financial demands. *All* available funds are absorbed by the routine costs of living. Indeed, the costs of living often require the borrowing of additional capital, and the cost of borrowing in turn further suppresses the family's financial position. Above the dividing line, a family finds it possible — increasingly possible as income exceeds the line — to satisfy financial demands, and often the family is left with a financial surplus. This surplus is of critical importance for it can be used in a number of ways to provide a net improvement in the family's financial position. The surplus may be placed into savings or into other types of investment. It is quite easy to use the surplus as security for borrowing money which in part becomes a further part of the family's surplus, thereby allowing for the possibility of using and re-using income perhaps several times over, while all the time the family's financial position improves. Obviously, as income increases beyond the dividing line of poverty, the family is able to assume much more freedom in the utilization of its economic surplus. The definition of poverty, then, is not suggested to be in terms of the raw dollar amount earned by a family, but in terms of the family's inability to accumulate a dollar surplus. It is the economic surplus which enables flexibility in such things as budget planning.

A great deal of poverty is less a function of income, and more a function of such things as subjective adherence to standards of consumerism which, perhaps even more than the ties of family and work, serve to keep people in their place.

When talking about poverty, to be kept in place is to be kept poor. As has been noted many times, social policy in search of a solution for poverty might concentrate on such things as low-interest consumer loans guaranteed by government in much the same way as certain mortgage loans are guaranteed, and more stringent legal protections for lower-income people, especially in areas such as protection for tenants, consumer legislation, and the provision of easy and cheap (if not free) access to legal remedies.

Macrodynamic: Language and Culture

> Even a great cultural language, even an international language like French, under certain sociological conditions, can wither away to the point where, for certain groups, it no longer expresses the essentials of contemporary civilization. In such a case the culture itself is in mortal danger; for nobody will maintain that a group still has a living culture, in the full sense of the term, when it is forced to use another language in order to express to itself the realities which make up a large part of its daily life (Royal Commission on Bilingualism and Biculturalism, Book I, 1967, p. xxxv).

This section discusses four subjects: the historical and contemporary situation as described by the Royal Commission on Bilingualism and Biculturalism, the "bilingual belt" thesis as developed by Joy, the "priority treatment" thesis as developed by Jones, and a brief statement of a tentative conclusion concerning language, culture and the future of Quebec in Canada.

The Royal Commission on Bilingualism and Biculturalism reviewed the evolution of language rights in Canada beginning as early as 1713 with the Treaty of Utrecht. The commissioners noted that the history of Canada, even prior to confederation, was very much a rivalry between the English and French languages. "Not only the history of Quebec, but the evolution of Canada, has been marked by the meeting of these two linguistic groups" (Book I, 1967, p. 42).

The present legal foundation of language rights in Canada is the British North America Act. Section 133 of the Act reads as follows. "Either the English or the French Language may be used by any Person in the Debates of the Houses of the Parliament of Canada and of the Houses of the Legislature of Quebec; and both those Languages shall be used in the respective Records and Journals of those Houses; and either of those Languages may be used by any Person or in any Pleading or Process in or issuing from any Court of Canada established under this Act, and in or from all or any of the Courts of Quebec. The Acts of the Parliament of Canada and of the Legislature of Quebec shall be printed and published in both those Languages."

Section 133 is the only comment on language rights contained in the British North America Act and, at that, the section is highly circumscribed. It is, however, entrenched in Canadian constitutional law, that is, it has been made extremely difficult to change. When the British North America Act was amended in 1949 to allow Parliament the power to further amend it, Section 133 was specifically excluded. Section 91(1), the enabling legislation passed in Britain, reads that the "amendment from time to time of the Constitution of Canada, except as regards ... the use of the English or the French language" is included as part of the exclusive legislative authority of the Parliament of Canada.

The Royal Commission on Bilingualism and Biculturalism asked the following types of questions of Section 133. Are the language rights it guarantees applicable to administrative law, the many rules and regulations which affect the rights and obligations of all citizens? Are the language rights it guarantees applicable in the lower courts of Canada? Do the prescribed language rights apply to various quasi-judicial bodies such as the National Parole Board or the Unemployment Insurance Commission? What of language requirements concerning the actual administrative conduct of government? The commissioners concluded in 1967 that Section 133

is not intended to secure fully the linguistic rights of the French-speaking or English-speaking minorities in Canada. At best it represents embryonic concepts of cultural equality, and it cannot be expected to provide for the many complex situations that must now be faced [in Canada]. Such language rights as are exercised in Canada are generally based [not on the constitutional or other law of the land but] on custom, practical considerations, political expediency, or result from the exercise of incidental jurisdiction. While we [the commissioners] do not underrate the role of custom or of incidental legislation in fleshing out the existing provisions of the Constitution, we must not forget that these rights are not entrenched and thus can be abrogated at will (Book I, 1967, p. 55).

Following a more detailed analysis of Canadian law and legal practice, the commissioners concluded further that their

brief survey of language rights in Canada reveals the wholly inadequate way in which present laws give effect to the concept of the country as an equal partnership between two linguistic communities. It is certainly true that language rights have been gradually recognized through the years and still continue to expand. But this evolution has been intermittent and has suffered numerous setbacks. There does not exist a fully developed linguistic regime expressing the bicultural character of the country as a whole and based on well defined and fully accepted legal rights (Book I, 1967, p. 69).

The Royal Commission strongly recommended the passage of new legislation to further guarantee language rights. The Official Languages Act was passed by Parliament in 1969. Section 2 of that Act specifies that the "English and French languages are the official languages of Canada for all purposes of the Parliament and Government of Canada, and possess and enjoy equality of status and equal rights and privileges as to their use in all the institutions of the Parliament and Government of Canada." The Official Languages Act carefully acknowledges languages other than those termed "official." "Nothing in this Act shall be construed as derogating from or diminishing in any way any legal or customary right or privilege acquired or enjoyed either before or after the coming into force of this Act with respect to any language that is not an official language" (Section 38). In other words, both the Royal Commission and the Official Languages Act acknowledged the cultural importance of other languages and language groups in Canadian society. Other groups are important by simple virtue of the census. English was given as the mother tongue by 58.5 percent of Canada's population in 1961, while French was given as the mother tongue by 28.1 percent of the population (see Table 8.5 which appears later in this section). The remaining 13.4 percent was distributed among a number of language groups: German (3.1), Ukrainian (2.0), Italian (1.9), Dutch

(.9), Polish (.9), Indian and Eskimo (.9), Scandinavian (.7), Yiddish (.5), with 2.6 percent of the population reporting a mother tongue other than those listed (see CANADA YEAR BOOK 1970-71, p. 240). While the language rights of these various language groups are guaranteed in law, there remain many questions concerning practical matters such as schooling.

One of Canada's social realities, then, is multilingualism. Insofar as it is possible to guarantee multilingual rights legally, legislators at the federal level and in some of the provinces have done so. If we think of Canadian social organization in terms of language, a number of topics of a sociological nature emerge and require further attention. These topics range from patterns of assimilation to futuristic-type questions concerning the potential of a formally bilingual or multilingual state. It seems fair to say that the Royal Commission on Bilingualism and Biculturalism succeeded in directing attention to the inevitable necessity of coping with the implications of bilingualism, if not multilingualism, in Canada.

One of the conclusions noted earlier from the Royal Commission's study is quite direct in its bias. The commissioners' standard was the "concept of . . . an *equal* partnership between two linguistic communities [thereby living up to] . . . the *bicultural* character of the country" (emphases added). That this was a standard for the study can be partly explained by the fact that the standard was contained in the Commission's terms of reference. The government had challenged the Commission to "inquire into and report upon the existing state of bilingualism and biculturalism in Canada and to recommend what steps should be taken to develop the Canadian Confederation on the basis of an equal partnership between the two founding races, taking into account the contribution made by the other ethnic groups to the cultural enrichment of Canada and the measures that should be taken to safeguard that contribution" (PRELIMINARY REPORT, 1965, p. 151).

This raises the question whether Canada in fact is a bilingual state. The logic seems to be that, given Canada as a bilingual state, action must be taken to increase the equality between Anglophone and Francophone Canadians so that, at the very least, the strength of the bilingual state is not diminished. At stake is the French language. Since language is the key element in culture, also at stake is French-Canadian culture.

Inspection alone shows that Canada is a bilingual state, that is, that Canada recognizes and encourages two languages as official languages. Although French and English have been termed "official" languages only since 1969, we have seen that they were explicitly recognized at the time of confederation in 1867. So it is not enough to ask whether Canada is a bilingual state; the significant questions concern the degree to which Canada is increasingly (or decreasingly) a bilingual state, and the degree to which Canadians are increasingly (or decreasingly) bilingual.

This brings us to a book which should be required reading for any person who studies the Royal Commission on Bilingualism and Biculturalism. Joy's LANGUAGES IN CONFLICT: THE CANADIAN EXPERIENCE (1972) was available as early as 1967, although its widespread distribution was limited until it was reprinted in the Carleton Library series. In a preface to the Carleton edition, Vallee acknowledged Joy as the "first to use age-specific data in assessing the rate of French language loss among Canadians of French origin. By so doing he showed that the *actual* rate of assimilation is higher than the *apparent* rate derived from census data which does not take generation into account" (p. xii). In addition to this, Vallee called Joy's work the "classic statement of the Two Unilingualisms divided by the Bilingual Belt" thesis (p. xii). Joy's analysis is based on census data up to and including the year 1961.

Joy concluded that unilingual areas are increasingly developing, and that assimilation to the majority language of an area is rapidly taking place. On the matter of the development of increasingly unilingual areas, Joy examined the data on language spoken for the Canadian population and for the urban areas of the province of Quebec for each of four census years (1931 through 1961, inclusive). The pattern for the Canadian population was exceedingly stable. In 1931 67.5 percent of the population spoke English only; in 1961 it was the same at 67.4 percent. In 1931 17.1 percent of the population spoke French only; there was a slight increase to 19.1 percent by 1961. In 1931 12.7 percent of the population spoke both French and English; there was a slight decrease in the bilingual population by 1961 to 12.2 percent (see p. 13).

Compare these national percentages to those for all adult males in urban Quebec. The pattern is not stable as before but lies in the direction of increasing unilingualism, with the majority language being French. In 1931 19.7 percent spoke English only; there was a decrease by 1961 to 13.0 percent. In 1931 21.1 percent spoke French only; by 1961 this percentage had increased to 33.2. Among adult males in the urban areas of Quebec a majority in each of the four census years up to 1961 was bilingual in both French and English. Whereas the percentage in 1931 was 58.5, it slowly eroded so that by 1961 it was 52.9 percent (see p. 13). Joy concluded from this evidence that "there is no mistaking the trend toward French unilingualism within the Province of Quebec; this is particularly noticeable in the urban areas" (p. 13). Joy also concluded that "language boundaries in Canada are hardening, with the consequent elimination of [linguistic] minorities everywhere except within a relatively narrow bilingual belt" (p. 21). This belt is located for the most part along the St. Lawrence River Valley of Quebec, although it also includes parts of the provinces of Ontario and New Brunswick.

Joy then considered the topic of language assimilation. By assimilation is meant the degree to which the first language learned in childhood corresponds to the majority language of the residence area and differs from the language associated with the ethnic origin of the person. Joy concluded that the "French language has been capable of surviving in those areas in which it is spoken by a majority of the population but that assimilation becomes increasingly severe as the proportion of French-speakers among the total population declines" (p. 33). He argued that "[a]ssimilation proceeds through contact" (p. 34), and that sociological factors are indeed more important in influencing assimilation than is legislation. To illustrate, Joy examined assimilation rates within Ontario and found that, while school laws and other legislation is constant, it is "only in the overwhelmingly-English areas of the province that high assimilation rates can be found" (p. 32). No significant assimilation is apparent in those areas which support French-speaking majorities.

It is interesting to look at the province of Quebec and to ask the fate of the English-speaking minority. It appears that more than three-quarters of the English-speaking Canadians who live in Quebec reside in the city of Montreal. We can ask whether the remaining English-speaking Canadians in Quebec are being assimilated to the French language. Apparently not. Joy's analysis suggested that the "gradual disappearance of Quebec's [English] minority is attributable to an actual departure of those who prefer to speak English. This is quite different to what has happened in all the other provinces (except Northern New Brunswick), where the fading-away of the French-speaking minorities is due to assimilation, rather than to any outward migration of those of French origin" (p. 97).

"The forecast . . . emerges of a Canada in which the relative strengths of the two major language groups may remain similar to those found today but within which there will be a much more pronounced linguistic segregation: French within Quebec and English elsewhere" (p. 135). Patterns of assimilation attest to this; so

TABLE 8.5

Percentages of Population Claiming Selected Spoken Languages as Mother Tongue for Provinces, Territories and Canada, 1961 and 1971

		English	French	Other	Total
Newfoundland	1961	98.6	.7	.7	100.0
	1971	98.5	.7	.8	100.0
Prince Edward Island	1961	91.3	7.6	1.1	100.0
	1971	92.4	6.6	1.1	100.1
Nova Scotia	1961	92.3	5.4	2.3	100.0
	1971	93.0	5.0	2.0	100.0
New Brunswick	1961	63.3	35.2	1.5	100.0
	1971	64.7	34.0	1.3	100.0
Quebec	1961	13.3	81.2	5.6	100.1
	1971	13.1	80.7	6.2	100.0
Ontario	1961	77.5	6.8	15.7	100.0
	1971	77.5	6.3	16.2	100.0
Manitoba	1961	63.4	6.6	30.0	100.0
	1971	67.1	6.1	26.8	100.0
Saskatchewan	1961	69.0	3.9	27.1	100.0
	1971	74.1	3.4	22.5	100.0
Alberta	1961	72.2	3.2	24.6	100.0
	1971	77.6	2.9	19.5	100.0
British Columbia	1961	80.9	1.6	17.5	100.0
	1971	82.7	1.7	15.5	99.9
Yukon Territory	1961	74.3	3.0	22.7	100.0
	1971	83.5	2.4	14.1	100.0
Northwest Territories	1961	35.6	4.3	60.1	100.0
	1971	46.9	3.3	49.8	100.0
Canada	1961	58.5	28.1	13.5	100.1
	1971	60.2	26.9	13.0	100.1

Source: STATISTICS CANADA DAILY, April 25, 1972.

do patterns of migration. "[T]he disappearance of linguistic minorities is a natural phenomenon," accorded Joy, and the public should be prepared for such developments since the "psychological shock when the minorities do disappear could be far more harmful to Canadian unity than will be the actual disappearance" (p. 136).

Joy later noted that up to the fall of 1971, "all the evidence still appears to indicate that Quebec Province is becoming increasingly French-speaking while the [French-speaking] minorities elsewhere are fading away at a rate that varies with their distance from Quebec. If anything, the trends noted in 1967 are accelerating, as the population of Quebec is purged of its non-French elements by outward migration that now considerably exceeds immigration" (p. 137). Analysis of the 1971 census will indicate the actual continuing trends in these respects.

Table 8.5 reports advance information from the 1971 census. It turns out that Quebec is not increasingly Francophone, there having been a slight drop in the proportion of the provincial population claiming French as both their language of speech and their mother tongue, the decrease being from 81.2 percent in 1961 to 80.7 percent in 1971. The proportion of the population claiming to speak a mother-tongue language other than French or English increased over the ten-year period, from 5.6 percent to 6.2 percent, suggesting immigration as the main reason for the slight decline in the proportionate number of Francophones in Quebec. This is speculation for the moment; detailed analysis must await the publication of the complete census data.

Has there been a decline in the size of Francophone minorities in other provinces of Canada? The general answer is in the affirmative, with British Columbia and Newfoundland being the only exceptions in that little or no change in the percentages between 1961 and 1971 appear for these provinces. Finally, has there been a decline in the size of language minorities other than the Anglophone and Francophone language groups? Except for the provinces of Newfoundland, Quebec and Ontario, the answer is again in the affirmative; the tendency is a significant one across the Prairie provinces, especially in Saskatchewan and Alberta, but also in British Columbia, the Yukon and Northwest Territories.

Many things point to the goal of government policy being to strengthen bilingualism in Canada. The only vehicle for strengthening bilingualism, at least from the perspective of government, is legislation, and the principle which is employed when legislating is *le principe de l'égalité*, or, in the case of language in Canada, equal partnership between the two founding races. And so it is that many of the recommendations of the Royal Commission on Bilingualism and Biculturalism take the form of proposals which seek to equalize *access* to participation across the different language groups. The commissioners, as they began their study in the mid-1960's, were firm in this regard for they believed that the "notion of equal partnership connotes a vast enlargement of the opportunities for Francophones in both private and public sectors of the economy. The Commission will give close attention to measures designed to create conditions of work which will equalize the chances and improve the career preparation of those whose first language is French" (Book I, 1967, p. xliv). It remained for Joy to question even legislation for, on the basis of the facts available to the historical demographer and notwithstanding the overtures of law, the French language will gradually replace English as the language of work in Quebec. If anything, the Royal Commission's effect might be to accelerate the process of change.

Equal treatment is not supported by all. For example, Jones (1972) argued

168

that the French language, not being on equal footing with English to begin with, must be treated unequally, indeed preferentially, if it is to survive. "Equality is the magic word and the solution to the national problem. Translated into the Canadian context, it means increased rights for French-speaking citizens in the English provinces and a more significant role for French Canadians at Ottawa. . . . [But] this kind of equality is insufficient to guarantee at least a chance to survive" (pp. xii-xiii).

Jones asserted that the "French language and culture actually need a priority treatment. The critic will immediately cry 'favoritism' and, superficially, he is quite right. This does *appear* to be a demand for more than equality. Still, such 'favoritism', if that is what some want to call it, is necessary to ensure that a Pee-Wee hockey team, obliged to play against one of the N.H.L. teams, can at least entertain the hope of scoring a few goals! Greater bilingualism outside Quebec . . . must be accompanied by a very definite priority treatment within Quebec. Such priority treatment may, in fact, be called 'unilingualism' " (p. xiii).

There may be something to this thesis, especially given the data for Quebec as presented in Table 8.5. Joy's observation concerning increasing unilingualism within the province of Quebec is accented all the more by the planned unilingualism argument contributed by Jones. Notwithstanding the extensive contributions of the Royal Commission on Bilingualism and Biculturalism, it is obvious that the debate has not ended, just as the actual distribution of language skills will continue to reflect the weight of political decisions in combination with the findings of the social demographer.

It would seem to be the case that English and French will persist as the majority languages in Canada and that, through such adjustments as intergenerational assimilation, the languages of Canada other than the two majority languages will slowly but steadily decline in terms of the numbers of persons using them. As these broad shifts take place, there will be increased pressure on the non-English immigrant to learn swiftly one or the other of the majority languages. Meanwhile, given the importance of language in culture, and especially given the importance of language maintenance for culture maintenance, the dynamic of language will continue to affect Canadian social organization. The specific effects of language largely depend upon the course of events in Quebec. Speculation suggests that there are two distinct possibilities. If the proportion of people who speak French in Quebec declines in the years to come, then there is sure to be a heightened sense of culture threat in that province, even to the degree that the level of social disruption in recent years will be greatly surpassed. On the other hand, if the proportion of people who speak French in Quebec should increase, even significantly, then cultural homogeneity at least in terms of language will be realized, although it may come at the expense of acute conflicts with other aspects of provincial or national society. Although the actual outcome cannot be prejudged, if only because the data are lacking, the model of the future for Quebec will be shaped by such factors as provincial economic growth, the birth rate among Francophone Quebecois, the extent of assimilation to the French language experienced by residents of Quebec whose mother tongue is other than French, the retention of the French language by residents of Quebec whose mother tongue is French, the success experienced by Quebec in bringing French-speaking immigrants to the province, and the relative isolation of Quebec from the other social regions of Canada.

Macrodynamics of Social Participation

Social groups . . . require organization, psychological unity, and a division of labor, however simple, whereby group members cooperate toward group goals. . . . An aggregate is thus not a genuine social group because it involves only the most rudimentary social relations and lacks most of the features of social groups (Lindesmith and Strauss, 1968, p. 62).

When we refer to Canada as a total society, we mean that the individual members of that society live and work as aggregates of people, and that most members of each aggregate share certain characteristic experiences. The majority of people are members of many different aggregates. For example, a man may be pegged as a blue-collar worker through his occupational aggregate (the status of those in his occupation) and yet be accepted as a middle-class citizen because of his residential aggregate (the status of those in his neighbourhood), or because he married a woman of middle-class background (the status of his in-laws and his wife's friends).

Generally, however, the macrodynamics of social participation pertain to the characteristic experiences of aggregates of persons rather than to the behaviours of the persons themselves. We are only interested in individual behaviour, to the extent that it is similar across a large number of persons who share common life circumstances. This chapter and Chapter 7 before it reviewed many such circumstances: the degree to which social regions within Canadian society define characteristic aggregates of people, and the characteristic experiences of such groupings of people as rural or urban dwellers, poor or affluent persons and Francophone or Anglophone Canadians.

At the level of macrodynamics, three topics which relate to social participation are discussed in this section: participation in the labour force, participation in associations and participation in the political process. Each of the discussions is cursory at best.

Let us first consider participation in the labour force. While there was a time when most able-bodied persons either sold or volunteered their labour as a requirement of pre-industrial society, participation in the labour force has generally been declining, although marked fluctuations are found by sex and certain age groups. The potential labour force is a "flexible resource whose growth tends to parallel that of the total population while responding to changes in technology and in levels of economic activity and opportunity" (Kalbach and McVey, 1971, p. 216). Table 8.6 indicates that the percentage of males in the labour force (although not their absolute numbers) steadily declined between 1911 and 1961, while the percentage of females (and their absolute numbers) steadily increased between the same years. That the total participation rate increased slightly between 1951 and 1961 is an indication that the absolute number of participating females increased by a marked degree. Kalbach and McVey indicated that these trends seem to have continued throughout the 1960's, especially with respect to part-time female workers (see p. 338).

TABLE 8.6

Canadian Labour Force Participation Rates by Sex, 1911 to 1961

	Males	Females	Total
1911	90.6	18.6	57.4
1921	89.8	19.9	56.2
1931	87.2	21.8	55.9
1941	85.6	22.9	55.2
1951	84.4	24.4	54.5
1961	81.1	29.3	55.3

Source: Kalbach and McVey, 1971, p.218. The participation rate is the percent of the population 14 years of age and above in the labour force.

When labour force participation is examined for males and females separately, the implication is that each sex group constitutes an aggregate, and that membership in one or the other aggregate implies a characteristic type of participation. The labour force participation rates for males and females are dramatically different. Chart 8.7 documents this difference and also makes it clear that, while females participate most when they are aged in their mid-20's, the greatest absolute increase in female participation between 1941 and 1961 occurred for females in mid-life, between 35 and 65 years.

Kalbach and McVey summarized other factors which influence female participation in the labour force. Urban females participate more than rural females (see p. 225). Single, divorced and widowed females participate more than married females (see p. 228). University-trained females participate more than females with secondary schooling; females with secondary schooling participate more than females with elementary schooling (see p. 230). Married women participate more when there are no children at home, but the higher the level of education attained by women the greater their participation in the labour force, notwithstanding the presence or age of children (see p. 231). "The evidence strongly supports an economic explanation for working wives, since they are more likely to choose housekeeping and child care as their husband's earnings reach a level high enough to provide for their family needs without the additional increment of income provided by the working wife" (Kalbach and McVey, 1971, p. 230).

Additional information on female participation in the labour force is available from a number of federal government publications, including Ostry, THE FEMALE WORKER IN CANADA (1968) and the Report of the Royal Commission on THE STATUS OF WOMEN IN CANADA (1970). The Royal Commission's report brought the data up to date by noting that 29.6 percent of all married women in Canada (who constituted 54.6 percent of the female labour force) were in the labour force in 1968 (see p. 56). That participation rate is higher than it was for *all* females in Canada in 1961, a fact which suggests that women are taking their rightful place in the economic marketplace.

One final note of interest with respect to female participation in the labour force. The unemployment rate pertains to those who cannot find employment and who wish it. It seems that in Canada the unemployment rate for women has tended to be lower than the unemployment rate for men. THE STATUS OF WOMEN IN CANADA (1970) reported that the rates were 3.6 percent for women and 8.1 percent for men in 1961, while in 1967 these rates were 3.0 and 4.6, respectively (see p. 55). The unemployment rate for women in the United States has tended to be higher than the unemployment rate for men (see p. 55). "It is not clear why women's unemployment rates have been lower than men's in Canada and not in the United States. Canada seems to be unlike a number of other countries in this respect. It may be that married women in Canada have been less committed to working than women in some other countries. If this has been the reason, the gap between men's and women's rates may well narrow in the future since there is some indication that married women are becoming increasingly attached to the labour force" (p. 56).

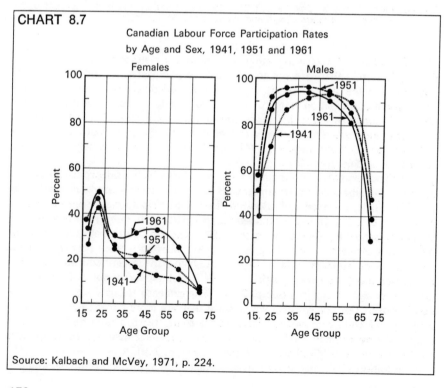

CHART 8.7

Canadian Labour Force Participation Rates
by Age and Sex, 1941, 1951 and 1961

Source: Kalbach and McVey, 1971, p. 224.

The discussion now turns to social participation in associations. The leading question is the degree to which Canadians are participants in voluntary associations, and not who participates for what reasons in which associations. Voluntary associations are not work organizations. Rather, they are associations that range from wine-tasting clubs to labour unions, youth organizations and business groups such as a Chamber of Commerce or the Kinsmen.

It has long been argued that Americans are joiners of voluntary associations. Such a claim does not mean that everybody belongs; it means that relative to other countries Americans belong more often than do the people of other countries. A recent analysis by Curtis (1971) suggested that the "scope and especially the u-niqueness of the American pattern may be somewhat overemphasized" (p. 873). Curtis was able to compare available Canadian data with data from five other countries: The United States, Great Britain, Germany, Italy and Mexico. He claimed with some confidence that "differences which obtain between countries are due to differences in national cultures and social structures and not nonequivalence of research procedures" (p. 873).

Table 8.8 supports two main conclusions. First, that Canada is as much (excluding union memberships) if not more (including union memberships) a nation of joiners than is the United States. Roughly one-half of Canadians and Americans report non-union memberships. In comparison, roughly one-third of the English

TABLE 8.8

Percent of Respondents Reporting One or More Voluntary Association Affiliations by Union Membership and by Sex, Six Nations

	Males		Females		Total	
	%	N	%	N	%	N
Including Unions						
Canada	73	1,388	56	1,379	64	2,767
United States	68	455	47	515	57	970
Great Britain	66	460	30	503	47	963
Germany	66	449	24	506	44	955
Italy	41	471	19	524	29	955
Mexico	43	355	15	652	25	1,007
Excluding Unions						
Canada	51		51		51	
United States	55		46		50	
Great Britain	41		27		33	
Germany	47		22		34	
Italy	36		17		25	
Mexico	21		12		15	

Source: Curtis, 1971, p.874. Consult the original source for information concerning data sources, sampling and questionnaire design.

and Germans report non-union memberships, while one-quarter or less of Italians and Mexicans report such memberships. Among western democracies, then, Canada joins the United States in leading in the proportion of residents who participate in various voluntary associations. Second, that participation is highest in Canada and the United States in large measure because women participate more in these countries than they do, especially, in Germany and Great Britain. Women participate in voluntary associations to an extent not much less than men, even when union membership is included. When union membership is excluded, the participation of women equals the participation of men in Canada (51 percent).

These findings suggest that Canada and the United States exhibit similar trends concerning participation in voluntary associations, although Canadian men and women show more similar patterns of participation than do American men and women. Curtis speculated on reasons at some length. "The comparatively high membership proportions reported for Canada are perhaps to be expected on the basis of other general social, structural, and cultural similarities between the U.S. and Canada. For example, Canada has a very similar, high level of economic development and is most similar with respect to associated processes of urbanization, industrialization, requirements for trained labor, expanded formal education facilities, social mobility opportunities, and expansion of middle-class strata. . . . [W]e might suggest that these processes of urbanization, increased industrialization, and changes in social stratification systems are likely to be highly correlated with differentiation — complexity of social organizational structures in general, and secondary social and economic organizations in particular — and perhaps directly related to the extent of adult affiliation and participation in voluntary organizations. Moreover, Canada is characterized by the following specific aspects of 'democracy' and the 'modern urban way of life,' all of which have been discussed as major impetuses for the proliferation of associations in the U.S.: (1) the change of function in the family, church, and state and the relative loss of control of these major institutions over the person, (2) the democratic and Protestant principle of the freedom of individual choice, (3) the articulation of minority groups, (4) the increased division of labor, and (5) secularization. . . . In short, social life in the U.S. is probably scarcely more [or less] 'modern,' 'urban,' or 'democratic' than in Canada, and perhaps the voluntary association membership findings are a reflection of this similarity. We could also speculate further about the overall national differences in terms of the points just made. While Great Britain and Germany are as urbanized and industrialized as the U.S. and Canada, they are slightly less economically developed, and some researchers have suggested that their political cultures are both less equalitarian and less participatory (lower levels of political participation) than the political cultures in the U.S. and Canada. . . . If such differences hold, they might provide a partial explanation of the lower overall rates of membership . . . in these countries, and this line of reasoning might also be followed in explanation of the still lower extent of association affiliation in Italy and Mexico. However, these arguments represent hunches which go well beyond our data. The precise relationship (if any) between such social and cultural differences, individuals' attitudes toward social participation, and association affiliation remain to be studied in large scale comparative research" (p. 878).

This section concludes with a brief discussion of participation in the political process. It is difficult to reconstruct participation at this level since voting, one likely indicator of participation, is a private affair. In addition, academic interest in voting behaviour usually pertains to the party, candidate or issue supported through the vote. This discussion is limited to voting participation in the political process, and in the degree to which membership in the sex aggregates implies a characteristic type of participation.

Table 8.9 indicates that better than two-thirds of eligible Canadians participated through voting in the 1965 federal election. This table is constructed from data gathered at different points in time. The election was held in November of 1965 while the population data derive from the 1966 census which was completed almost seven months after the election. The population data are therefore not accurate representations of the population as it numbered in November of 1965. Nevertheless, the participation rates reported in Table 8.9 are likely accurate to within one percentage point.

The table indicates that considerable variation in voting participation exists across Canadian regions. Almost 86 percent of the eligible persons in the Atlantic region voted in 1965. This high participation rate compares with a participation of just 64 percent in the province of Quebec. The national participation rate for the 1965 general election was 68.5 percent. It is not easy to develop participation rates for provincial elections. Engelmann and Schwartz (1967) reported that the average turnout of eligible voters in eleven Quebec provincial elections between the years 1923 and 1960 was 76 percent. The average turnout in eleven Ontario provincial elections between 1923 and 1959 was 63 percent, while in twelve provincial elections in British Columbia between 1920 and 1960 the average turnout was 70 percent (see p. 40). It would be frivolous to compare any of these participation rates with those contained in Table 8.9 since there are no bases for comparison.

The Royal Commission on THE STATUS OF WOMEN IN CANADA (1970) noted that in a "study of the 1965 general election [Van Loon, CANADIAN

TABLE 8.9

Voting Participation in the Canadian Federal Election by Region, 1965

	Eligible Population	Popular Vote	Participation Rate
Atlantic	1,023,631	878,123	.8578
Quebec	3,164,038	2,037,312	.6438
Ontario	4,051,603	2,743,783	.6772
Prairie	1,886,198	1,313,192	.6962
British Columbia	1,113,382	725,984	.6520
North	21,350	14,922	.6989
Total	11,260,202	7,713,316	.6850

Sources: Dominion Bureau of Statistics, Catalogue No. 92-610 (March, 1968), and No. 92-611 (January, 1968). Population data for June 1, 1966. Voting data from Beck, 1968, p.397. Voting data for November 8, 1965.

POLITICAL PARTICIPATION, 1968] it was reported that: ' . . . about 3 percent more men than women vote regularly and the difference is constant in both federal and provincial elections. However, when we look at the differences by province, some interesting findings appear. In Quebec and Ontario more men than women vote, but in the Maritimes the position reversed . . . ' " (p. 353).

The Commission noted that an "analysis of voting . . . in Canada shows a very slight difference between women and men. Voting turnout was examined in a recent study of voters in the 1968 federal election [Meisel]. The study included 1,388 men and 1,379 women eligible to vote. Of these, 86.8 percent of the men, or 1,205, said they had voted in that election. Among the women, 84.2 percent, or 1,161, said they had voted. The same degree of similarity emerged when they were asked whether or not they had voted in all federal and all provincial elections for which they had been eligible" (pp. 352-353).

There is a difference, of course, between voting *per se* and higher levels of political participation. Here the amount of participation by women declines. In the extreme, of 264 members in the House of Commons in 1969 there was only one woman. In the same year just four of the 102 members of the Senate were women, while fourteen of the 634 members of provincial legislatures were women (see p. 343).

In conclusion, the three dimensions of social participation outlined above do not exhaust the possible dimensions of participation for various Canadian aggregates of persons. Some aggregates not represented in this chapter seem to have more visible effects for introducing change to Canadian society. Various provincial governments have played such a role. For example, the Quebec government under Bourassa followed earlier provincial initiatives when it vetoed the constitutional charter negotiated at Victoria in 1970. While many Canadians accepted that veto as one of malice, the intent behind it was to win concessions from the federal government in certain areas of social welfare administration. Bourassa's government has since won concessions from Ottawa. It is now possible to view the original veto without malice but with a broader political strategy in mind; support for constitutional revision became a pawn in the larger matter of provincial autonomy in certain areas of administration. The crisis when viewed in the short run becomes a substantial social change when viewed in the long run. The villain becomes the victor. What is more, the victor may be representing, in spirit if not in fact, a circle of potential victors. THE GLOBE AND MAIL made this suggestion in a questioning editorial entitled "The Rise of Premier Power?" "What is different about the present [federal-provincial] conference is that it is possible to see the beginning of solidarity among the provinces, the beginning of distinct provincial policy as opposed to Ottawa's, and that policy being put forth in a credible fashion." That the provincial premiers are starting to be more demanding of Ottawa, especially in areas such as economic policy planning and program co-ordination, can be construed as an extension of the strategies played out for some time by Quebec. It is not that Quebec is the thorn in the side of Canada, but that there is "common sense in the provincial insistence upon consultation and co-ordination, upon the joint discussion of economic priorities and when and how they are to be achieved" (November 17, 1971).

If the argument has merit, provincial governments are major sources of change in the patterns of Canadian social organization. They are aggregates through which persons can participate in the affairs of their society, and through which some persons can participate with considerable impact. There are other aggregates which have significant effects for Canadian society: the Front de Libération du Québec or the National Farmers' Union, for example. However, to say that such aggregates occupy a foremost position in channeling social dynamics is likely deception, for their importance is more a function of special times and circumstances.

References

Beck, J. Murray, PENDULUM OF POWER: CANADA'S FEDERAL ELECTIONS, Scarborough, Ont.: Prentice-Hall of Canada, Ltd., 1968.

Benson, E. J., PROPOSALS FOR TAX REFORM, Ottawa: Queen's Printer, 1969.

Curtis, James, "Voluntary Association Joining: A Cross-National Comparative Note," AMERICAN SOCIOLOGICAL REVIEW, 36 (October, 1971) 872-880.

Durant, Will and Ariel Durant, THE LESSONS OF HISTORY, New York: Simon and Schuster, 1968.

Economic Council of Canada, THE CHALLENGE OF GROWTH AND CHANGE, Ottawa: Queen's Printer, 1968.

Engelmann, Frederick C. and Mildred A. Schwartz, POLITICAL PARTIES AND THE CANADIAN SOCIAL STRUCTURE, Scarborough, Ont.: Prentice-Hall of Canada, Ltd., 1967.

Jones, Richard, COMMUNITY IN CRISIS: FRENCH–CANADIAN NATIONALISM IN PERSPECTIVE, Toronto: McClelland and Stewart Limited, 1972.

Joy, Richard J., LANGUAGES IN CONFLICT: THE CANADIAN EXPERIENCE, Toronto: McClelland and Stewart Limited, 1972.

Kalbach, Warren E. and Wayne W. McVey, THE DEMOGRAPHIC BASES OF CANADIAN SOCIETY, Toronto: McGraw-Hill Company of Canada Limited, 1971.

Lenski, Gerhard E., "American Social Classes: Statistical Strata or Social Groups?" AMERICAN JOURNAL OF SOCIOLOGY, 58 (September, 1952) 139-144.

Lindesmith, Alfred R. and Anselm L. Strauss, SOCIAL PSYCHOLOGY, Third Edition, New York: Holt, Rinehart and Winston, Inc., 1968.

Munro, John, INCOME SECURITY FOR CANADIANS, Ottawa: Queen's Printer, 1970.

Ostry, Sylvia, THE FEMALE WORKER IN CANADA, Ottawa: Dominion Bureau of Statistics, 1968.

Podoluk, Jenny R., INCOMES OF CANADIANS, Ottawa: Dominion Bureau of Statistics, 1968.

Porter, John, THE VERTICAL MOSAIC: AN ANALYSIS OF SOCIAL CLASS AND POWER IN CANADA, Toronto: University of Toronto Press, 1965.

Royal Commission on Bilingualism and Biculturalism, PRELIMINARY REPORT, Ottawa: Queen's Printer, 1965.

Royal Commission on Bilingualism and Biculturalism, THE OFFICIAL LANGUAGES, Book I, Ottawa: Queen's Printer, 1967.

Royal Commission on the Status of Women in Canada, THE STATUS OF WOMEN IN CANADA, Ottawa: Information Canada, 1970.

Seeman, Melvin, "On the Meaning of Alienation," AMERICAN SOCIOLOGICAL REVIEW, 24 (December, 1959) 783-791.

Smith, David C., INCOMES POLICIES: SOME FOREIGN EXPERIENCES AND THEIR RELEVANCE FOR CANADA, Ottawa: Queen's Printer, 1966.

Special Senate Committee on Poverty, POVERTY IN CANADA, Ottawa: Information Canada, 1971.

Warner, W. Lloyd, DEMOCRACY IN JONESVILLE: A STUDY IN QUALITY AND IN-EQUALITY, New York: Harper Torchbooks, 1964.

For Further Reading

Adams, Ian, William Cameron, Brian Hill and Peter Penz, THE REAL POVERTY REPORT, Edmonton: M. G. Hurtig Limited, 1971.

Duke Law Journal, THE LEGAL PROBLEMS OF THE RURAL POOR, Chicago: American Bar Foundation, 1969.

Gordon, Milton M., ASSIMILATION IN AMERICAN LIFE: THE ROLE OF RACE, RELIGION, AND NATIONAL ORIGINS, New York: Oxford University Press, 1964.

Lenski, Gerhard E., POWER AND PRIVILEGE: A THEORY OF SOCIAL STRATIFICATION, New York: McGraw-Hill Book Company, 1966.

Lieberson, Stanley, LANGUAGE AND ETHNIC RELATIONS IN CANADA, New York: John Wiley & Sons, Inc., 1970.

Ostry, Sylvia, PROVINCIAL DIFFERENCES IN LABOUR FORCE PARTICIPATION, Ottawa: Dominion Bureau of Statistics, 1968.

Rosenberg, Morris, "Perceptual Obstacles to Class Consciousness," SOCIAL FORCES, 32 (October, 1953) 22-27.

Royal Commission on Bilingualism and Biculturalism, VOLUNTARY ASSOCIATIONS, Book VI, Ottawa: Queen's Printer, 1970.

Part IV
Social Action

Chapter 9

Social Consciousness and Responsibility

This chapter could very well be subtitled "Take Off Shoes and Pluck Blueberries." Its content is offered as a critical appraisal of professional responsibility, especially with respect to the social science professions. Its content is also a guide for citizen responsibility. The overriding thesis of the chapter is that social consciousness is a necessary prerequisite for both professional and citizen responsibility.

The suggested subtitle indicates that the subjects to be discussed are controversial, sometimes uncharted and usually bound up in endless philosophical debate. The issues are sufficiently complex that one must approach the various subjects as one would cultivate an unploughed field. This approach necessarily implies that we must be content with questions in place of solid answers, and that we must be creative while being critical of the traditional ways of determining social consciousness and responsibility.

The subjects discussed include the sociologist and his values, the development of social policies and programs and their evaluation, and both the study and prospect of the future for Canadian society. There is a concluding section on consciousness and responsibility.

The Sociologist and Values

> But data do not interpret themselves. Quantity is not quality. Knowledge is not wisdom. Nor can we truly see without insight, hear without listening, count without comprehending. The question we have to direct to the social scientists is this: Has your work significantly contributed to the improvement of self-understanding and of human civilization? (Drews and Lipson, 1971, p. 79).

Sociologists and anthropologists over the years have conducted numerous studies which describe social and cultural settings. Description is the most basic method they have employed. Sociologists have prepared descriptive studies of communities, while anthropologists have preoccupied themselves with descriptions of primitive cultures. Noteworthy contributions include the Lynds' studies MIDDLETOWN (1929) and MIDDLETOWN IN TRANSITION (1937), Malinowski's CRIME AND CUSTOM IN SAVAGE SOCIETY (1959; first published in 1926), and Warner's A BLACK CIVILIZATION (1964; first published 1937).

In part because of this traditional concern, it is widely held that social scientists are victims of their own enculturation experiences, and that the best and perhaps only medicine is the intellectual one whereby personal and cultural value-biases are made explicit and held in open respect, thereby decreasing the possibility that social observations and descriptions are influenced in some unwitting fashion by personal and cultural standpoints. The key word is "unwitting," for to commit error without knowledge of it is taken by many to be the most unforgivable error in observation. At least there is more sympathy for those who commit error while being aware of both the nature and extent of that error. To unwittingly accept value-biases and to have one's analysis significantly affected by such unknown-to-the-observer influences seems to be the cardinal sin of the intellect.

The sociologist must come to confront and to challenge those value-biases which may, or indeed do influence studies and comments concerning Canadian society. There are a number of them which can be classified into two broad categories. There are those value-biases which derive in the first instance from the cultural experience, from the fact of persons being socialized within a given setting which itself encompasses certain value-biases. There are also those which are learned through professional socialization.

In the broadest sense, we learn the values of our culture. The young person comes into contact with institutions such as the family and kinship organization, the church and school; in each case of contact the value-biases which are embodied by institutions may become value-biases learned and accepted by the individual. Contact with institutions is extensive in that persons are subject to a great many

182

and varied number of institutional influences which embody values of primary importance in the given culture. After all, these influences are representative of those things which have been expressed and legitimated in the culture in the past. In this respect, institutions embody traditional orientations to objects and attitudes in the culture. The contact with institutions is also intensive in that persons often find themselves integrated so deeply within some institutional order that emotional commitment is demanded of them.

The institutions, during the process of socialization, communicate value-biases to persons, sometimes directly but often covertly. The biases are usually premised upon some value commitment, where "value" refers to those matters which are given such importance that they come to significantly affect the things done or aspired to be done in culture and society.

On the other hand, some value-biases are learned through professional social-ization. These biases can be just as forceful and problematic as those just discussed. More often than not, they are extensions of cultural values, their difference being their incorporation within professionalized standards for defining specific problems. For example, scepticism may be an important value for a culture-at-large, but scepticism receives its greatest accent within the professionalized orientations of the sciences.

The value-biases learned in professional socialization are often most obvious since, being a function of specific disciplines or groups of disciplines, they are more visible to critical outsiders, even while being less visible to those on the inside. Visibility depends so much upon contrast. Thus, as such things as interdisciplinary contact and wider experience increase, it is likely that persons become more aware of the biases which are embedded in their own professional orientation.

Again, the argument is that some biases are learned through professional socialization, and that such biases in the main are reflections of those matters within the professional group and, more generally, in the culture which are given such importance that they come to affect the things done or aspired to be done in the profession. For purposes of illustration, let us note several of the value-biases — biases premised upon value commitments — which seem to characterize the discipline of sociology in Canada.

One example comes from a number of subject-biases which were most evident in sociology during the 1950's and 1960's, biases which are still to some degree with us. Rural sociology was of prime importance at one time in both Canada and the United States. This subject's popularity is not surprising, given the once prevailing importance of agrarian activities. Likewise, it is not surprising that, as urbanization became a process to be reckoned with, the bias of sociology shifted to a concentration upon the processes and problems of cities.

There is some merit in the argument that sociology's shift in orientation (rural to urban) was too swift and too complete. While three in four people in Canada, roughly speaking, reside in urban areas, there remains the fourth person and the relative loss of professional interest in the study of *ruralization*. (Rogers (1960) used the word "rurbanization" to indicate the "exchanging and merging of rural and urban social values" (p. 7). While it is true that ruralization, urbanization and rurbanization are interrelated social processes, they are also in some measure distinct processes. Ruralization and urbanization occur in the contexts of different social space, while rurbanization suggests sociocultural interchange in social space.) For present purposes ruralization is a choice use of terms, for processes of change are always with us, where change implies nothing more complicated than necessary adaptation to changing conditions. Some would argue that to use the word "ruralization" is a contradiction in terms, given such facts as the decline of the rural population. After all, why talk about ruralization when everyone knows, they would say, that rural areas are on the decline. A reply would be that one reason behind sociology's (and perhaps society's) disinterest in the strengths and problems of rural areas may well be sociology's (and society's) decidedly urban bias. The media reinforce the subject-biases of professionals and other people. We must argue here that there is little meaningful relationship between population decline and ruralization, and to pretend that such a relationship exists is to confuse the proper pursuit of the social science community. A similar argument can be waged concerning a number of other topics: female (as compared with male) social participation, conformity (as compared with deviance), the social organization of affluent (as compared with lower socio-economic) classes of persons, and so forth.

A second example is the professional value-biases learned by sociologists in Canada, especially English-Canadian sociologists. In a keynote address to the Canadian Sociology and Anthropology Association in 1970, Davis put the problem as follows. "Generally speaking, anglophone social scientists in Canadian universities have presented an abstract, bland, fragmental and static picture of Canadian society. They see the world through a middle-class lens. They underestimate conflict. They do not see the whole picture. They abstract their variables from time and place — hence the images they present are largely timeless and placeless. Above all, they have little to say to ordinary people, even about limited and local problems. For the most part, anglophone sociologists appear to be talking to each other about esoteric topics. . . . [M]ost sociologists are as culture-bound and class-bound as everyone else" (Davis, 1970b, p. 32). These allegations are sweeping, but they should not be dismissed on that score since they may be partially or even significantly correct. Davis was not wanting to imply that the work of English-Canadian sociologists is of no consequence, but simply that intellectual effort often needs to be focused in other directions as well, including the direction of more critically appraising the influence of value-biases when doing sociology.

Value-biases are learned during professional socialization in two central ways: during formal education, and in the exercise of professional responsibility. Professionals, whether they are medical doctors or architects or sociologists, are groomed during many years of university training. During that time they are indoctrinated with a mass of material which seeks, in the abstract, to transform a heterogeneous group of new recruits into a homogeneous group of budding professionals who share a certain core of skills as well as similar value orientations and commitments. Skills, orientations and commitments are strengthened by the direction and control of professional organizations after the phase of formal training has been completed. While significant value cleavages often develop within professional groups, it is rather homogeneity of viewpoint that characterizes professional organizations.

Let us turn to an example of a rare critical commentary by a social scientist. In a colloquium presentation at The University of Alberta in 1970, Seeley proved himself as a critic of his own earlier contributions. He was concerned with outlining reasons for his belief that many things he once accepted must now be questioned. In most instances, Seeley's object of criticism was a book he co-authored, CREST-WOOD HEIGHTS: A STUDY OF THE CULTURE OF SUBURBAN LIFE (1956).

"There is a sense," said Seeley, "in which everything or almost everything I

have done, said and written since CRESTWOOD HEIGHTS is a response to CREST-
WOOD HEIGHTS — to the total experience, to the report, to reflection on both, to
reflection on the reflection." He suggested that it was not easy to rebuild the
assumptions and beliefs associated with the original enterprise. "Many or most of
these [assumptions and beliefs] I now doubt or disbelieve, and yet, looking back, I
not only do not think we were naive for our day, but suppose that if anything, we
were in advance of it."

Seeley once believed that there was time enough for tackling pressing problems, and that interests would be served best by "letting social scientists severally
choose the problem or problems they wanted to 'work' on, guided by their assumed
capacities and perceived intellectual interests and varying senses of what was or
wasn't theoretically and practically important." Seeley has come to wonder about
time, whether there is time to "stave off a network of connected catastrophes," or
whether there is time to "build a discipline that can either stay ahead of events or
perhaps cohere at all." Furthermore, the "luxury of letting each social scientist
study whatever strikes his fancy . . . is something we can no longer afford."

Seeley once believed that the "system-as-a-whole was sufficiently good (or so
little in need of radical question) that enterprises that succeeded in permitting
institutions to function 'better' were either themselves good or harmless, and perhaps sufficient to justify their social costs." After several decades of experience, "I
think there are now acute questions for anyone operating — even, or especially if
successful — to aid the institutions to function better. . . . The critical question . . . is whether any and every institutional improvement does not go to shore
up a system that is in one or more respects fatally destructive or more destructive
than it need be to human nature or even to itself; and, if the answer to this is
'no' . . . which ones are exempt?"

Seeley once believed that the discovery of social-scientific knowledge through
the development of social-scientific theory and research would "inure to the general
good." Again, experience has altered his view. "I have come to believe that the
more we know and report about most of the concrete social situations available to
us for study . . . and the more precise and refined our instruments of uncovering
and discovering, and the more coherent and powerful and general our theory, if
any, the more does the benefit inure, not to the general good, but to those occupy-
ing positions at the upper tail of the distribution curve on all goods in distributions
— and that indeed the general effect is that we become part of the power-structures
[sic] early-warning or advance-intelligence system, or that finally, having learned all
they can from us, they develop an 'independent research capability' to study
everything we studied, including us studying it."

Seeley once believed that heightened self-awareness was in the personal or
public interest. "I have come gravely to doubt that heightened self-awareness or
increased knowledge is, in general, or necessarily an intrinsic good," especially in
the sense of information-overload as repression, and in the sense that "new knowledge as it accrues seems to present us with ever-more-dangerous and perhaps in-
soluble problems, before we even have time to solve the old ones, so that unsolved
urgent problems multiply in the culture of discovery."

Seeley has come to question many other assumptions and beliefs. He now
doubts that society "remains largely independent of the fact and manner of studying it." He now doubts that "there was and would be no connection, or no problematic connection . . ., between the problems social scientists studied or tried to

185

study, what they reported, and the reward-structure, internal to and external to, the profession or the consequent social positions in which different social scientists would thus find themselves." He now doubts that the "study of social problems (and even the desire to solve them) or of social misery (even combined with the desire to relieve it) would generally leave the student at least sufficiently free of a vested interest in perpetuation of the problem as to render him at worst harmless, at best, useful." He now doubts that a "certainly possible and probably probable outcome of our [social-scientific] studies might be at best a reduction in the dispersion of various goods (wealths and incomes, material and immaterial)." He now doubts his earlier belief that "science in general — including social science — was benign or beneficent, since in application it seemed to promise universal release from the majority of pre-existent major ills, without necessarily exacting unreasonable prices in new ills or new forms of old ones."

"All of these [and more], in some degree, and some of these in every degree, I now doubt."

Looking back to the discussion of social reality and sociological concepts in Chapter 1, recall the two logical possibilities which can be applied to Seeley's present beliefs and disbeliefs. Things once believed must often be questioned at some later time either because the initial belief was erroneous, or because reality itself has significantly changed in the interim. These two possibilities are difficult to weigh in terms of their relative effects, but it cannot be denied or overemphasized that both are important to some degree, given the forever-changing relationship between reality and concepts of reality. Every person will not be able to agree with Seeley's observations, but everyone should find his comments at least challenging. It may be that Seeley's present convictions are the more accurate ones, his former value-biases being the product of a distorted professional background. On the other hand, perhaps his convictions concerning both past and present are accurate, being nothing more than changed orientations to changing times and conditions. Of course, Seeley is not unlike the rest of us in that his conception of social reality has likely changed along with passing time and circumstance, while he also has become more aware of the value-biases learned through professional training and experience.

A rich overlay of subjective meanings is the context of all social action. It is usually the politician's delicate task to assess the convictions of men and women, to draw from available knowledge, to establish policies and to formulate programs to achieve priorities, all in the name of managing society. Given that a policy is a "set of principles for the guidance of actions, including the act of deciding how to act," and that a program is a "regimen of assorted actions adopted as an instrument of purpose" (Nettler, 1972, p. 5), let us examine social policies and programs in more detail.

Social Policies and Programs

> A ... perplexing failure in Canada ... is the failure to apply more effectively various pieces of the existing and well-established body of ... knowledge that are both available and relevant for policy (McQueen, 1971, p. 27).

We start with the question of how a society can solve its social problems. A tentative answer is that the society establishes social policies which support programs designed to achieve various goals and thus to solve various problems. Toss in some assumptions, work hard, and with a little luck problems may be resolved. Of course, the problems also may be exacerbated or left unaffected.

It is not that easy, even though the above represents the paradigm for action employed by most government and other agencies. It is not that simple for at least the two following reasons. The first is that social problems like crime and delinquency are usually taken as fact rather than as symptom. Thus, the treatment which is prescribed is often related to the behaviour rather than to the cause. In part, this tendency derives from our rationalistic legal and legislative systems which are biased — they must be — in favour of overt conduct. Secondly, our human condition makes us believe that social problems are contemporaneous. We tend to pass over historical roots and cycles. It is too easy to assume — even if in part it is to assume correctly — that the present is a unique situation. However, just as yesterday was shaped in part by persons of that day reacting — sometimes revolting — to an even earlier situation, so today we are shaping the present partly through our reactions to yesterday. Our revisions, too, will be overthrown by our children, if not by our brothers and sisters.

Many of us have come to live with what we believe to be a certainty of knowledge and an immediacy of technological culture, and thus a twenty-first-century capability to solve all problems encountered. It may be difficult for such believers to realize that the finite nature of human life and experience is such as to guarantee that the history of the past and tomorrow's history of the present will show what man's language already shows, that "volution" and "vitalization" become "revolution" and "revitalization" when viewed across time. Alinsky (1972) noted that history "is like a relay race of revolutions; the torch of idealism is carried by one group of revolutionaries until it too becomes an establishment, and then the torch is snatched up and carried on the next leg of the race by a new generation of revolutionaries. The cycle goes on and on, and along the way the values of humanism and social justice the rebels champion take shape and change and are slowly implanted in the minds of all men even as their advocates falter and succumb to the materialistic decadence of the prevailing status quo" (p. 78). The cycle described by Alinsky is moving much faster now than it did in past centuries, even to the degree that revolutions and counterrevolutions are occurring within generations rather than between them. The generation gap, if ever it was real or important, is becoming a fragment of yesteryear.

Social policy in the area of technology seems to respond to a multitude of causes and consequences associated with its expansion. Technology is a catch-all term if ever there was one. The dictionary says that technology is the science of the industrial arts. But there is more to technology than that, for it involves so many different means whereby ends are achieved. Technology is represented by text-books on engineering, physics and chemistry, just as well as it is represented by the computer, cantilever bridges and spacecraft. In the so-called developed countries industrial technology — which in large part means scientific technology — is king. The chief problem encountered when talking of industrial technology is that we may tend to exclude many facets of technology which are every bit as important as industry, for example, the technical means of transportation and communication. No matter how inclusive, technology today is so dominant that we are justified in calling Canadian society a technocracy.

Can there be control over technology? Of course not, for it is outside the jurisdiction of everybody. It moves with the tide of development and change. The most that can be said — and there is no certainty even of this — is that perhaps some aspects of technology can be channeled. In this respect, we are talking of at least two distinct types of subjects: the sequencing and timing of decision making, and the future possibilities for governing the application and use of technology. Outside of vagaries such as these, to think of setting anything but general policy with respect to technology may be wishful fantasy.

Consider the sequencing and timing of decision making. The time a decision is to be made or implemented can be a real question even though the inevitability of making the decision is assumed. For example, Canada intends to bring its northern residents into the twentieth-century communications network by using a satellite to beam telecommunications to remote settlements which are equipped with the appropriate receiver. The political pressure behind such a decision makes the decision inevitable. In ways such as this communications technology continues to expand.

Before Newfoundland entered the Canadian union the land was backward and the people, especially the rural people, were ruled by merchant kings. After confederation, the technologies of building roads, electrifying settlements and expanding communications facilities were more than adequate to cause a revolution of expectations among the people and to create one developmental crisis after another, as seen especially in the massive community resettlement program which began in the early 1950's and continues to this day. Many persons and communities in Newfoundland have experienced a degree of social change in a period of less than twenty years which by rough guess matches the same degree of change spread over hundreds of years in other lands. Problems associated with change "go far beyond finding a house, a job, and possibly a school or church for, in numerous instances, those who move live in a radically different society. They move from a subsistence economy to an industrial market economy. Many are ill-prepared to make the necessary adjustments, particularly adjustments to the economic institutions of mortgages, banks, and credit as well as to the demands of industrial work on a year-round basis" (Iverson and Matthews, 1968, p. 143). The point of this example is that, while such a degree of social change did not have to occur during the past twenty years, for many reasons it did occur and did so in response to the introduction of new technologies. In the perspective of 1949, drastic social and cultural change was sooner or later inevitable in Newfoundland.

Perhaps technology will never cease expanding. There will always be reason to search for new means to achieve ends. The major question of the immediate future concerns the kinds of shift in values which may or must occur in Canadian society to allow technology to be channeled in ways which are consistent with man's desires. There are signs that shifts are occurring. One study of the future, to be discussed shortly, concluded that the "value of quantity is giving way to the value of quality" and the "importance of individuality in the future" appears entrenched (Dyck, 1970). These projections may turn out to be valid for the immediate future, but conclusions such as these point to one of the difficulties encountered when doing futurology, namely, falling victim to an assumption which implies that the social pattern of the future will be homogeneous or uniform.

For those who argue that civilization is on the verge of collapse because of a combination of demographic and ecological factors, what is needed is a new priority of social values within and between societies so that social policy can be framed which might facilitate man's release from the threatening grasp of industrial technology. Social policy may help to channel the present industrial technology into a new and more advanced form which protects rather than exploits man and his environment. Some recent suggestions for policy to fit a redirected postindustrial society include continuing efforts to reduce the rate of population growth and new tax programs which, for example, would penalize industries that deplete nonrenewable resources and favour those that employ people. Another kind of tax

TABLE 9.1

Composition of the Canadian Labour Force by Age and Sex Groups, Selected Years

Age and Sex Group	Percentage of Labour Force in Each Group				
	1950	1955	1960	1965	1970
Males, 14 to 24	16.1	14.3	13.4	14.0	15.0
Males, 25 to 64	58.3	59.7	57.8	54.5	51.0
Females, 14 to 24	8.9	8.5	8.6	9.5	10.7
Females, 25 to 64	12.2	13.7	16.7	19.0	20.9
Males and Females, 65 and over	4.4	3.8	3.6	3.1	2.4
Total Male	78.4	77.4	74.2	70.9	67.9
Total Female	21.6	22.6	25.8	29.1	32.1

Source: Economic Council of Canada, 1971b, p.61.

TABLE 9.2

Growth of the Canadian Labour Force by Age Groups, Selected Years

Age Group	1960	1970 (Thousands)	1980	Percentage Change in Labour Force 1960-70	1970-80
14 to 19	627	861	926	37.3	7.5
20 to 24	777	1,286	1,703	65.5	32.4
25 to 34	1,506	1,825	2,921	21.2	60.1
35 to 44	1,445	1,733	2,094	19.9	20.8
45 to 54	1,152	1,515	1,815	31.5	19.8
55 to 64	674	948	1,220	40.7	28.7
65 and over	230	206	247	−10.4	19.9
Total	6,411	8,374	10,926	30.6	30.5

Source: Economic Council of Canada, 1971b, p.46.

frequently discussed would increase in inverse proportion to the expected life of a product. Thus, an automobile designed and built to last fifteen years or 250,000 miles would be taxed much less, if at all, in comparison to one destined to collapse within five years or before 75,000 miles.

Let us turn to manpower policy as a specific example of social policy. The Economic Council of Canada (1971a) suggested that since 1966 the development of manpower policy has become much more important as a federal policy area. We should note aspects of the Council's appraisal of some of the manpower programs in relation to the policy behind them.

The manpower stage is set by Tables 9.1 and 9.2. Since 1950 males have made up a decreasing proportion of the labour force, while the proportion of females has increased. At the same time, the age of persons in the labour force is projected to increase. Whereas the greatest percentage increase between 1960 and 1970 was for workers aged 20 to 24 years (65.5 percent), between 1970 and 1980 the greatest percentage increase (60.1 percent) is projected for workers aged 25 to 34 years. These facts alone suggest that changes in the labour supply require the establishment of manpower policy. "Canadians face a formidable task of job creation in the decade ahead — proportionately as great as in the 1960's, and even greater in terms of actual numbers of new jobs that need to be opened up" (Economic Council of Canada, 1971b, p. 45).

The Economic Council estimated that 1.4 million new jobs must be created in Canada during the five-year period 1970 to 1975 (see 1971b, p. 50). Some of these jobs are needed to reduce unemployment to an acceptable level. It should be noted that an acceptable level of unemployment is not a finite quantity; chances are that an acceptable level of unemployment for Canada as a whole would not be an acceptable level for certain Canadian regions. Some unemployment data are pro-

TABLE 9.3

Regional Unemployment Rates Expected at Different Levels of the National Unemployment Rate, and Estimated Unemployment Rates for January, 1972

Canada	Atlantic	Quebec	Ontario	Prairie	B.C.
Expected Unemployment Rate in Region (%)					
2.5	4.3	3.8	1.4	2.0	2.3
3.0	5.1	4.4	1.8	2.3	3.0
3.5	5.9	5.0	2.3	2.6	3.6
4.0	6.8	5.6	2.7	2.8	4.2
5.0	8.4	6.8	3.6	3.3	5.5
6.0	10.0	8.0	4.4	3.8	6.8
7.0	11.7	9.1	5.3	4.3	8.0
Estimated Unemployment Rate in Region (%)					
7.7	12.9	9.8	5.8	5.8	8.7

Sources: Expected rates from Denton, 1966, p.6; estimated rates for January, 1972 from THE GLOBE AND MAIL, February 9, 1972.

vided in Table 9.3. This table suggests that there is a remarkable stability and predictability in the pattern of regional unemployment rates for January of 1972, as premised upon Denton's (1966) average 1961 to 1964 relationships.

Denton summarized this problem of disparity by saying that the "achievement of a relatively low rate of unemployment for Canada as a whole would by no means assure similarly low unemployment rates in every section of the country. Moreover, there is evidence to suggest that even if a relatively low national unemployment rate were to be achieved and maintained over a long period of time, this by itself would leave the interregional disparity of income levels essentially intact" (pp. 5-6).

Like many government policies, the broad objectives of manpower policy are growth, equity and stabilization. The Economic Council quoted the Minister of Manpower and Immigration as declaring that the "main objective of the Department [of Manpower and Immigration] is to further the economic growth of Canada by endeavouring to ensure that the supply of manpower matches the demand qualitatively, quantitatively and geographically" (1971a, p. 96; see pp. 87-98).

There are many ways of evaluating programs which are designed to meet manpower policy (see Economic Council of Canada, 1971a, pp. 97-165). Two evaluations are noted here. Tables 9.4 and 9.5 comment on the distributional effects of manpower training programs. For example, a policy goal of increasing equity can be evaluated by an examination of income data. The data suggest that fewer persons earned smaller amounts of income after manpower training than the

TABLE 9.4

Pre-Training and Post-Training Annual Earnings Distributions, 1969

Income Class	Percentage of Trainees in Income Class before Training	Percentage of Trainees in Income Class after Training
Less than $1,000	10.8	7.5
$1,000 to $1,999	17.0	14.0
$2,000 to $2,999	20.6	19.3
$3,000 to $3,999	18.0	18.6
$4,000 to $4,999	12.0	13.7
$5,000 to $5,999	8.7	9.7
$6,000 to $6,999	5.3	6.2
$7,000 to $7,999	3.3	4.4
$8,000 to $8,999	1.5	2.8
$9,000 to $9,999	.9	1.6
$10,000 and over	1.9	2.2

Source: Economic Council of Canada, 1971a, p.116.

TABLE 9.5

Net Dollar Transfers Under the Canada Manpower Training Program, Fiscal Year 1969-1970

Region	Net Fiscal Transfers
Atlantic	$ +22,700,000
Quebec	+ 33,000,000
Ontario	− 38,600,000
Prairie	− 4,100,000
British Columbia	−13,000,000

Source: Economic Council of Canada, 1971a, p.117.

amounts earned prior to training. A second aspect of equity concerns the redistribution of manpower training resources across Canadian regions. The data here suggest that taxpayers in Ontario, the Prairie region and British Columbia pay for manpower programs in Quebec and the Atlantic region.

This brief discussion has been included for the general purpose of introducing policies and programs, and for the specific purpose of stressing the importance of evaluation. There is a great need for evaluational research, not just to find out whether goals are being achieved, but to feed the ongoing debate concerning the setting of meaningful social goals and for revealing the reasons why programs fail or only partially succeed. Many persons have argued that evaluational research should be a central if not the central activity of social scientists. "Where public policy is clear and programs have been invented to fulfill it, the social scientist comes into his best use. His expertise . . . is that of society's accountant. Where the counts are reliable, the accountant may be graduated to the role of societal actuary, calculating the odds on the results of alternative courses of action" (Nettler, 1972, p. 6).

Projections of the Social Future

> Futurology involves clarification of values and goals as well as description of trends, and it includes projections of alternative futures as well as explanations of existing routines of interdependencies. The sociology of the future promotes planned intervention in social processes through the invention, evaluation, and selection of policy alternatives (Huber and Bell, 1971, pp. 293-294).

Just a few years ago the majority of sociologists cried treason to those in their profession who dared to speak of applied sociology. They usually spoke with reason. Many continue to support Nettler's (1970) warning that to call "studies of economies, governments, personalities, and societies 'sciences' is to express either aspiration or arrogance. Individuals and governments that would purchase such 'science' are advised to consume it with caution" (p. vi).

In addition, there are the warnings of Moynihan (1969). "We constantly underestimate difficulties, overpromise results, and avoid any evidence of incompatibility and conflict, thus repeatedly creating the conditions of failure out of a desperate desire for success. More than a weakness, in the conditions of the present time it has the potential of a fatal flaw" (pp. xii-xiii). Moynihan continued, saying that "this danger has been compounded by the increasing introduction into politics and government of ideas originating in the social sciences which promise to bring about social change through the manipulation of what might be termed the hidden processes of society" (p. xiii).

These social scientists are careful with — indeed critical of — social science because they are well acquainted with applied problems. They join others who realize that social science knowledge is limited and sometimes erroneous, and who caution against the often indiscriminate advice which is peddled by sociologists and others who display limited and sometimes badly-biased conceptions of society and of its processes.

Such conservatism must be placed against the potential for a different sort of fatal flaw. While it is sometimes wrong to act, or to act indiscriminately, likewise it is often wrong to fail to act. According to Rosenberg (1968), social problems "suddenly become big and real for no other reason than that we have acted when it would have been advisable not to act" (p. vii). He concluded that "[w]hen to do something and when not to are the major questions of our time" (p. viii).

The real fatal flaw is not too far off, according to many experts. Its importance is such that it has become increasingly more difficult to remain calm and to simply observe. Given the potential for bypassing tolerable limits of growth, the comfort of armchair philosophizing may soon become a luxury of the past. For

194

example, the sober end to civilization as we know it has been concluded by the Meadows team of researchers at the Massachusetts Institute of Technology (1972). "If the present growth trends in world population, industrialization, pollution, food production, and resource depletion continue unchanged, the limits to growth on this planet will be reached sometime within the next one hundred years. The most probable result will be a rather sudden and uncontrollable decline in both population and industrial capacity" (p. 23).

The Meadows research, published for laymen in THE LIMITS TO GROWTH (1972), has been described as a "remarkably successful venture in the mass marketing of neo-Malthusian economics" (Gillette, 1972, p. 1092). "Never mind that hardly a reputable economist can be found who thinks these [the Meadows] projections amount to more than a fascinating exercise in model-making. Never mind that not a shred of this has yet been exposed to critical review in a scientific journal. There's not enough time to fiddle with stodgy publications and their interminable lead times. And anyway the economists are only grimacing from sour grapes, what with the very foundation of their profession — the assumption of inevitable growth — threatened by a band of computer-wielding upstarts" (p. 1088).

Works such as THE LIMITS TO GROWTH invite criticism, no doubt! Some of Gilette's comments reflect a certain defensiveness in science, but other criticisms seem well-founded in the assumptions and procedures of the investigation. Abelson (1972) noted that behaviour and technology both will change, and thus through tomorrow's change catastrophe *may* be averted. In addition, Abelson and others have argued that it is oversimplification to examine variables such as population on a global scale, since there are so many significant variations by state and region. We must judge for ourselves the validity of the basic study and of criticisms directed toward it. We must judge whether the study and/or its criticisms are the product of, or can be placed in the service of ideology (see Gillette, 1972, p. 1091). In the final analysis, however, even well-founded scientific criticism will be laid bare by disparities ongoing in the world. As Abelson noted, "although Meadows predicts hell in 50 years, hell is already present on Earth in places such as Calcutta" (p. 1197).

We are trying to study the future more often. It is perhaps an indication of our anticipation of the changing foundations of society. Things, as they say, are likely to be different a few years from now, just as present-day industrial society is different from some earlier form such as feudal society. It would be wise for us to anticipate that the differences between today and the tomorrow of a few decades from now will be just as dramatic as are the now-known differences between feudal and industrial society.

One project to ascertain the social future was recently undertaken by the Alberta Human Resources Research Council and the Commission on Educational Planning (Dyck, 1970). The study was premised upon expert panel opinion, a doubtful technique for studying the present, but likely as good as any technique for tackling the future. Some selected panel opinions follow.

In terms of social divisions in Canadian society, the study concluded that during the 1970's and 1980's "each of the current major divisions in Canadian society will grow wider. Opposing groups — the English and French, East and West, rich and poor, Red and White peoples, young and old, political extremist and moderate, and labour and management — will draw further apart. Although the widening of these divisions will not likely cause a demise of the Canadian nation during the next 35 years, the extent of Canadian unity and well-being depend largely on how effectively and how quickly these divisions can be arbitrated and narrowed. . . . It is along the cultural, regional, economic (income) and color lines that the most serious widening of divisions will take place in the future. In many respects, the seriousness of these divisions results from the fact that they reinforce each other. The rich-poor division is reinforced by the Red-White and Anglo-French division. To counter reinforcing cleavages with 'criss-crossing' solidarities is, perhaps, this nation's highest priority" (p. 15).

Concerning value change and ideology in Canada, a "complete shift in our value system and ideological orientation may occur in the very near future. Over the next 35 years, we will begin to notice a sharp upgrading in values pertaining to personal well-being, i.e., personal liberty and freedom, individuality and self-respect, health care, etc. Those values pertaining to the social well-being of the individual, i.e., social consciousness, welfare and humanitarianism, civil rights and legal equality, aesthetic and environmental appreciation, and a greater access to knowledge, will also be sharply upgraded. Values pertaining to personal material welfare, privacy, economic security and national prosperity will also be upgraded, although somewhat less sharply. . . . Values related to nationalism, cultural pride and cultural identity will rise slightly only to diminish again after the 1980's. Values related to patriotism, capitalism and notions of private ownership will decrease considerably. In essence, what we can probably anticipate by the turn of the century is a government that is extremely devoted to the needs of the individual within that individual's social context. Such a transition will not come easily to the members of present-day society" (p. 31).

Finally, the report included among its many projections a statement on leisure and recreation. "Two broad alternative concepts of leisure emerge in this forecasting exercise. In one view, the present work-leisure dichotomy will be maintained; in the second, this distinction will lose most of its significance. The first view anticipates that no foreseeable change in economic development will permit the restructuring of job tasks or work situations sufficiently to allow a change in the differentiation between work and leisure. It also assumes that the present rate of economic growth and technological progress is not sufficient to permit any radical reduction of the labour force before the year 2000. . . . The second view postulates considerable economic development and technological innovation; enough, in fact, to create a drastic reduction in the size of the labour force. This reduction will produce concomitant changes in the amount and distribution of leisure and work time" (p. 101).

In terms of the amount of time devoted to the selling of one's own labour, the study projected that work will increasingly take less time, that the duration of vacations will increase, that persons will enter the labour market at a later age and leave it at an earlier age, and that both leisure time and involuntary unemployment time will increase. The study anticipated differences across occupational groups, for example, the changes outlined will affect skilled and unskilled labour groups more dramatically than professional, managerial and white collar labour groups. In terms of unemployment, the study estimated that the rate of unemployment will be 9.2 percent in 1975, 10.0 percent in 1980, 18.4 percent in 1990 and 32.7 percent in 2005 (see pp. 102-103).

These unemployment estimates can be interpreted in the following way. We can expect the rate of unemployment to increase in the decades ahead because patterns of work participation will significantly change. Work participation patterns will change because of changes in the productive foundations of society. The rate of unemployment will increase as these productive foundations change, not because greater unemployment is inevitable, but because society, for a long time to come, will be insufficiently equipped to handle the massive task of worker retraining and reassignment. It is possible, however, that even with efficient retraining and reassignment programs there will still be an increase in the unemployment rate.

An increase in the rate to the extent that one in three or four members of the labour force are out of work will not necessarily mean that times are harder, as they say. Other value shifts which may occur will have their effects also. It is quite possible, for instance, that a broadened concept of the welfare state will emerge and be accepted. If political values become more socialistic, it is likely that valued goods will be distributed somewhat more closely toward the mean, that is, there will be greater homogeneity of such things as income within the population, or there will be more income equality.

All of these possible shifts are logically tied to the transition of the industrial state. Industrialization will likely persist, but greater stress upon such things as the quality of the environment and equality of opportunity suggest the possibility that the distribution of industrial versus postindustrial functions will be significantly altered. Industrial functions — most importantly the tasks of manufacturing — will be relegated to what we call hinterland areas. These areas more often will be the equivalent of the sovereign state of today. States as such will likely decline in number through political and economic amalgamations, both friendly and forced. Postindustrial functions — those social tasks associated with human welfare — will come to consume more and more of the time and other resources of politicians and laymen alike.

The rationale for at least some of these developments can be found in the writings of those who view capitalism in terms of a metropolis-hinterland structure. We have already seen that Davis (1971; see also 1970a) argued this viewpoint with respect to Canadian society. A well-known statement with respect to Latin America is Frank's CAPITALISM AND UNDERDEVELOPMENT IN LATIN AMERICA (1969; first published 1967). Frank emphasized the need to "encompass the structure and development of the capitalist system on an integrated world scale and to explain its contradictory development which generates at once economic development and underdevelopment on international, national, local, and sectoral levels" (p. xv). The implication, of course, is that the hinterland will increasingly assume the functions of the industrial state, while the metropolis will increasingly centre its activities around postindustrial concerns associated with managing human rather than technical resources.

As we sit in our finite environments, we cannot hope to see the full significance for the future of present-day trends and observations. Even some knowledge of history may not make us any more aware of future possibilities. Political leaders are usually accountable for coping with the immediate pressures of the present and for finding rationalizations of yesterday's actions. The politicians of tomorrow may, in addition, be responsible for defining their tomorrows. As the comedian Dick Gregory has said, if man could only get a little older a little later, and a little wiser a little younger! These words may contain a forecast in their own right, for shifts in values may soon allow man to comprehend future possibilities and thereby, simply through comprehension, to deal more adequately with the social future.

Canada as a postindustrial society is difficult to comprehend at this point in time because of regional and other disparities in development, because the rate of social change is so rapid, because that rate is accelerating and because many of our own actions themselves contribute to the transition of the industrial state. The onset of postindustrialism can follow pre-industrialism by matters of decades and generations, not centuries. The complete turnover of knowledge in many disciplines occurs every twenty to thirty years, and that period too is decreasing. Automation and other factors of technology continually redefine the labour force. Our very concern for these and other problems may be of the greatest consequence in terms of drawing us more quickly to the achievement of the status of a postindustrial society.

It seems necessary, in conclusion, to reiterate a caution concerning any enterprise which aims to project the social future. There are two essential aspects to this caution: the one which says that to use past experience to predict future structures and processes is a dubious activity; and the other which says why it is a dubious activity — because the emergence of new conditions in the future may make past experience obsolete. This caution is implied by Abelson when he suggested that data from the past "are far more relevant to the past than to the future" (1972, p. 1197).

Consciousness and Responsibility

> Unlike . . . puppets, we have the possibility of stopping in our move-
> ments, looking up and perceiving the machinery by which we have been
> moved. In this act lies the first step towards freedom. And in this same
> act we find the conclusive justification of sociology as a humanistic
> discipline (Berger, 1963, p. 176).

Nettler (1970) argued that we should not "confuse art with science, and appreciation with knowledge" (p. 75). To build upon this caution, there is both an art and a
science of society which incites, respectively, either artful appreciation or scientific
knowledge. Art and science are different pursuits, but art and science taken together, and not separately, are the only means for developing what Grant has
termed the "educated imagination."

Grant discussed the educated imagination in a short preface to HERITAGE
(1971; no pagination), a volume of prose (by Symons) and pictures (by de Visser)
on Canadian furniture. Grant suggested that a glimpse at furniture "leads us out
into the complexities of lived traditions. The man of intellect without sensibility
does not bother to look at furniture; the man of sensibility without intellect cannot
know fully what is given to him in his looking."

So it is that the sociology of Canadian society beckons personal resources of
intellect and sensibility. Consciousness and responsibility can be viewed at two
levels: The one concerning methods and abilities for observing and interpreting
facts and relationships; the other concerning methods and abilities for understanding facts and relationships within their many contexts. Responsibility follows consciousness. For example, the young child is presumed by common law not to be
responsible for his acts, even if these acts should contravene the law. Responsibility
also follows consciousness at the level of sociological study, for the limits of what
we can see and do are defined by whether we are aware of what is there, and
whether such awareness helps to define our possible courses of action.

The subjects of this book have been considered without any claim that sociology is, or can be, a value-free pursuit. Quite the contrary. True, facts and relationships should be observed and interpreted in a context which allows for replication
and verification. But the context itself cannot always be described as neutral or
objective, for ideology and fiction penetrate social reality. When we do scientific
studies, perhaps the most that we should want is that somebody else can do as we
have, and possibly find what we have found. Which is to say, another person has the
chance to replicate and to verify our research and its conclusions, or to voice
negation.

That is the science side of sociology. The subjects of this book may have demonstrated also that there is vision and art in sociology. Sociology is not all craft. Indeed, art and craft are interlocking work-forms. The sociologist Mills (1959) provided us with valuable instructions in this respect. "Scholarship is a choice of how to live as well as a choice of career; ... you must learn to use your life experience in your intellectual work: continually to examine and interpret it" (p. 196). When Mills bound man up in his craft, he took the first step toward achieving Grant's educated imagination. The educated imagination, for Mills, was THE SOCIOLOGICAL IMAGINATION (1959), a "quality of mind that will help [men and women] ... to use information and to develop reason in order to achieve lucid summations of what is going on in the world and of what may be happening within themselves" (p. 5).

In any other context it might be surprising to find reference made to an illustrated book on furniture. But, like laws and the birth rate, traffic accidents and the consumer price index, furniture serves us as a social indicator. "If we know what our furniture is," argued Symons, "then we know who we are, in the profoundest sense — and we cannot escape with a counterfeit identity. Documents, newspapers, books, men's words — these may lie. But furniture does not lie. It presents to our naked eye, we ourselves — if we dare but see." Symons may not have wished his furniture referred to as a social indicator, for it sounds degrading and unkind. But social indicator it is, and Symons has managed to relate pieces of furniture to periods and contradictions in Canadian social history. His stage was the historical story of Canada's coming together into confederation. His indicator became furniture. For example, he saw in French-Canadian furniture (and culture) a "fundamental experience of celebration." "French Canadiana is a case of the Medieval world trying to include the Renaissance mind, but defending itself against mere-mind. French Canadiana is a case of the Catholic Baroque."

Turning to English Canada and its furniture, the historical tradition is not as unitary as it is in the case of French Canada. "English Canadian furniture styles do not derive uniquely from England. The basic English Canadiana style is *American* ... via the Loyalists." Add to this political fact the religious fact: a "push towards the Protestantism of Progress, which is English North America. And a recoil back to some original English, catholic, millenial sources. This is the swing against American Puritan extremism."

All of this may sound beside the point, either to furniture in general or to Canadiana in particular. It isn't! What we witness in this brief story of Anglo-American culture and design (and religion) is the birth of the mere-mind at the expense of every other element of reality! The birth of utilitarian rationality and the correlative decline of body, substance, flesh, sheer animal intuition, and — in religion — Real Presence. In short, the rise of reason and the decline in capacity for joy.

In furniture, then, Symons saw history and society, unity and difference. His argument may not be convincing at the level of craft and science, for the relations between different furniture designs and different historical events are tenuous at best. But the argument has been noted here precisely because it does not have to be convincing at the level of craft and science. The canons of scientific adequacy are perhaps beside the point. The argument is convincing because intuitively it is interesting and plausible, and because Symons has tackled a subject which in art lends support to our understanding of facts and relationships within their historical contexts.

200

So much of the argument in the above debate and throughout this book has focused upon the need to question social reality, the need to avoid assuming its existence *ad infinitum*. Perhaps it is permissible to make such an assumption consciously, through deliberation; but to placidly assume a *status quo* means that rarely, if at all, do we capitalize upon opportunities to see social things as they are, to envision things as they might be, to compare one pattern with another and so forth. If sociology offers any exciting challenge to its students, it is to broaden our imaginations so that we can cope more adequately with subjects as varied as policies for the more equal distribution of income, if it is our wish to do so, and alternative conceptions of the social future. The very nature of these subjects requires a joining of art with craft, for such questions and their answers are equally the claim of committed moralists and methodological scientists.

If consciousness must come first, we must do whatever we can to introduce it in one another. But if and when it materializes within us, we are moved to the point where there must be accountability for actions. Most persons become accountable or responsible for their actions. In the end, a common belief in western cultures is that education is the chief means for developing consciousness, and further, that responsible appraisal and action generally leads to improved conditions through more effective decisions. It is our belief.

References

Abelson, Philip H., "Limits to Growth," SCIENCE, 175 (March 17, 1972) 1197.

Alinsky, Saul, "Playboy Interview: A Candid Conversation with the Feisty Radical Organizer," PLAYBOY, 19 (March, 1972) 59ff.

Berger, Peter L., INVITATION TO SOCIOLOGY: A HUMANISTIC PERSPECTIVE, Garden City, N.Y.: Anchor Books, 1963.

Davis, Arthur K., ed., CANADIAN CONFRONTATIONS: HINTERLANDS AGAINST METROPOLIS, Edmonton: The University of Alberta Printing Services, 1970a.

Davis, Arthur K., "Some Failings of Anglophone Academic Sociology in Canada: The Need for a Dialectical and Historical Perspective," in Jan J. Loubser, ed., THE FUTURE OF SOCIOLOGY IN CANADA, Montreal: Canadian Sociology and Anthropology Association, 1970b, pp. 31-35.

Davis, Arthur K., "Canadian Society and History as Hinterland Versus Metropolis," in Richard J. Ossenberg, ed., CANADIAN SOCIETY: PLURALISM, CHANGE, AND CONFLICT, Scarborough, Ont.: Prentice-Hall of Canada Ltd., 1971, pp. 6-32.

Denton, Frank T., AN ANALYSIS OF INTERREGIONAL DIFFERENCES IN MANPOWER UTILIZATION AND EARNINGS, Ottawa: Queen's Printer, 1966.

Drews, Elizabeth Monroe and Leslie Lipson, VALUES AND HUMANITY, New York: St. Martin's Press, 1971.

Dyck, Harold J., SOCIAL FUTURES ALBERTA: 1970 2005, Edmonton: Human Resources Research Council, 1970.

Economic Council of Canada, DESIGN FOR DECISION-MAKING: AN APPLICATION TO HUMAN RESOURCES POLICIES, Ottawa: Information Canada, 1971a.

Economic Council of Canada, PERFORMANCE IN PERSPECTIVE: 1971, Ottawa: Information Canada, 1971b.

Frank, Andre Gunder, CAPITALISM AND UNDERDEVELOPMENT IN LATIN AMERICA: HISTORICAL STUDIES OF CHILE AND BRAZIL, New York: Modern Reader Paperbacks, 1969.

Gillette, Robert, "The Limits to Growth: Hard Sell for a Computer View of Doomsday," SCIENCE, 175 (March 10, 1972) 1088-1092.

Huber, Bettina J. and Wendell Bell, "Sociology and the Emergent Study of the Future," THE AMERICAN SOCIOLOGIST, 6 (November, 1971) 287-295.

Iverson, Noel and D. Ralph Matthews, COMMUNITIES IN DECLINE: AN EXAMINATION OF HOUSEHOLD RESETTLEMENT IN NEWFOUNDLAND, St. John's: Institute of Social and Economic Research, 1968.

Lynd, Robert S. and Helen Merrell Lynd, MIDDLETOWN: A STUDY IN AMERICAN CULTURE, New York: Harcourt, Brace & World, Inc., 1929.

Lynd, Robert S. and Helen Merrell Lynd, MIDDLETOWN IN TRANSITION: A STUDY IN CULTURAL CONFLICTS, New York: Harcourt, Brace & World, Inc., 1937.

Malinowski, Bronislaw, CRIME AND CUSTOM IN SAVAGE SOCIETY, Paterson, N.J.: Littlefield, Adams & Co., 1959.

McQueen, David L., "The Modes of Feeding Research into Policy," in Gwynn E. Nettler and Karol J. Krotki, eds., SOCIAL SCIENCE AND SOCIAL POLICY, Edmonton: Human Resources Research Council, 1971, pp. 25-38.

Meadows, Donella H., Dennis L. Meadows, Jorgen Randers and William W. Behrens, THE LIMITS TO GROWTH, New York: Universe Books, 1972.

Mills, C. Wright, THE SOCIOLOGICAL IMAGINATION, New York: Oxford University Press, 1959.

Moynihan, Daniel P., MAXIMUM FEASIBLE MISUNDERSTANDING: COMMUNITY ACTION IN THE WAR ON POVERTY, New York: The Free Press, 1969.

Nettler, Gwynn, EXPLANATIONS, New York: McGraw-Hill Book Company, 1970.

Nettler, Gwynn, "Knowing and Doing," THE AMERICAN SOCIOLOGIST, 7 (February, 1972) 3, 5-7.

Rogers, Everett M., SOCIAL CHANGE IN RURAL SOCIETY: A TEXTBOOK IN RURAL SOCIOLOGY, New York: Appleton-Century-Crofts, Inc., 1960.

Rosenberg, Bernard, "Editor's Forward," in Richard R. Korn, ed., JUVENILE DELINQUENCY, New York: Thomas Y. Crowell Company, 1968, pp. vii-viii.

Seeley, John R., R. Alexander Sim and Elizabeth W. Loosley, CRESTWOOD HEIGHTS: A STUDY OF THE CULTURE OF SUBURBAN LIFE, Toronto: University of Toronto Press, 1956.

Symons, Scott, HERITAGE: A ROMANTIC LOOK AT EARLY CANADIAN FURNITURE, Toronto: McClelland and Stewart Limited, 1971.

Warner, W. Lloyd, A BLACK CIVILIZATION: A STUDY OF AN AUSTRALIAN TRIBE, New York: Harper & Row, Publishers, 1964.

For Further Reading

Alinsky, Saul D., RULES FOR RADICALS: A PRACTICAL PRIMER FOR REALISTIC RADICALS, New York: Vintage Books, 1972.

Braden, William, THE AGE OF AQUARIUS: TECHNOLOGY AND THE CULTURAL REVOLUTION, Chicago: Quadrangle Books, 1970.

Commission on Educational Planning, A CHOICE OF FUTURES, Edmonton: Queen's Printer, 1972.

Denzin, Norman K., ed., THE VALUES OF SOCIAL SCIENCE, Chicago: Aldine Publishing Company, 1970.

Duncan, Otis Dudley, ed., WILLIAM F. OGBURN ON CULTURE AND SOCIAL CHANGE: SELECTED PAPERS, Chicago: Phoenix Books, 1964.

Hughes, H. Stuart, CONSCIOUSNESS AND SOCIETY: THE RECONSTRUCTION OF EUROPEAN SOCIAL THOUGHT 1890-1930, New York: Vintage Books, 1958.

Lerner, Daniel, ed., THE HUMAN MEANING OF THE SOCIAL SCIENCES, Cleveland: Meridian Books, 1959.

Stein, Maurice and Arthur Vidich, eds., SOCIOLOGY ON TRIAL, Englewood Cliffs, N.J.: Prentice-Hall, Inc., 1963.

Toffler, Alvin, FUTURE SHOCK, Toronto: Bantam Books of Canada Ltd., 1971.

Chapter 10

Postscript

There is a sense in which scholarship is not a function of citizenship but more a function of empathy and understanding. The irony of this judgment is illustrated by a group of women sociologists who attended the annual meeting of the Pacific Sociological Association in 1972. They observed "no women . . . on the panel on the future of sociology" and they questioned whether this meant there were "no women in the future of sociology?" Their question may indeed have been a conclusion! Being Canadian does not guarantee contribution any more than being female; being anything else does not exclude the possibility of contribution. Just as participation does not guarantee contribution, in many if not most situations nonparticipation does not exclude it.

To be caught up compulsively in one's status as a woman or as a Canadian may mean to wear blinkers concerning a lot of other things. This seems increasingly true as trends become global rather than local or regional or national. But global trends have always abounded, as, for example, when one civilization challenged another during expansion and conquest. Scholarship often reveals such trends which otherwise might pass unnoticed. Of course, something more than scholarship is usually required to stimulate political action. And so, as this book was being written, it coagulated an emergent bias in its author's mind: that the people of Canada must demand the setting of social goals, that they must demand a regular accounting of progress toward such goals, and through such means they must come to change patterns of growth so that the warnings of today do not become the misfortunes of tomorrow. Our society has only reached the threshold of such commitments; we will never pass on to genuine social progress until these commitments are made in the form of nothing less than a national commitment. Recently, the Economic Council of Canada termed such subjects as social goals and social reporting "new approaches" (1971, pp. 17-34). Such a declaration is just the beginning. If we do not require our tomorrow to yield such commitments, then our scholarship and all else are for naught.

Prophecies of doom have been preached on more than one occasion. One of the most eloquent and sympathetic of such prophecies, THE PEOPLE OF THE TWILIGHT by Jenness (1959; first published 1928), is one which is relevant for Canada and Canadians during the 1970's, especially as we push to develop the northern frontier and as we *must* push to settle the claims of the first Canadians. Every adult Canadian could benefit from this book, and if we were to all read it together we might well gain a common consciousness that otherwise is continually dimmed by idiosyncratic actions. While our consciousness need not be directed toward regaining the past, it could open our eyes about preserving what we now value for the future. By an odd twist of word meanings, to so argue is not to fight for conservatism, but is to fight the radical fight in support of a meaningful social future. The people of the twilight are gone, but their legacy is a lesson worth learning. Jenness lived with the Dolphin and Union Strait Eskimos before their traditional culture was swallowed up by the advance of the new-world trader. But his experience and knowledge told him that the real question for the Eskimos was then, as it is now for all of us, the choice which faces all systems not permanently at rest. "Fifty years ago the cyclone [of the white man's ways, including his sicknesses] swept over the Eskimos of the Mackenzie River delta, and of its two thousand inhabitants a scant two hundred survive. Fifty years earlier it struck Baffin Island with a similar result. Will history, fifty years hence, record the same fate for this twilight land where for two years we carried on our mission? Were we the harbingers of a brighter dawn, or only messengers of ill-omen, portending disaster?" (p. 247).

There seem to be at least two conclusions worth mentioning. One is the fact that relative unacquaintance with historical knowledge and interpretation is a weakness which the author and many of his readers must overcome if a mission indeed is to be conceived and consummated. The other is a related deficiency which many if not most of us share. Its complexity derives from the fact that it is less a deficiency and more a trait of psychological character. We look at things too indirectly and too uncritically. We fail to see the causes and consequences as they are patterned. We fail to demand accountability in others, and we too infrequently demand it of ourselves. Education of the young involves a very serious responsibility. We must expand the debate in our schools so that young Canadians are led past the provincialism of attitude and inquiry which the author still finds great difficulty in overcoming.

References

Economic Council of Canada, DESIGN FOR DECISION-MAKING: AN APPLICATION TO HUMAN RESOURCES POLICIES, Ottawa: Information Canada, 1971.

Jenness, Diamond, THE PEOPLE OF THE TWILIGHT, Chicago: The University of Chicago Press, 1959.

For Further Reading

Mowat, Farley, PEOPLE OF THE DEER, New York: Pyramid Books, 1968.

Author Index

The letter "r" following page
numbers indicates a bibliographical
reference.

Frank, Andre Gunder, 25r, 57, 69r, 197, 202r.
Fraser, Blair, 85, 93r.
Freud, Sigmund, 72, 73.

Gajda, Roman T., 35, 36, 52r.
Gantcheff, Helene, 93, 93r.
Gardner, John W., 119, 121, 125r.
Gardner, R. C., 93, 93r.
George, M. V., 53r.
Gillette, Robert, 195, 202r.
Ginsberg, Morris, 154.
Godfrey, Dave, 69r.
Gonick, Cy, 93r.
Gordon, Milton M., 178r.
Gorer, G., 74.
Gosselin, Emile, 139, 140, 150r.
Gouldner, Alvin W., 89, 93r.
Grant, George, 85, 93r, 199.
Gwyn, Richard, 126r.
Gwyn, Sandra, 116, 125r.

Hall, Edward T., 25r.
Hall, Jerome, 63, 69r.
Harp, John, 150r.
Hauser, Philip M., 90, 93r.
Hein, R. N., 92, 94r.
Hénaut, Dorothy Todd, 117, 118, 125r.
Henderson, Edmund H., 93, 93r.
Herman, Kathleen, 22, 25r, 122, 123, 124, 124r, 125r.
Hill, Brian, 178r.
Hoebel, E. Adamson, 31, 32, 33, 52r.
Hofley, John R., 150r.
Homans, George C., 9, 10, 13r, 73, 93r.
Honigmann, Irma, 126r.
Honigmann, John J., 126r.
Horowitz, Gad, 85, 93r.
Howe, Joseph, 140.
Huber, Bettina J., 194, 202r.
Hughes, Everett C., 53r.
Hughes, H. Stuart, 203r.

Inkeles, Alex, 16, 25r, 74, 75, 76, 91, 93r.
Innis, Harold A., 37, 52r, 101, 125r.
Iverson, Noel, 126r, 188, 189, 202r.

Jenness, Diamond, 104, 125r, 151r, 204, 205, 205r.
Jesperson, Ivan F., 114.
Jones, Frank E., 25r, 94r.
Jones, Richard, 140, 150r, 168, 169, 177r.
Joy, Richard J., 45, 52r, 165, 166, 167, 168, 169, 177r.

Kalbach, Warren E., 42, 43, 52r, 141, 150r, 170, 171, 172, 177r.
Kanungo, Rabinda N., 93, 93r.
Kelner, Merrijoy, 123, 125r.
Kelsen, Hans, 69r.
Kilbourn, William, 85, 94r.
Kinden, Stan, 115, 125r.
Korn, Richard R., 151r, 202r.
Krotki, Karol J., 202r.
Krueger, Ralph R., 150r.
Kuhn, Thomas S., 4, 13r.

Lambert, W. E., 92, 94r.
LaPierre, Laurier, 25r.
Laskin, Bora, 69r.
Lazarsfeld, Paul F., 93r.
Leacock, Stephen, 128, 150r.
Lenski, Gerhard E., 11, 13r, 153, 177r, 178r.
Lerner, Daniel, 203r.
Levinson, Daniel J., 74, 75, 76, 91, 93r.
Levitt, Kari, 25r, 57, 58, 69r.
Levy, M. G., 55, 69r.
Lieberson, Stanley, 178r.
Lindesmith, Alfred R., 170, 177r.
Lindzey, Gardner, 93r.
Lipset, Seymour Martin, 25r, 53r, 65, 66, 69r, 80, 81, 82, 83, 86, 92, 94r.
Lipson, Leslie, 7, 13r, 182, 201r.
Lithwick, N. H., 151r.
Lloyd, Trevor, 34, 52r.
Long, Barbara H., 93, 93r.
Loomis, Charles P., 22, 25r.
Loosley, Elizabeth W., 202r.
Lotz, Jim, 119, 120, 125r, 151r.
Loubser, Jan J., 201r.
Lower, Arthur R. M., 82, 94r.
Lower, J. A., 34, 52r.
Lubart, Joseph M., 126r.
Luckmann, Thomas, 5, 13r.
Lynd, Helen Merrell, 182, 202r.
Lynd, Robert S., 182, 202r.

Malinowski, Bronislaw, 182, 202r.
Martindale, Don, 68, 69r, 75, 94r.
Matthews, D. Ralph, 126r, 188, 189, 202r.
Maxwell, James D., 123, 125r.
Maxwell, J. W., 143, 144, 145, 150r.
Maxwell, Mary Percival, 123, 125r.
McGee, Reece, 14r.
McLeod, Jack, 25r.
McQueen, David L., 187, 202r.
McVey, Wayne W., 42, 43, 52r, 141, 150r, 170, 171, 172, 177r.
Meadows, Dennis L., 202r.

Subject Index